Jotería Communication Studies

Critical Intercultural Communication Studies

Thomas K. Nakayama and Bernadette Marie Calafell
General Editors

Vol. 26

The Critical Intercultural Communication Studies series
is part of the Peter Lang Media and Communication list.
Every volume is peer reviewed and meets
the highest quality standards for content and production.

PETER LANG
New York • Bern • Berlin
Brussels • Vienna • Oxford • Warsaw

Robert Gutierrez-Perez

Jotería Communication Studies

Narrating Theories of Resistance

PETER LANG
New York • Bern • Berlin
Brussels • Vienna • Oxford • Warsaw

Library of Congress Cataloging-in-Publication Data

Names: Gutierrez-Perez, Robert, author.
Title: Jotería communication studies: narrating theories of resistance /
Robert Gutierrez-Perez.
Description: New York: Peter Lang, 2021.
Series: Critical intercultural communication studies; vol. 26 | ISSN 1528-6118
Includes bibliographical references and index.
Identifiers: LCCN 2021016791 (print) | LCCN 2021016792 (ebook)
ISBN 978-1-4331-6461-3 (hardback) | ISBN 978-1-4331-6462-0 (paperback)
ISBN 978-1-4331-6458-3 (ebook pdf) | ISBN 978-1-4331-6459-0 (epub)
Subjects: LCSH: Queer theory—United States. | Hispanic Americans. |
Identity (Psychology)—United States. | Marginality, Social—United
States. | Intersectionality (Sociology)—United States. | Oppression (Psychology)
Classification: LCC HQ76.16.U6 G88 2021 (print) | LCC HQ76.16.U6 (ebook) |
DDC 306.7601—dc23
LC record available at https://lccn.loc.gov/2021016791
LC ebook record available at https://lccn.loc.gov/2021016792
DOI 10.3726/b18436

Bibliographic information published by **Die Deutsche Nationalbibliothek**.
Die Deutsche Nationalbibliothek lists this publication in the "Deutsche
Nationalbibliografie"; detailed bibliographic data are available
on the Internet at http://dnb.d-nb.de/.

For those we lost
For those in the struggle
For those still to come
and for me

Contents

Acknowledgements

The task of acknowledging those who have made this work possible is difficult because I believe that reality is socially constructed and radically interconnected to everyone and everything, so I couldn't be here without you (the reader) or without so many others in my life. However, I would like to acknowledge Gloria Anzaldúa as a guiding theoretical and philosophical light for me throughout my academic journey and this book. Thank you for your scholarship, activism, art, and life. You are a light in the dark for so many. Additionally, I am incredibly proud of my academic lineage and academic family. Thank you Bernadette Marie Calafell for your friendship, mentorship, and for being a fierce Chicana. You are a role model, and I am and will forever be part of the House of Calafell. With that said, I want to thank Haneen Al-Ghabra, Shadee Abdi, Miranda Olzman, Pavithra Prasad, Anthony Cuomo, Shinsuke Eguchi, Fatima Zahrae Chrifi Alaoui, Richard Jones Jr., Sophie Jones, Kathryn Hobson, Dawn Marie McIntosh, Raquel Moreira, and Sara Baugh for your support during this project. Thank you to Jessica Johnson, Nivea Castaneda, and Brendan Hughes! You three have saved me so many times. I love you. Lore LeMaster, Michael Tristano Jr., Cypress Amber Reign, Salma Shukri, Kate Willink, Lacey Stein, Jared Vasquez, Leandra Hernández, Amanda Martinez, Gust Yep, Jeffrey McCune Jr., and Godfried Asante, I will forever be grateful and appreciative of you. Kristen Foht

Huffman, thank you for your careful reading and suggestions of prior drafts of this book. You are amazing! Luis Manuel Andrade, mi esposo academico, te amo mucho. Also, right after graduation with my doctoral degree, two of the committee members from my dissertation passed away, but this book and my intellectual orientation to inquiry is forever informed by Roy Wood and Luis León. Luis, this book is especially for you. Thank you for every moment of your life that you gifted to me. Your mentorship, love, and faith in me led me here. Finally, I want to thank Deanna Fassett, Rona Halualani, Kathleen McConnell, Wenshu Lee, and David Terry for their mentorship and support during my undergraduate and master's program. San José State University and the department of Communication Studies at this university empowered me to move beyond my poor and working-class roots through its commitment to an affordable, accessible, and excellent world-class education. I am forever indebted to this institution and to the city of San José.

On a more personal note, I want to thank my husband and best friend: Juan Carlos Perez. Our journey has only begun, and I am grateful and blessed to be able to witness your radiant and beautiful spirit in this life. As one of the 18,000 couples married before Proposition 8 passed in California, ours is one of the first queer unions acknowledged by law in the United States, and I will always cherish our queer marriage. Regardless of what form our union takes in the everyday, you are my angel, and indeed, I am the man I am because of your love, care, and commitment. I love you.

To my found family, I love you so much! Patricia Corrolla, Carlos Ramirez, Mark Cardiel, Francisco Clavel, Matthew Kopec, Kimberly Carrasco, and Melate Bekele Tolossa. To Luis Armendariz, thank you for being my muse throughout this project. When I saw you, I knew we were meant to meet, and you will always hold a special place in my heart. I wish you nothing but happiness, love, and Chicano soul. Further, I want to thank my wonderfully talented, intelligent, and social justice-engaged siblings that have become the core of what I know to be my roots. Thank you to my siblings and to my parents for always loving me just as I am. To Kevin, Derek, Tony, and Carly, I cherish each of you so much. Melissa Perez, you are the best sister-in-law that a guy could ask for, so thank you for your years of support and friendship. I would also like to thank my grandfather, Dwayne Weatherby, for being a wonderful father figure to me. Also, I want to thank my grandmother, Mary Weatherby; you are indeed a miracle and a blessing. I love and cherish you deeply and always. There are many others that have been part of this journey, and there may not be space to place all your names on this page or in this book, but please know that I love you. Thank you.

Introduction: Theories in the Flesh as Resistance in Everyday Communicative Life

There is something very powerful about a story. Once you tell a story or a narrative, it becomes alive, wild, and hungry.[1] What traumas, secrets, and intimate wanderings will I feed to this story? What narratives of power and resistance can I share? If I refuse the process, then will this theory made from my flesh starve and die? It has taken me many years and decades to reach this moment in life. This location right here on the page where I am finally able to believe that my story or my theorizing is worthy—I am valid, I am enough, I matter. Gloria Anzaldúa, in *Light in the Dark/Luz en lo Oscuro*, describes theory as a story about the world, and as a story, it emerges out of a historical and political context.[2] It is not a dead object as understood within the Western gaze, but rather, these theories (re) perform every time the images, symbols, and metaphors on the page are utilized in the everyday.[3] For example, I envision you reading this somewhere—possibly for a class assignment, for a manuscript you are working on for publication, for inspiration for some poem, some song, some cultural artifact or performance in process—and hopefully, you are someone who has been searching for *this* book. The Black and Brown immigrant cook on the line making salads or washing dishes; the primo or sobrino that your gay tío or tía has been wanting to talk to you about something; or the Chicanx and Latinx LGBTQ everyday person riding the bus, working and chasing sueños, surviving, and sometimes thriving in their truths. Yes, the text is frozen on the page, but every word you read enacts, performs, and re-performs an "equipment for living."[4] The performativity of the utterance of a story moves through the everyday world of communicative behavior and shows how we can make meaning of our experiences of history, society, and culture.

For example, "joto" is a derogatory label used to discipline, describe, categorize, and hurt Jotería, as joto roughly translates as "faggot" or "queer."[5] As a homophobic slur in the Spanish language, joto is beginning to be reappropriated by Jotería as a "dramatic gesture toward resignifying the term and refuting the negative connotations that it has carried historically."[6] Like the Chicanos, Chicanas, and Chicanxs that came before them, Jotería draw on the myths, history, and politics of Aztlán and other Latinx or Mestizx cultures to challenge master narratives of invisibility and disempowerment, and this labor is undertaken within an intersectional, hegemonic system of control.[7] Jotería studies emerged out of Chicana/o studies and "can be considered a critical site of inquiry that centers on nonheteronormative gender and sexuality as related to mestiza/o subjectivities."[8] Yet, Jotería studies is interdisciplinary because jotos and jotas have found spaces to survive and thrive across the disciplines, so this story of joto is complex, circular, and oftentimes, misunderstood and made monstrous.

Aye gente, I feel myself slipping into the academic training that compels me to cite more, explain deeper through complex vocabulary and complex sentences, and in general, separate myself from the masses by writing in a specialized language. Throughout this book, I've struggled to clearly articulate the theories of power and resistance that I have collected and analyzed through multiple communication research methods and methodological approaches. I want to show the rigor and validity of these methods and this scholarship with Jotería; yet, my audience for this book is not solely scholars and practitioners from communication studies, gender and sexuality studies, performance studies, cultural studies, or even, Latinx and Chicanx studies in education, sociology, history, literature, media, arts, and humanities. I envision this book to be the handbook that I never had. This book speaks to and with those nonheteronormative mestizas/os who perform their sexuality and gender in queer practices and queer communicative forms—Jotería. This book is for those Jotería and their allies who are creating spaces of survival within a system that wants them silenced, on the margins, and/or in their graves. How can I make it clear that in order for me to survive in the world of the everyday that I had to write this book? I needed you as my reader—desperately.

Why Do You Want to Write This Book?

I want   to look
in the obsidian mirror
and smile
be grateful

Now   I see a monster
Brows furrowed trying to see past the fangs
wolf pack mentality
silver and blue hungry
post-apocalyptic crawling through downtown
I want to be eaten, chewed on slowly
wiggling to contain desire, my will
begging to transform   scream in ecstasy
finally open   receptivity

I runneth over

Over the borders of acceptability
questions of authenticity
politics of merit and civility
the imposter syndrome kicks in again
Where do I belong?
What am I?

I am searching for others like me
Demanding   we will never die
lone princes of flowers
sitting on creativity
imagining desire like a mushroom
creating liberation with soul
work, believing we deserve space

When I was an elementary school student, my mom and dad allowed me to buy a big thick book at la pulga called *Greek Mythology* by Edith Hamilton.[9] For a young person sent to a private Christian preschool, kindergarten, and first grade in Milpitas, California, the stories reminded me of those we heard in the Bible readings that I experienced weekly and sometimes daily. In my mind, the stories of Athena, Artemis, Atlanta, Apollo, Zeus, Medusa, Venus y más played out on the same fabric board and in the same paper cutouts of my Bible-reading storytelling sessions. I took these stories and reimagined them. I constructed telenovelas for all my toys on the carpet or in the bathtub with my brother. My everyday communicative life became a place where I discovered I could escape by going on "flights of the imagination." When I spent my recesses alone because I was separated out for my intelligence, I wove my cuentos. When I was reading my books while my primos played at the family reunion, I gathered more narratives to help me live my life.[10] The point is that these mitos y leyendas awoke and were (re)performed by my body, and the way I did those stories was by doing them in particular ways, under particular circumstances, and toward a particular horizon. The historical and political context of these narratives place them into the public and private spheres, which becomes encoded into the culture and the society of a geographic location. And like water to fish, culture becomes the air we breathe, and these atmospheres of influence we inhabit become like Venn diagrams where we co-create culture and society endlessly in our co-constructed images. In the busyness of an ever-growing, interconnected, neoliberal capitalism and globalization, it is easy to forget the underground reservoir of images and symbols that flow, move, and bubble up from the subterranean spaces of shadow (the cave).[11] These archetypical images, metaphors, and symbols continue to breathe through our breath; narratives are an everyday performance with performatives that can be observed and shared in the everyday acts of telling the told or through everyday communicative life.

Jotería Communication Studies

I specifically remember when I first felt shame for exhibiting my sexuality. I was sitting on a tall stool at the kitchen peninsula at my grandparent's home in Milpitas.[12] I was young, perhaps 3 or 5. I was rubbing my privates—to scratch or to adjust or to learn about the body I was inhabiting for the first time. My grandmother was aghast. She scorned me, "Don't touch yourself! If you touch yourself, Jesus will make your hands fall off!" The image of two bloody stumps for hands revisits my mind sometimes when I masturbate or have sex with other men. Shame. In this micro moment, the story that was being communicated to me was: "Sex is bad. Sexuality is a sin." Even to this day, my grandma earnestly approaches me to tell me that her only goal left in life is to make sure all her children and grandchildren will join her in heaven. The unstated assumption being that, currently, I will not be joining her. I am bad. I am a sin. In writing this book, I am not only conflicted with who you are as the reader/audience, but I've also struggled because writing this book means taking risks and being vulnerable, as I am in fact an imperfect person and scholar. It will mean telling secrets. Like Anzaldúa writes: "One of my biggest fears is that of betraying myself, of consuming myself with self-castigation, of not being able to unseat the guilt that has ridden on my back for years."[13] I want to shock the reader and myself shitless.[14] In this book, I shake the foundations of my reality in the service of articulating the immense labor undertaken by people on the periphery of society and culture, and I am nervous because I will have to tell stories that I have never told before. Stories that my family, colleagues, community, and culture may not want me to tell—labeling me traitor, queer, unmentionable, untouchable, sinvergüenza—but I have to do the work, la tarea.[15] I am compelled to write this book because there are too many of us that are forced into silence, into the margins, into death.[16] I write because there are too few of us here in academia.[17] I write because too many of us have lost our lives before our scholarship, art, and activism was complete. I write to heal myself and others traumatized and hurt by White supremacist, capitalist, cisheteropatriarchy.

Like the old adage goes, history is written by the victors. So, what of the marginalized? Do they not have a story about power, culture, and history worthy of (re)membering? Or, as Gayatri Chakravorty Spivak asks, "Can the Subaltern speak?"[18] The book currently in your hands is about how gay, bisexual, transgender, queer, and questioning (GBTQ) Chicanos and Latinos generate theories of resistance to carve out spaces to live and sometimes thrive. The focus on GBTQ Chicanx interlocutors is not meant to ignore the histories, politics, narratives, cultural artifacts and productions, or experiences of the rest of the Jotería community; instead, it is an acknowledgement that the beauty, intellect, creativity, and bravery of our community cannot and should not be attempted to be encapsulated in its complete entirety within one single book. This does not mean this space isn't for you or that I am not speaking with you.[19] For example, the scholarship, theorizing, experiences, and cultural representations of women of color are critical to any understanding that this book on power, history, culture, communication, and resistance may offer to the reader. Further, given the radical interconnectedness of identity, culture, and power, the data that was collected itself points to, implicates, questions, gives insight into, and engages multiple communities, because GBTQ Chicanxs, like all interlocutors, form their identities in difference.[20] That is, I am this because I am not that.

Communicating across difference, living in and with difference, embracing monstrosity, and narrating these experiences on the margins is a central focus of this book. Discussing identity negotiation, De Los Santos-Upton notes how identity construction is interpersonal, cultural, contextual, historical, and structural as identities are constructed in relationship to others.[21] In other words, the process of identity construction is political because:

> our handling of difference varies tremendously—the ways we react to difference, and the ways we speak of difference. Sometimes, we deliberately accentuate and exaggerate differences; at other times, we suppress them, either by trivializing them or by pretending that they are not there at all.[22]

Drawing on scholarship from communication studies, cultural studies, and performance studies, I offer an interdisciplinary study on how GBTQ Chicanxs and Latinxs make sense of their own difference, how people interpret their assumed or perceived difference, and ultimately, how difference is managed as an emancipatory tool toward the goal of queer of color world making.[23]

Language and communication are the lynchpin that holds together this book on identity and difference, culture and society, and power and narratives. For instance, Ronald Jackson II and Jamie Moshin draw on Fanon, Sartre, and Foucault to describe the process of "naming the other" as intimately connected to language and the "I-Other Dialectic," which I quote here at length:

> The clearest way to explain the I-Other dialectic is to point to its most explicit analog—the sentence. Sentences are structured so that there is a subject, verb, and object. The subject is the predicate nominative; it is what controls the sentential arrangement. The object is either controlled by the subject or is indicated by the subject as the "what" in the sentence. The verb signifies the character of the relationship or situation. If I say, "I love her," the "I" occupies the subject position, as always. "Love" is the verb that carries action and shows what is done to something or someone else; and "her" is the object. In the English language "her" does not get to be "she." "She" would signify autonomy and perhaps even control over the encounter. When "her" is placed in the object position it is an object waiting to be acted upon.[24]

Language and communication is about power and control whether discussing identity as avowed or ascribed in social scientific forms;[25] as constraining and challenging;[26] as agency, resistance, and relating;[27] as a process of inner work, public acts,[28] identity negotiations with dominant cultural norms, values, and beliefs; or ideological and repressive state apparatuses.[29]

This book articulates Jotería Communication Studies as a subdiscipline and articulates a praxis for resisting multiple forms of oppression by focusing on how everyday performances of identity and culture challenge master narratives of power and control. Specifically, I am interested in locating those "theories in the flesh" that are utilized to survive the multiple oppressions encountered at the intersection of race, gender, class, sexuality, and nation. I want to tell a story about my community and the things we do to survive, love, and live our best lives—now.[30] Theories in the flesh are located within the everyday lives of Jotería and are done/made to push back on master narratives of identity, culture, and history. Indeed, consejos or advice are an example of a narrative form that is shared throughout this book from interviewees, research poems, scholarship, and the author to connect experiences in everyday communicative life with navigations of intersectional structural oppression. Theories in the flesh are epistemologically connected to the experiences and scholarship of nonheteronormative mestizas/os dwelling in the borderlands of race, class, gender, geography, ethnicity, sexuality, and citizenship.[31] However, the lived experiences of GBTQ Chicanxs over the past 500 years are rarely if ever archived, considered, or heard, and therefore, the experiential knowledge of Jotería is underrepresented, marginalized, and silenced in popular, historical, and academic texts and culture. As such, the personal and political experiences of Jotería are "lived legacies of colonialism, racism, xenophobia, homophobia, sexism, and heterosexism."[32] When and where experiential, embodied, and intersectional knowledge is centered in everyday life is the critical location for collecting and remembering a theory in the flesh.

Chip on My Shoulder

I woke up kinked
forced to love myself
everyday   an exercise
Like the first day at the gym
Are you sure you want to live?
You have to answer correctly

Fire in my belly
I hide it from everyone
gazing into my eyes
you see it   something inside me
inhabiting my body   hurting
ablaze through space
transiting Taurus
toward destiny
no longer fighting

resistance is futile
a bull charging at you
ojos salvajes
drooling into your mouth
you swallow

Smile,
You get to run.
Just like every   body.

Mirrored worlds faultlines apart
Tragedy incomplete
You must choose
a comedy of errors
To fail, To succeed

That is the question

Opening books
you practice gratitude and affirmations
you concoct ceremony and masturbations
like hooks, it is *All About Love*
knotted   lost   Searching   no feeling
blackmailed   choosing my karma
Venus in retrograde
you're at the decision

Do I continue reading the poem?

writing out our existence
together hoping to understand
a rhythm in the song   or maybe
a rhyme   a flower
cementing a beat
calling for a response

Alive, the poem takes space
Conjures a context   a magic
breathing like an animal
a lifeline when you wake up in bed alone
an outlet, a receptive agency of retribution
on my best days, I hit the alarm
take my pills and repeat
on my worst days, I reach into the void
to touch you, to feel something   anything

spiritually-encountered, mixing
a never-ending voice that stops, resists
on the page, here
I can't make up my mind
a pen continuing beyond me
a story out of control
a narrative with everything to lose

There is a kink in my neck
It feels   like reason
Or, is it just a gaze
Taking each word
signifying decoding encoding
meaning   I want to mean
know   I want to know
heavy   tired   sat on   left broken
Why won't you invest in my infrastructure?
Why won't I invest in myself?
Like Anzaldúa writes, I'll have to do
Do it alone   Do it for my survival
Do it because
the chip on my shoulder
my good morning
my reminder
my blessing
my choice to live   one more day

Locating Theories in the Flesh within Borderlands Narratives

Although theories in the flesh can be collected from analyses of poetry, literature, theatrical performance, paintings, dance, music, cultural artifacts, and autobiographies,[33] this book focuses on locating theories in the flesh within the borderlands narratives of GBTQ Chicanos. These borderlands narratives weave in and out of everyday performances of identity, culture, and history, and, oftentimes, these narratives address embodied experiences of fragmentation and hybridity, such as the transgression of crossing "boundaries of genre, of method, of content, of disciplines."[34] Anzaldúa describes this experience as a mestiza consciousness, where one develops a "holistic, nonbinary way of thinking and acting that includes a transformational tolerance for contradiction and ambivalence."[35] As a form of experiential knowledge, theories in the flesh emerge "where the physical realities of our lives—our skin color, the land or concrete we grew up on, our sexual longings—all fuse to create a politic born out of necessity."[36] Therefore, theories in the flesh utilize the traumas experienced in/on the body to create and enact a form of resistance or agency that is at once verbal, nonverbal, physical, psychological, emotional, and spiritual—it is praxis turned theory turned praxis.[37]

For example, many GBTQ Chicanos and Latinos do not have any stories (cuentos) from GBTQ elders and ancestors to help them make sense of themselves to others or to themselves,[38] so when we are at our most dire need, we have no one to turn to for advice (consejos); for a safe space to engage in talks or chats (pláticas) about who we are; or for a positive image of ourselves in myths, legends, or folklore (mitos). Our testimonios go unheard and unrecorded, and separated from each other by time, space, and cultural norms/values/beliefs, our narratives are only known to others through chismé (gossip) and harmful stereotypes. Theories in the flesh are shared through these narrative forms because narratives erupt out of embodied experiences within specific cultural, geopolitical, relational, and economic circumstances embedded in everyday life. These often hidden, invisible, or forgotten Jotería-historias express experiences that can aid other LGBTQ Chicanos and Latinos in understanding their identity and culture in the present.[39] Given that GBTQ Chicanx experiences are intimately connected to the history and politics of the geographic regions currently known as the U.S. Southwest and Mexico, it is not an accident that GBTQ Chicanxs know little to nothing about our Jotería-historias. This project focuses on Chicanismo; however, given the proliferation of the pan-ethnic identity of Latina/o, this work at times implicates and offers insights into both communities. Patricia Hill Collins, speaking on the individual and group experiences of U.S. Black women, discusses "standpoint theory," which explains how a group can "face similar challenges that result from living in a society that historically and routinely derogates ... [yet] this neither means that individual African-American women have all had the same experiences nor that we agree on the significance of our varying experiences."[40] In other words, there are "points of connection" or "patterns of intersecting oppression" that articulate a "standpoint," and the goal of this book is to reflect on these standpoint experiences throughout each chapter.[41]

As forms of subjugated knowledge, theories in the flesh are committed to understanding power as operating simultaneously at the intersection of multiple identity and socio-cultural constructs. Kimberly Crenshaw first theorized the term "intersectionality" within critical race theory to explicate the particular struggles of Black women trying to receive justice in the U.S. legal system.[42]

As a theory of oppression that reveals the (in)visible, interlocking, and multiple levels of power operating within an identity, a performance, or an interaction in a particular time and place,[43] intersectional knowledge generation and critique requires an acknowledgement of one's relationality to power through an understanding that we each occupy spaces of privilege and oppression simultaneously.[44] Within this intersectional understanding of power, relations of oppression and resistance are viewed as fluid, contextual, and complex.

Indeed, understanding theories in the flesh as experiential, embodied, and intersectional becomes a useful tool for collecting and remembering the narratives of GBTQ Chicanos and Latinos toward the goal of honoring their embodied experiences in the borderlands. For example, this book is essentially a methodological intervention into the study of marginalized and subaltern communities. By providing research on the Jotería community from specific geographic regions of the U.S. Southwest, this book provides a cultural map or political snapshot of a particular time and place from a particular point of view or location. Further, by providing research utilizing multiple methods, such as ethnography, auto/ethnography, oral history performance, archival research, rhetorical criticism, and interviewing, this book generates knowledge with and for the Jotería community by providing thick descriptions of history, culture, and communication practices. However, a third goal of this book aims at performing the culture under analysis in the very process of writing about research. In other words, this book is meant to be a roadmap for other Jotería struggling to find their voices and their place in a society and culture that would rather they be silent, invisible, or dead.

Narrating Theories and Methods of Resistance

In "Part One: Borderlands Narratives and Snapshots of Jotería-Historias," I argue that narrative theory necessitates an ontological shift when collecting and remembering historical narratives of GBTQ Chicanos and Latinos. For instance, in Chapter 1, this borderlands approach to narrative theory is explicated through the narrative forms of cuentos, pláticas, chismé, mitos, testimonios, and consejos, and to demonstrate these "borderlands narratives," I provide a literature review and example for each to flesh out how these narrative formats intersectionally engage with theories of power, history, culture, and identity. To provide snapshots of Jotería culture, identity, and communication and to provide a macromicro context for the historical narratives collected and remembered throughout the book, I utilize autobiographical performance and performative writing in

Chapter 2 to explore issues of fathering, spirituality, loss, and cultural inheritance through an interrogation of my grandfather's funeral. Further, I include a testimonio from a family member to layer this exploration of fathering and memory with a borderlands narrative where I attempt to talkback with rather than for the testimonialista. In Chapter 4, I utilize this same methodology of autobiographical performance and performative writing to critique higher education spaces and places and to explicate the theory of nepantla, which I argue is not a painless process of healing and transformation but one filled with confusion, uncertainty, and movement.[45] By examining the intersectional privileges and potential for agency embodied by a queer, Chicanx male educator and student, I offer my own personal experiences and history as a way of remembering and understanding borderlands narratives and Jotería resistance.

Additionally, throughout the book, I share personal and political poetry created from the research processes and projects undertaken. Together, these poems serve as ethnographic fieldnotes that share theories in the flesh with the reader and "attempt to bridge the contradictions in our experience" by "naming our selves and by telling our stories in our own words."[46] Further, utilizing poetry as research offers what Sandra Faulkner describes as "research poetry" meant "to enlarge understanding, resist clear undemanding interpretations, and move closer to what it means to be human."[47] Research poetry references poems that "are crafted from research endeavors, either before a project analysis, as a project analysis, and/or poems that are part of or constitute an entire project."[48] Each poem offers an opportunity for the reader to experience the lived experience of GBTQ Chicanos and Latinos, and further, these research poems demonstrate the utility of poetry for capturing communicative interactions and performances of identity, culture, and power. In order to collect and (re)member historical narratives of GBTQ Chicanos and Latinos, arts-based research approaches are integral to shifting research toward performative, queer, and decolonial scholarship.

In "Part Two: Narrating and Staging Theories and Methods of Resistance," I utilize my own borderlands positionality to demonstrate an approach to social science research that researches and analyzes communication, culture, history, and identity through a decolonial, cyclical, and creation-centered ontology and methodology. For instance, in Chapter 5, I engage with and extend the work of Amira de la Garza's "Four Seasons Approach" to social science research.[49] Specifically, by utilizing the Four Seasons ethnographic approach, I describe and analyze the performances and performativities of a LGBTQ Latino night club in the Rocky Mountain region of the United States. By focusing on "Drag Night," this chapter argues that nonheteronormative mestiza/o performances of gender

and sexuality create homeplaces for Jotería through Muñoz's theory of disidentification.[50] Furthering this germinal work, I argue that Jotería audience members
act as co-performative witnesses who make meaning through and with the mate-
rial/ideological space of the LGBTQ Latino night club to disrupt in the form of
embodied aesthetics, or disruptive ambiguities, the heteronormative, national-
ist, and cissexist dominant scripts to express and to practice nonheteronormative
desire, gender, mestizaje, and homeplace on their own terms.

In Chapter 6, I explicate the method of the Four Seasons of Oral History
Performance (FSOHP) to critically collect and (re)member the theories in the
flesh of GBTQ Chicanxs and Latinxs. In the early stages of this project, it became
clear that a decolonial, cyclical, and creation-centered approach to the collection
and (re)membering of the historical narratives of GBTQ Chicanos was essential
to speaking with/to this marginalized and underrepresented community, and as
an insider/outsider, I had to put my body on the line just like my interviewees.
So to further introduce the reader into this queer of color world, I share personal
journaling, poetry, drawings, affirmations, and field notes to offer a glimpse into
the everyday life of a GBTQ Chicanx and Latinx interlocutor. Moreover, this
chapter stages the collected cuentos, pláticas, mitos, chismé, testimonios, and
consejos that were collected and (re)membered through the FSOHP method. The
methods of poetic transcription and performative writing are utilized to poetically and rhetorically present my research findings in an accessible and engaging
format that could be performed on a stage or in a theatre.

In "Part Three: Jotería Performance Rhetoric," I continue to mark and critique
the socio-cultural marginalization, violent manifestations, and tactical resistance
experienced by GBTQ Chicanos and Latinos through the sharing of personal and
research poetry. In Chapter 7, I selectively analyze the cuentos collected during
FSOHP fieldwork to highlight the multiple inter-/intra-generational silences
within GBTQ Chicano communities. Further, the traumas and subsequent theories in the flesh created from coming out as a GBTQ Chicano and the multiple
vectors and levels of identity, culture, and power GBTQ Chicanos navigate are
explicated. In order to make sense of themselves and to make sense of themselves
to others, Jotería undertake a labor of intelligibility,[51] which is the principle focus
of this chapter as it has implications for all the collected works within this book.
Essentially, this book seeks to address the following research questions:

(1) What are the historical narratives and communicative processes that shape how
GBTQ Chicanos and Latinos understand and perform their identities? (2) How
do these narratives and processes inform how GBTQ Chicanos and Latinos make

sense of their relationships with others and themselves? (3) What theories in the flesh do GBTQ Chicanos and Latinos utilize in their everyday lives to survive and resist on the peripheries of multiple, oppressive, power structures?

As a final offering to the reader, I undertake a radical approach to concluding scholarly work by inviting Dr. Luis Manuel Andrade to interview me as a way of providing a conclusion without an end. This conclusion covers topics from same-sex marriage and queer unions to the massacre at Pulse nightclub in Orlando, Florida, as well as pointed questions about the content of this book and my prior work on LGBTQ Chicanxs and Latinx interlocutors.

When I was growing up as Jotería in California, I wish I had a survival guide or something/anything that told me I wasn't a monster.[52] As a political and historical snapshot of Jotería culture, history, and politics, this project is not a complete picture of this complex and nuanced cultural community, but it offers several insights into theories in the flesh, generational dis/continuities, identity, politics of coming out, disidentification, and the labor of intelligibility. Drawing on and dialoguing with Latina/o Communication Studies, this work navigates the borderlands between intercultural communication, rhetoric, and performance studies to argue for a critical/performative turn that highlights reflexivity, cultural/queer nuances, and decolonial acts of resistance. In the end, I hope that this project recognizes the power of narrative, imagination, and self-love to create radical acts of resistance. From historical/political erasures, traumas, and violence, GBTQ Chicanos and Latinos create theories in the flesh to carve out spaces to survive and thrive on the fringes—this work collects their histories and their struggles.

> I am not a victim
> I am a not a champion
> I have thrived
> Overcoming every obstacle
> It has felt like survival
> Hopeless, yet
>
> Agency, change, changing,
> mentor, role model, scholar,
> poet, performer,
> teacher
> This didn't just happen
> someone hurt me
> on purpose, but

It happened.

Transforming, ripping
off my own arm
beating, reattaching
the new and unexpected
fighting, advocating

History

It happened.
We happened.
Do you believe me?

Notes

1. Gloria Anzaldúa, *The Gloria Anzaldúa Reader*, ed. AnaLouise Keating (Durham, NC: Duke University Press, 2009).
2. Gloria Anzaldúa, *Light in the Dark/Luz en lo Oscuro: Rewriting Identity, Spirituality, Reality* (Durham, NC: Duke University Press, 2015).
3. Anzaldúa, *Light*.
4. Kenneth Burke, *The Philosophy of Literary Form: Studies in Symbolic Action* (Baton Rouge, LA: Louisiana State University Press, 1941).
5. Xamuel Bañales, "Jotería," *Aztlán: A Journal of Chicano Studies* 39, no. 1 (2014): 155–66.
6. Bañales, "Jotería," 156.
7. Shane T. Moreman, "Rethinking Dwight Conquergood: Toward an Unstated Cultural Politics," *Liminalities: A Journal of Performance Studies* 5, no. 5 (2009): 5.
8. Daniel Enrique Pérez, "Jotería Epistemologies," *Aztlán: A Journal of Chicano Studies* 39, no. 1 (2014): 143.
9. Edith Hamilton, *Mythology* (Boston, MA: Little, Brown, and Company, 2013).
10. Burke, *The Philosophy of Literary Form*.
11. Anzaldúa, *Reader*; Anzaldúa, *Light*.
12. Milpitas translates as "Little Cornfields," and it is a California city that was incorporated in 1954.
13. Anzaldúa, *Reader*, 39.
14. Ibid, 23.
15. Ibid, 121–23.
16. Ibid., 26–35; Robert Gutierrez-Perez, "Editor's Introduction: Deconstruction as a Simultaneous Act of Reconstruction," *Border-Lines: Journal of the Latino Research Center* 11, (2019): 9–15.

17. Tara J. Yosso and Daniel G. Solórzano, "Leaks in the Chicana and Chicano Educational Pipeline," *Latino Policy & Issues Brief* 13 (2006): 1–4.

18. Gayatri Chakravorty Spivak, "Can the Subaltern Speak?," in *Marxism and the Interpretation of Culture,* eds. C. Nelson and L. Grossberg (Urbana and Chicago: University of Illinois Press, 1988): 271–313.

19. Linda Alcoff, "The Problem of Speaking for Others," *Cultural Critique* 20 (1991): 5–32.

20. Ron L. Jackson and Jamie Moshin, "Identity and Difference: Race and the Necessity of the Discriminating Subject," in *The Handbook of Critical Intercultural Communication*, eds. Thomas K. Nakayama and Rona Tamiko Halualani (Malden, MA: Wiley-Blackwell, 2013), 348–63.

21. Sarah De Los Santos Upton, "Communicating *Nepantla*: An Anzaldúan Theory of Identity," in *This Bridge We Call Communication: Anzaldúan Approaches to Theory, Method and Praxis*, eds. Leandra Hinojosa Hernández and Robert Gutierrez-Perez (Lanham, MA: Lexington Books, 2019), 30.

22. Crispin Thurlow, "Speaking of Difference: Language, Inequality and Interculturality," in *The Handbook of Critical Intercultural Communication*, eds. Thomas K. Nakayama and Rona Tamiko Halualani (Malden, MA: Wiley-Blackwell, 2013), 227.

23. Robert Gutierrez-Perez and Luis Manuel Andrade, "Queer of Color World-Making: <Marriage> in the Rhetorical Archive and the Embodied Repertoire," *Text and Performance Quarterly* 38, no. 1–2 (2018): 1–18; José Esteban Muñoz, *Cruising Utopia: The Then and There of Queer Futurity* (New York: New York University Press, 2009); José Esteban Muñoz, *Disidentifications: Queers of Color and the Performance of Politics* (Minneapolis: University of Minneapolis Press, 1999).

24. Jackson and Moshin, "Identity and Difference," 351.

25. Nilanjana Bardhan and Mark P. Orbe, "Introduction: Identity Research in Intercultural Communication," in *Identity Research and Communication: Intercultural Reflections and Future Directions*, eds. Nilanjana Bardhan and Mark P. Orbe (Lanham, MA: Lexington Books, 2012).

26. Sara Baugh-Harris and Bernadette Marie Calafell, "A Tolerance for Ambiguity or the American Dream: Utilizing Anzaldúa to Disrupt and Reclaim Latina Lives from Multicultural Feminism," in *This Bridge We Call Communication: Anzaldúan Approaches to Theory, Method and Praxis*, eds. Leandra Hinojosa Hernández and Robert Gutierrez-Perez (Lanham, MA: Lexington Books, 2019), 213–25.

27. "Satoshi Toyosaki and Hsun-Yu (Sharon) Chuang, "Critical Intercultural Communication Pedagogy from Within: Textualizing Intercultural and Intersectional Self-Reflexivity," in *Critical Intercultural Communication Pedagogy*, eds. Ahmet Atay and Satoshi Toyosaki (Lanham, MA: Lexington Books, 2018), 238–43.

28. Anzaldúa, *Light in the Dark*, 117–59.

29. Richard Delgado and Jean Stefancic, *Critical Race Theory: An Introduction* (New York: NYU Press, 2001); Rachel Alicia Griffin, "Navigating the Politics of Identity/Identities and Exploring the Promise of Critical Love," in *Identity Research and Communication: Intercultural Reflections and Future Directions*, eds. Nilanjana Bardhan and Mark P. Orbe (Lanham, MA: Lexington Books, 2012).

30. Anita Tijerina Revilla, personal communication, August 17, 2018.

31. Gloria Anzaldúa, *Borderlands/La Frontera: The New Mestiza* (San Francisco: Aunt Lute Press, 1987); Alicia Arrizón, *Queering Mestizaje: Transculturation and Performance* (Ann Arbor: University of Michigan Press, 2006); Shane T. Moreman, "Memoir as Performance: Strategies of Hybrid Ethnic Identity," *Text and Performance Quarterly* 29, no. 4 (October 2009): 346–66; Kate G. Willink, Robert Gutierrez-Perez, Salma Shukri, and Lacey Stein, "Navigating with the Stars: Critical Qualitative Methodological Constellations for Critical Intercultural Communication Research," *Journal of International and Intercultural Communication* 7, no. 4 (October 2014): 289–316.

32. Michael Hames-García, "Jotería Studies, or the Political Is Personal," *Aztlán: A Journal of Chicano Studies* 39, no. 1 (2014): 136.

33. Aida Hurtado, "Sitios y Lenguas: Chicanas Theorize Feminisms," *Hypatia* 13, no. 2 (1998): 134–61.

34. Aída Hurtado, "Theory in the Flesh: Toward an Endarkened Epistemology," *International Journal of Qualitative Studies in Education* 16, no. 2 (2003): 215.

35. Anzaldúa, *Reader*, 321.

36. Cherríe Moraga and Gloria Anzaldúa, eds., *This Bridge Called My Back: Writings by Radical Women of Color*, 4th ed. (New York: Kitchen Table, 2015), 19.

37. D. Soyini Madison, " 'That Was My Occupation': Oral Narrative, Performance, and Black Feminist Thought," *Text and Performance Quarterly* 13, no. 3 (July 1993): 214.

38. Ernesto Javier Martínez, *On Making Sense: Queer Race Narratives of Intelligibility* (Stanford, CA: Stanford University Press, 2013).

39. Daniel Enrique Pérez, "Jotería Epistemologies," *Aztlán: A Journal of Chicano Studies* 39, no. 1 (2014): 143–54; Anita Tijerina Revilla and José Manuel Santillana, "Jotería Identity and Consciousness," *Aztlán: A Journal of Chicano Studies* 39, no. 1 (2014): 167–80.

40. Patricia Hill Collins, *Black Feminist Thought: Knowledge, Consciousness, and the Politics of Empowerment* (New York: Routledge, 2000), 28–9.

41. Hill Collins, *Black Feminist Thought*, 289.

42. Crenshaw, Kimberle, "Mapping the Margins: Intersectionality, Identity Politics, and Violence Against Women of Color," *Stanford Law Review* 43 (1991): 1241–99.

43. Michael Hames-García, *Identity Complex: Making the Case for Multiplicity* (Minneapolis: University of Minnesota Press, 2011).

44. Bernadette Marie Calafell, "(I)dentities: Considering Accountability, Reflexivity, and Intersectionality in the I and the We," *Liminalities: A Journal of Performance Studies* 9, no. 2 (April 2013): 6–13; Hill Collins, *Black Feminist Thought*; Haneen Ghabra, "Disrupting Privileged and Oppressed Spaces: Reflecting Ethically on my Arabness through Feminist Autoethnography," *Kaleidoscope: A Graduate Journal of Qualitative Communication Research* 14 (2015): 1–16; Richard G. Jones and Bernadette Marie Calafell, "Contesting Neoliberalism Through Critical Pedagogy, Intersectional Reflexivity, and Personal Narrative: Queer Tales of Academia," *Journal of Homosexuality* 59, no. 7 (August 2012): 957–81.

45. Anzaldúa, *Reader*; Robert Gutierrez-Perez, "Monstrosity in Everyday Life: Nepantleras, Theories in the Flesh, and Transformational Politics," *The Popular Culture Studies Journal* 6, nos. 2 & 3 (2018), 345–368.

46. Moraga and Anzaldúa, *This Bridge*, 19.

47. Sandra Faulkner, *Poetry as Method: Reporting Research Through Verse* (Walnut Creek, CA: Left Coast Press, 2009), 16–7.

48. Faulkner, *Poetry as Method*, 20.

49. María Cristina González, "The Four Seasons of Ethnography: A Creation-Centered Ontology for Ethnography," *International Journal of Intercultural Relations* 24, no. 5 (2000): 623–50.

50. Muñoz, *Disidentifications*.

51. Martínez, *On Making Sense*, 13–14.

52. Bernadette Marie Calafell, *Monstrosity, Performance, and Race in Contemporary Culture* (New York: Peter Lang, 2015).

Part One:

Borderlands Narratives and Snapshots of Jotería-Historias

Remembering Jotería

Voyagers
gather the blood vessels
pumping arteries into capillaries
spongy foreskin   pulled back
brown tasting
like caterpillar nights
inching up a cool blade of grass
fingers   stroking up and down
a pre-Columbian
milky way

Sacred fire
bring white-hot charcoal dreams
bring shamanic might
scald us
red

burning
heartbeats cracking
purple twilight
glowing

la luna voyeuristic
tall grass like the sea
nibbling my two-spirit
feathers
daring to pluck
each one gently
rolling down hillsides
our bodies in a turbulent cycle
    cresting waves
        barely missing destruction
        noses above water
        salt tightening throat
around memories
corrupted
made far-fetched
made un-American

It feels right
trusting myths of Joto elders
who tell their own histories:
                stoned dead
                made into slaves
                stricken with plague
                picking your grapes
                sin papeles
because they give you pride
in your holes
chords stretched open
a chorus singing
burdened
libre

1

Decolonizing Communication Studies—A Borderlands Lens to Narrative Theory

Sitting on an Amtrak train, my mind, like this transportation vehicle, is racing through landscapes and feelings while carrying people and their problems. Burdened with my own issues, I am heading to visit my mother in the central valley of California. She just kicked out my stepfather and is applying for a divorce (or is she?). I have reflected before on the intersectional power structures that undergird the law and everyday life when it comes to <marriage>.[1] Although I should feel love, I don't—I feel anger. Old fears of abandonment and betrayal have reared their head because you (my mother) are still being selfish, and as the oldest, it is my job to snap you out of your self-destructive denial. The weight of growing up too soon because you are my friend but not my parent reminds me that navigating my "racial/ethnic mestizaje alongside my bisexual-gay-queer identities in tandem with my working-class positionality [makes] performing and understanding my particular manifestation of masculinity a difficult and nearly impossible task."[2] My whole life has been affected by your bipolar disorder and YOUR choices not my stepfather's, and I refuse to let you be a victim. Yet, I can't let him off the hook either.

This isn't a new route for me physically or metaphorically. As a Chicano, there is a political and historical ideological overlap with indigenous peoples, so my ancestors have always moved from north to south and back following familial lines of power across the U.S. Southwest, or Aztlan.[3] This is not my land; how-ever, Chicanismo has a connection to this migratory pattern. After several hours of drinks and singing sad love songs in a local gay bar called Alibi, you told me that you were afraid of me coming to visit you. I told you that I was afraid to come, but we need to have this plática. As I wrote in my letter to you on March 17, 2019 (St. Patrick's Day):

> I feel like I have barely any communication or commitment from you, yet you want me to listen to you cry over this selfish liar? You are feeling suicidal over a man who couldn't put food on the table, who couldn't provide a roof over your head, who brought out and fed off the worst parts of you (addictive behavior, stealing, drug use, physical, mental, and verbal abuse, anger, neglect, and depres-sion), whose own two children hate him and will probably not let him have a relationship with his grandchildren, who broke your trust in a way that he knew would hurt you the most,[4] who can't admit when he is wrong, who doesn't sleep next to you or share resources with you, who demanded 100% of your attention at the expense of missing your two youngest children's childhood, and who you chose over a relationship with me. I can't begin to explain the pain that our relationship for the past 20 years and longer has caused me. I can handle being kicked out of my house one week after turning 18, but I refuse at this point to feel sad that this leech/virus/parasite is no longer freeloading off of you in your parents' house.

You may feel like this cuento should not be told or that my (un)intentional choices have formed our relationship into a structure not of your design, but there is a risk and vulnerability when it comes to telling cuentos. A part of me hopes that my mom never reads this book.

Indeed, there is an ethical dilemma that occurs when speaking for the other.[5] Mom, how can I speak with you and not for you? How can I speak about myself in ways that acknowledge my privileges and oppressions? My shadows obscure how power moves through my body, yet I am empowered in this location in space and time as a communicative interlocutor creating various realities with my symbol making.[6] In the end, storytelling, narratives, and other oral traditions are about power, culture, and history.[7] In discussing the turn to performance in narrative theory, Peterson and Langellier note how narratives are embodied in the practice of communication that "requires bodily participation in listening and speaking, reading and writing, seeing and gesturing, and feeling and being touched."[8] Further, narratives are "constrained by situational and material condi-tions,"[9] as well as "embedded in and ordered by fields of discourse."[10] This means that narratives are "strategically distributed to reproduce and critique existing relations of power and knowledge."[11] Telling stories or narratives is essential to how human beings communicate, and, therefore, the stories that are told and not told (and how they are told) become the everyday materials in which socio-cultural reality is created.

Mom, I feel neglect and abuse, so I am naming our relationship as a culture of lovelessness.[12] It is because "narrative is a communication practice, a conduct of the lived body and not something the body records, processes, or contains"[13] that I am writing and telling this cuento. I do this not out of spite, but in order to heal, we have to open the wound; clean it out; feel the stinging, icy taste of air hitting our vulnerability and pain (our humanity); stitch it up like a flesh shoelace; and then, accept that it will be a scar (a process of mental and psychic healing in its own right!).[14] I'm tired. I feel cynical and nihilistic about our future and the future of the world. No one said that loving each other would be easy, but here we are on the page together. What path will you choose? I hate that you don't know me.

Shifting into the Borderlands of Narrative Theory

Focusing on borderlands narratives, I locate theories in the flesh within the every-day lives of Jotería to remember the embodied performances of resistance dynam-ically created, shared, and remembered through cuentos, pláticas, chismé, mitos, testimonios, and consejos, all of which I will define and describe in more depth below. Narrative theory and criticism have developed from multiple perspectives across the subdisciplines of rhetoric, organizational communication, health com-munication, and critical/cultural communication,[15] and as a dialogic, contested, and aesthetic performance, narratives are embodied acts of storytelling that involve a performer and audience whether in person, published, spoken, or via the Internet.[16] However, as Horacio N. Roque Ramírez, the late LGBTQ Latino oral historian, discusses: "You get very hungry to know more of the history . . . because we're dealing with a community of color in the U.S. where a lot of them are immigrants, many of them are undocumented, and they're queer bodies."[17] Given the community and the theoretical commitment to locating theories in the flesh in everyday life, this project shifts to a borderlands lens for the collection and (re)membering of historical narratives, and as such, GBTQ Chicanx and Latinx narratives are theorized throughout this project as performative, intersec-tionally queer, and ultimately, decolonial acts.

Shifting to performance means that narrative is both a doing and a making.[18] I quote Eric Peterson and Kristin Langellier at length to describe the performance/performative of narrative that I am discussing:

> Narrative is performative in that the bodily capability for narrating constitutes or realizes a narrative (what is done) by its exercise (the doing); and narrative is performance in that the bodily ability to narrate brings into existence or actualizes one possible narrative rather than others (something made) and that is distinct from the activity itself (the making).[19]

In the case of this book, the bodies performing narratives of resistance and agency are historically marginalized within an intersectional structure whose vectors and kinesis are difficult to navigate and survive in every life. Collecting and remembering the historical narratives of queer of color bodies means coming to terms with the fact that this community is under attack but is powerful, and the situational and material conditions of this community are ordered by intersectional structures of power. Indeed, intersectionality is a "critical hermeneutics that register[s] the copresence of sexuality, race, class, gender, and other identity differentials as particular components that exist simultaneously with one another."[20] Meaning narratives not only do and make, but also "they recite, repeat, and represent . . . narrative forms already circulating in local communities and in popular culture."[21] Narratives circulate through the participation of the body in the communicative acts of listening, speaking, reading, writing, seeing, gesturing, feeling, and being touched.[22]

Through this viewpoint, the storyteller (me), narrator (interviewees), characters (people and institutions), and audience (you) are always already embedded socially and culturally in communication practices. A queer approach to identity and narrative research is necessary because the narratives included in and between (and beyond) this book are not neutral, transparent, or fixed.[23] These narratives are historical and just as much queer as they are raced, classed, and gendered. Acknowledging these narratives as a queer act is also about putting my own body on the line with/for the GBTQ Chicanxs and Latinxs that I researched because I *am* a GBTQ Chicano. I am Jotería. Additionally, the intersectional nature of storytelling acknowledges that narrative can reinforce *and* resist master narratives simultaneously and in a multiplicity of forms and contexts.[24] Thus, this ontological shift aligns narrative theory with theories in the flesh in that both can serve as forms of oppositional discourse or counternarrative.[25] Specifically, I contend that GBTQ Chicanx/Latinx historical narratives can be understood as decolonial acts of resistance and agency. What do we lose when we refuse to (re) member our Jotería?

(Re)membering as a Decolonial Act

(Re)membering a history of conflict and coalition is an active act that draws tactics of resistance from historical narratives "dis-membered by a history of ideological violence."[26] In the case of Jotería, these narratives of the subaltern disrupt the "habitual and habituating [colonial] patterns of behavior" that are constrained by modern "situational and material conditions," which are "ordered by multiple and dispersed discursive practices and conventions."[27] Therefore, locating Jotería theories in the flesh emerges from an "understanding [that] something as vast as the colonial/modern world system can begin with the glances exchanged between two cholos at a bar."[28] Remembering historical and cultural expressions of postcolonial queer subjectivities articulates a borderlands space in experiential, embodied, and intersectional configurations, and further, remembering is about pervasively proliferating, multiplying, consolidating, and dispersing these historical articulations toward the goal of social justice.[29] Lisa Flores, a rhetorician focused on race and gender, explains, "remembering the past is not about cultural separatism but about reenvisioning the future through the past so as to assure survival."[30] As a purposeful act focused on the goal of "connecting bodies with place and experience, and, importantly, people's responses to that pain,"[31] remembering the borderlands narratives of Jotería is a decolonial act that pushes back on master narratives of culture, history, and identity.

Moreover, as a decolonial act of resistance and agency, remembering is equally concerned with membering those marginalized or subaltern voices with an ethic of care that speaks to/with subaltern voices and not for.[32] As an example, in colonial Mexico, a mestizaje culture emerged where Spanish, African, and Indigenous American ideologies and biologies intermingled yet never fully integrated. Maricón is a derogatory Spanish word for a gay man, similar to the English word "fag," and it is often utilized in speech acts to insult, threaten, assault, or question the sexuality of Jotería. After the first contact, the conquest of Mexico became synonymous with not only religious conquest but also with sexual conquest.[33] Quoting Esteva-Fabregat, Alicia Arrizón writes,

> in countries ruled by Spain, conquistadors, motivated by their insatiable sexual appetite for Indian women and their incredible sense of power as colonizers,

frequently accumulated large numbers of concubines ... by the end of the six-
teenth century, mestizos were a new majority.[34]

Further, "before the conquest, there were twenty-five million Indian people in
Mexico and the Yucatán. Immediately after the conquest, the Indian population
had been reduced to under seven million."[35] The combination of mass penetra-
tion/rape/concubinage of Native women and increased indigenous death due to
disease and violence created a racial mixing that led to the emergence and proliferation of the mestiza/o.[36] As an epicenter of transculturation and violent conquest,
this historical moment of multiple worlds negotiating, contesting, and breathing
culture and co-creating society indicates the utility of gathering Jotería-historias
and the intersectional and multiplicitous topography Jotería interlocutors have
had to navigate in order to avoid murder and violence. This is our story but
not our story, so remembering Jotería-historias is a decolonial act that critically
speaks back to this history of violence, which includes demanding the membership of Jotería in places of knowledge production and leadership.

From a historical perspective, this topography included the Spanish empire
and their implementation of a complex and intricate racial caste system that
increased from six categories to more than 16 racial categories by the end of
Spanish rule in the early 1800s.[37] This racial, ethnic, religious, and cultural mixing or mestizaje also grappled with several sexual ideologies during the times of
conquest and colonialism. There are few glimpses into what nonheteronormative
mestiza/o life would have been like in Spanish colonial times, yet through court
records, it's known that homosexuality and sodomy were punished by stiff fines,
spiritual (Catholic) penances, public humiliation, floggings, or death. "Thus
a different identity was born in the minds of the Hispanized Nahuas. Now a
hybrid figure that combined the Hispanic puto, the seductive African man, and
perhaps the Nahua cuiloni emanated from the fulcrum of the colonial enter-
prise."[38] Murray explains how, during the Spanish Inquisition between 1656 and
1663, mass executions of homosexuals occurred in Mexico City in a part of the
city called San Lázaro. After the Mexican independence from Spain in 1821, "the
intellectual influence of the French Revolution and the brief French occupation
of Mexico (1862–67) resulted in the adoption of the French legal code, in which
sodomy was not a crime."[39] Although this did not allow for overt homosexuality,
a covert underground sub-culture for maricones did emerge during the neocolonial Porfirian regime (1876–1911).[40]

Given that narrative "moves away from singular, monolithic conception[s] of
social science towards a pluralism that promotes multiple forms of representation

and research,"[41] this book embraces a borderlands lens to narrative theory that remembers and members Jotería historical narratives to better reflect the cultural complexities of the community from which these narratives originated. Jotería borderlands narratives do not simply need to be included in popular and scholarly conversations surrounding culture, history, and power, which is a decolonial act in and of itself, but additionally, membering these narratives means allowing the cultural norms, beliefs, and values of the subaltern to dictate the theories and methods of analysis and presentation on their own terms. This commitment to genuine conversation to and with Jotería is a stance that is dialogic in nature as a means to navigate the "performative plunder, superficial silliness, curiosity-seeking and nihilism" of research.[42]

Intersectionality in the Micro, Meso, and Macro

In the following sections, I define and provide an example for each of the narrative forms under analysis across this project's collected chapters to further explicate my borderlands lens to narrative theory; yet, my understanding of borderlands narrative theory is heavily influenced by intersectional theory developed by women of color feminisms, critical and cultural theory, and communication as performance theory. By this, I mean that I view power as fluid, dynamic, and contested across multiple dimensions of identity and discourses and at multiple levels of hegemonic systems of oppression and privilege (micro, meso, and macro) that move through communication to create societies, cultures, and identities of predication, control, and domination. An intersectional "matrix of domination"[43] that functions as if natural, normal, and everyday when, in fact, it is voluntary, abnormal, and embodied in our collective and individual choices about how to communicate reality to each other. In this section, I explicate this theory of intersectionality, as it is key to every theoretical lens utilized by each method offered to study Jotería communication studies within this book. After this critical discussion of power and communication, I apply intersectionality to shift and remember narratives of borderlands interlocutors as emerging from and inscribed into the body, (re)producing knowledge in particular forms of oral tradition, and intrinsically involved in power, identity construction, and cultural production.

Intersectionality is a method, a disposition, a heuristic, and an analytic tool.[44] Additionally, it is a "way of understanding and analyzing the complexity in the world, in people, and in human experience" and clarifies six core ideas: inequality, relationality, power, social context, complexity, and social justice.[45] For this book, I envision intersectionality as a theory of oppression and privilege that allows a rhetor or critic or researcher to analyze power as it fluidly and dynamically moves through communication to exert control and domination. Intersectionality, as a contested and socially constructed process, understands power as mutually constructed, as operating across relations via their intersections and across structural, disciplinary, cultural, and interpersonal domains of power.[46] An intersectional relationality shifts away from difference-based approaches rooted in either/or binary thinking to a both/and approach that locates interconnections within a communication context.[47] Further, I deploy intersectional analyses from a distinctly queer intercultural communication lens, which reorients toward a focus on "thick intersectionalities" or relationalities in/through multiple registers of power difference, such as queering/quaring/kauering/crippin'/transing.[48]

As a theory and method, intersectionality is multidimensional; meaning, intersectionality is rooted in a deep understanding and appreciation for body epistemology, or embodied knowledge. Following Fassett and Warren, embodied knowledge recognizes that there is no body/mind split, and in fact, the mind/brain is an intimate and essential part of the body.[49] Further, according to the authors, the body knows and contains knowledge, the body is constantly communicating to others and to oneself, and regardless of whether one listens to the body or not, the body learns and gathers knowledge about reality. Given the immense amount of literature that validate the existence of body epistemology or embodied knowledge,[50] intersectionality as it is deployed here interrogates identity and identity construction, including the historical/political processes in which norms, values, and beliefs about race, gender, sexuality, religion, nation, and class are socially constructed and deeply connected to the conquest and colonization of indigenous lands and peoples.[51] This process is articulated as a modern-colonial gender system that perpetuates these socially constructed categories and the hegemonic systems of control that are overtly and covertly deployed by this system of social organizing. According to philosopher Maria Lugones, who termed this process, this "categorial, dichotomous, hierarchical logic [is] central to modern, colonial, capitalistic thinking about race, gender, and sexuality,"[52] so in my theorizing of intersectionality, I focus on the body as a site of knowledge and knowledge-generation because the body is multidimensional with multileveled influence yet remains mobile, fluid, and dynamically contested. If one has a body, then given the modern-colonial gender system, one is interpellated into the politics of identity, including the internal-external contestation of managing personally avowed and socially ascribed identities.

In this living matrix of domination,[53] the micro level is a multidimensional nucleus of identity and identity negotiation, specifically race, class, gender, sexuality, religion, ability, nationality, and age. Further, after teaching intersectionality for a decade in public speaking and intercultural, gender, and critical communication undergraduate and graduate courses, my students have (depending on the object or subject of study) included ethnicity, educational level, language, and geographic location as other possible dimensions within this micro level of intersectional analysis. The micro level as an analytic lens locates an object or subject of study within relations of power because "people find themselves encountering different treatment regarding which rules apply to them and how those rules will be implemented . . . power operates by disciplining people in ways that put people's lives on paths that make some options seem viable and others out of reach."[54] As a critical/cultural communication studies scholar, I know that the everyday communicative lives of interlocutors are a complex, enduring, and contested phenomenon. Take the dimension of race within this matrix of domination, and you will immediately encounter scholarship showing how this dimension is a hegemonic process of indoctrination into White supremacist ideology, which is a fundamental, consequential aspect of identity yet also a source of cultural pride and social organizing.[55] Interlocutors are vulnerable to internal oppression and pervasive systemic violence not only because of this socially constructed hierarchy of race, but also because this process is mitigated and radically interconnected to all other dimensions and levels.[56] This is all to say that narrative and performance theory are well-positioned theoretical lines of thought to intersectionally analyze and research interlocutors and social phenomenon in the microlevel as identity and identity construction are vital to communication theory.

In the meso, I draw on the work of Antonio Gramsci to flesh out this level of intersectionality as hierarchies of hegemonic control. Hegemony is defined as "domination through consent" or a process of struggle, a "war of position," a "reciprocal siege," and as a philosophy-enabling and constraining social agents in historically situated contexts and social self-understandings that have material and symbolic sociopolitical power manifestations.[57] The meso level embraces the fact that "power relations are about people's lives, how people relate to one another, and who is advantaged or disadvantaged within social interaction."[58] Like Gramsci, I view hegemony as different from dominant ideology in that hegemony "presupposes an active and practical involvement of hegemonized groups, quite unlike the static, totalizing and passive subordination implied by the dominant ideology concept."[59] Further, hegemony is the "process of granting a group with more power and privilege the ability to shape our worldviews, attitudes, beliefs, expectations, and actions."[60] Specifically, I am addressing the social construction of racism, classism, sexism and cissexism, heterosexism and heteronormativity, religious intolerance, ableism, nationalism, and ageism as hierarchies of hegemonic control. Given the connection between the body and identity, the meso level draws on the critical theory of hegemony to explain how hierarchies of control develop individually yet collectively across each dimension of identity in the micro. Because interlocutors within bodies with identities must negotiate and/or consent to their own domination to navigate the various restrictive and ideological state apparatuses that each communicative context demands of their flesh, the meso is about relationality and how these hierarchies of hegemonic control are socially constructed through human communication.

Another way to think about this meso level through language and communication is how I know and identify myself as Chicanx. The historical existence of Latino and Hispanic identities operating in popular culture and media construct our racial identities in forms that reinforce hegemonic systems of racial and ethnic hierarchies that silence and erase how one might know and understand oneself as Chicanx. Raced understandings of Latino/Chicano/Xicano sexuality, gender, class, ability, age, and more move fluidly and contextually in tandem with how Others who do not claim these identities perform their own identities (and vice versa).[61] This example shows how identity and identity construction in the micro interact in a bidirectional process where meso-level hierarchies of control intersectionally are communicated through language and relationality.

For me, the choice to utilize the method of performative writing to hail multiple interlocutors is another example of the meso in language and communication. Writing about research names oneself and claims a space for empowerment for Jotería through the act of self-identification and claiming voice. Performative writing, which sometimes includes getting rid of grammar and style rules, is also deployed in this book as a decolonial move meant to blur the performance of writing and to do something on the page that changes how images and metaphors function. Decolonization "entails dismantling colonial systems of power and knowledge. Colonial systems take many forms; they structure and shape the economy, educational institutions, churches, and the food system."[62] Even the choices about whether or when to italicize Spanish words or not is part of the performative writer's rhetorical and discursive politics doing work at the meso level with bidirectional implications at the micro, meso, and macro level. In general, I like to not italicize Spanish words, but inevitably, I cite quotations with Spanish that do italicize, and in that case, I will typically leave the italics. This cultural contestation through language and style choice is essentially about identity and how italicizing Spanish words in English publications makes Spanish appear as different or Other, which continues racial practices of exclusion in the very writing of research. This is a process of hegemonic control to establish hierarchies and either/or thinking within the production of knowledge. The practice of not italicizing is a means to push back on this modern-colonial practice of how knowledge is constructed and who is a knowledge producer in Western systems of knowledge generation. Yet, Spanish is a colonial language of conquest and domination, so either way both English and Spanish are colonizing forces in writing and research. It is only by blurring genre/identity/social boundaries, breaking and remaking temporality, and playing language games in the very writing of research that you can enact a decoloniality through the act of writing. I am trying to achieve a borderlands (both/and/neither/or) aesthetic throughout the book. The historical impulses and affective registers that catalyzed the politics of Jotería are revealed in the telling and retelling of borderlands narratives. This book highlights how narratives of identity construction are vehicles for transmitting theories in the flesh that help Jotería navigate the historical/political hegemonic terrain of decoloniality in the meso.

Intersectionality embraces complexity, and the macro level "highlights the significance of social institutions in shaping and solving social problems."[63] This macroscopic level is focused on social organizations, including hidden and destabilizing historical, social, and political aspects of the cultural context.[64] As Halualani, Mendoza, and Drzeweicka write,

> culture needs to be understood both in its enduring sedimentations (the deposits and traces left by historical contestations) and in its radical transformations and itineraries as it travels and enters into translations within specific localized contexts and toward differing goals.[65]

To do this, I utilize the work of Louis Althusser to name these social institutions within what he terms "restrictive state apparatuses" (RSAs) and "ideological state apparatuses" (ISAs), which I also connect to Critical Race Theory (CRT).[66] Over the course of a decade, my students have added other social institutions to their understanding of intersectionality, specifically medical institutions like hospitals, clinics, and other health service organizations. Specifically, RSAs are heads of state, police, military, prisons, courts, and government, which are social structures that can literally grab your body and force it to do things. Whereas, ISAs are schools, banks, churches, family, friends, law, and media, which are insidious social structures that discipline ideology into bodies toward the goal of hegemonic control. I name these ISAs and RSAs throughout the book to critique, resist, and name the macro structures under analysis. I encourage the reader to connect these borderlands narratives to the micro, meso, and macro as a means to relate and generate new relationalities to language, communication, and written text. Moving intersectionally between identity, culture, and society, the remainder of this chapter is dedicated to explicating the borderlands narratives of cuentos, pláticas, chismé, mitos, testimonios, and consejos, which will be the primary vehicles of knowledge-generation throughout this book—sometimes noted for the reader and other times left for the reader to note for themselves.

Borderlands Narratives

"Let us not be afraid of who we are. We were made exactly the way we were meant to be."[67]

As of late, this consejo has meant a lot to me because the current historical and political moment requires that all of my low self-esteem issues and fears of abandonment need to finally be handled. Because of my relationship with my parents, I am a person who is especially sensitive to and afraid of betrayal and abandonment. Mom, I realize now that I hold a lot of resentment toward you. In not sharing my hurt and perspective, I did not allow you to share your hurt and perspective. We have lost so much time with all these expectations. For too long, I have blamed my mother for "kicking me out of the house" just a few short days after turning 18 in the month of May. That memory of a June graduation from high school without a home to return to after the ceremony haunts me. I am a Taurus, and like my sign, I can be very stubborn and set in my ways; and, here I am twenty years later still holding onto this moment of trauma like an old friend. Didn't I also co-construct this moment when, instead of letting things cool down, I cut school at lunch and packed all my stuff in the '92 Ford Escort that used to be my grandmother's and left? I am your son after all. How did you think I would react? Mom, I hope you will never read this, but if you do, I am sorry for sharing our secret cuentos. I hope you understand that I am trying to articulate the need for a shift in narrative theory to the borderlands. I am trying to embody research in the writing of research.

Cuentos

Cuentos are cultural stories told and retold as a form of collective memory that often serve a pedagogical function. As deployed in this book, cuentos are stories of survival and resistance for and to marginalized people that often challenge master narratives about a community. For example, in many Chicana/o communities, the corrido, or the revolutionary ballad, is a musical/lyrical form of telling stories about the everyday experiences of being Mexican, Mexican-American, and/or Chicana/o. These cuentos told through song are lessons that re-interpret, re-member, and re-tell history through a borderlands lens that reflect the values, beliefs, and norms of the culture. Stereotypes that Mexicans are lazy, dumb, and/or dirty are directly challenged through the highly accessible cuento, and stories of hardworking campesinos, struggling first-generation college students, and respected elders and ancestors are passed down as correctives to dominant master narratives of a community or group of people.[68] Cultural stories, like the opening narrative of this section, share how we survive, who and why we love and hate, how we feel joy and fear, and how we deal with violence and trauma in our lives. In this book, narratives that invoke cultural identity and/or the process of cultural identity construction are considered cuentos.

As a kind of folk history, these cuentos are cultural in that they describe how the interlocutor came to understand and name themselves. Additionally, these cuentos are historical in that one's identity is mutually constitutive. Hames-García describes mutual constitution as "rather than existing as essentially separate axes that sometime intersect, social identities blend, constantly and differently, expanding one another and mutually constituting meanings."[69] When encountering a cuento, the narrative hails and must be interpreted through the aforementioned matrix of domination that includes Latino, Xicano, Anglo, Black, and Native American identities (and more). Further,

> while making our stories known, it is poignant to remember that our stories do not exist by themselves and are instead interconnected to those who could not previously tell their stories due to either shame, silence, lack of agency, blackmail, discrimination, embarrassment, or any combination thereof. As such, stories illuminate the oftentimes painful experiences that we would rather have remain in the margins of history.[70]

Indeed, the reader/listener of cuentos and her/his/their positionality to the cuento can only be understood through this characteristic of mutual constitution in the

formulation of an intersectional identity. Cuentos offer an avenue for the reader/
listener to enter Jotería worlds that exist alongside the master narrative.

For example, as I have written about elsewhere, conceptions of passivo and
activo are often conflated with effeminacy and class positionality where skin pigmentation (i.e., race and ethnicity) is a perceived determinate of the performed
sexual or gender role.[71] Passivo (passive) and activo (active) describe positions
during anal sex, and further, a passivo is considered the more effeminate of the
coupling.[72] To be passivo is an ultimate shame (within this cultural logic) because
it is believed that you are less than a woman. Unlike a woman who has "no
choice," you had a choice, and you chose effeminacy. Chicana and Mexicana
women are often locked in a virgin-whore dichotomy that restricts the possibilities for women within Latino culture. Moreover, men are expected to be macho,
central in all aspects of life, and deeply sexual, while women are supposed to be
self-sacrificing, passive, and without sexuality.[73] The history of conquest and colonialism in which Indigenous and Mestizo men and women were made passive
and subordinate to the Spanish furthers the cultural dislike of passivity in men.[74]
Whereas the passivo is shamed, reviled, and open to physical/emotional/spiri-
tual violence from the heteronormative structure, the conflation of effeminacy
with a specific sexual position creates an interesting gender-inflected hierarchy for
Jotería to navigate where the activo can maintain a masculine identity and avoid
affronts to their social standing.

Essentially, there are two sexual ideologies operating contextually that create
a complex landscape to navigate. Irwin explains that one ideology defines male
homosexuality "according to sexual object: men, whether masculine or effeminate, who desire other men, whether masculine or effeminate, are regarded as
homosexuals."[75] This ideology is in line with dominant constructions of homosexuality in the U.S., yet this second sexual ideology does not compete with this
dominant construction but rather coexists alongside it in hegemonic tension.[76]
Irwin continues his explanation,

> the other view defines it [homosexuality] according to sexual aim: men who
> wish to be women, who want to play "the woman's role" in sex, who desire to be
> penetrated by other men, are homosexuals, while men who penetrate other men
> remain men, untainted by homosexuality.[77]

In this ideological construction, an activo as the "agent of action" is thought to be
"an hombre macho, a real victor, and to him went the spoils of his conquest, that
is, sexual dominance of a passive object."[78] As stated earlier, sexual domination

of a passive object is deeply connected to the conquest of Mexico and machismo, and, therefore, "the sex (male or female) of the object of penetration is immaterial" as long as one is the activo penetrator.[79] Under these circumstances, homosexuality is acceptable in certain contexts, yet the activo is only able to avoid stigmatization on the basis of gender; he is still seen as a male, but only by other males, rarely from women, and never from mainstream society.[80] Chicanos/Xicanos and members of the Jotería community have internalized these viewpoints and externally perform varying degrees of this ideological continuum, depending on the environment, the people, and the dominant cultural logic.

In other words, I've met, been desired by, and been physically intimate with men who, afterward, still consider themselves straight because of the sexual act performed during sex, yet other men who do not accept this ideology have deeply questioned their sexual orientation with all the confusion and self-exploration that this questioning entails. In this case, coexisting sexual ideologies maintain patriarchy by adhering to gendered understandings of dominance and/or internally defending the status quo to maintain a dominant perception of oneself in society. Jotería must navigate this fluid and contextual terrain every day as part of their labor of intelligibility. While maintaining performances of masculinity and sexuality that keep us safe, we must still find ways to express our sexual desire. This is a labor of survival and resistance that Jotería have undertaken throughout history. In the telling and remembering of Jotería cuentos throughout this book, I am engaging in queer of color critique in that I am offering queer of color worldmaking that exists alongside the hetero/homonormative master narrative.

Pláticas

Pláticas translates as "chats/talks," and many Chicana feminists have engaged these "intimate conversations" as a method for locating resistance in the everyday lives of the subaltern.[81] Pláticas gather familial and cultural knowledge through the act of communication, and oftentimes, this narrative form produces knowledge by sharing thoughts, memories, ambiguities, and new interpretations through personal and group conversations.[82] For example, as an insider/outsider, I am aware that my communication with Jotería are intimate affairs because there are certain topics, areas of interests, and performances that only emerge when in communication with other Jotería. These pláticas reveal not only areas of mutual recognition with other cultures and identities, but in this historical moment, these narrative forms also showcase the communicative spaces where Jotería and

Latinas/os generate knowledge and where/how they choose to politically and materially push back on master narratives.[83]

This project highlights pláticas as a tactical space where Jotería mobilize for political projects; critically interrogate silence, silenced bodies, and experiences of voicelessness; and create intimate connections. Jotería and Jotería studies are connected and participate in the historical and political context of the U.S. Southwest and beyond, and in this book, the pláticas or chats/talks from the everyday life of Jotería are considered knowledge and spaces of knowledge generation. For example, Jotería studies in the field of education showcases the utility of pláticas as a research method, a theoretical framework, and a communicative space where knowledge is created.[84] Further, within the tradition of Curanderismo, there is special place for consejeras who utilize heart-to-heart chats or pláticas as a primary means through which care and healing is mediated.[85] In a plática amongst senior scholars discussing Latina/o/x communication studies, Calafell writes: "We need to turn to theories that help us understand lived experiences intersectionally and allow us to deal with colonial trauma."[86] Pláticas, like those collected and shared in this book, contribute to this emerging theoretical and methodological conversation in Latina/o/x communication studies and Chicana/o and Latina/o studies.

Chismé

For Jotería, some of the only ways we learn about each other, especially in our early years, is through chismé (gossip/rumor), and, in many ways, chismé contributes to and constructs our daily labor of intelligibility. As one Jotería explains, "What we enjoyed most was the chismé, the gossip we could share with each other."[87] The labor of intelligibility is the "everyday labor of making sense of oneself and of making sense to others in contexts of intense ideological violence and interpersonal conflict."[88] The labor of making Jotería bodies and performances intelligible to others and to oneself is challenging because of "the systemic erasure of queer people of color from the social imaginary (i.e., they are simply not represented and therefore rarely thought of as important)."[89] Because of this absence, chismé becomes an important borderlands narrative that Jotería utilize to open up possibilities beyond the socio-cultural contexts in which our identities emerge. Further, chismé is a transport/conduit/connection from which historical knowledge is transmitted to and through Jotería across time and space. As a vehicle for narrating theories in the flesh, chismé or gossip/rumor is a narrative form that "allows for an infinity of other truths, whether or not these counter truths are substantiated."[90] Therefore, chismé can be emancipatory in that it can imagine other possibilities for Jotería, yet as a narrative form, gossip/rumor can be constraining for Jotería interlocutors.

Chismé has the potential to be harmful to Jotería when their bodies and performances are distorted or exploited in popular culture or the historical record through a "diminutive incorporation."[91] In other words, Jotería experiences are trivialized through a process of coercion in which, as long as they "remain entertaining, marginal, witty, and benign," they are allowed visibility.[92] This labor of intelligibility performed by Jotería is not motivated by a desire to "be recognized or accepted by society on society's terms," but rather, this labor is a form of resistance to dominant structures to insist that we are a people with agency—that we are not chingados (fucked ones).[93] As queer people of color struggle to be seen as "legitimate bearers of knowledge," we create theories in the flesh to "interpret [our] lives accurately," to "find community backup and solidarity," and to resist/survive multiple, interlocking oppressions that incite confusion and fear, normalize ridicule and violence, and actualize displacement through social isolation.[94] Chismé, analyzed through the labor of intelligibility undertaken by Jotería, becomes a historical/political battleground over the sign—who gets to define what it means to be a GBTQ Chicano? to be Latina/o? to be Jotería?

As an example of what researching Jotería-historias could potentially offer, I briefly recount the events surrounding the infamous "El Baile de los 41 Maricones" also known as the Dance of the 41 Faggots. Prior to 1901, Mexican male homosocial bonds were not viewed as homoerotic (in the modern sense), and gender was socially constructed into a binary of masculine and feminine with no other options. Heterosexuality and homosexuality, as medical terminology, were barely being introduced and forced onto the public from the scientific community, so erotics and affection between men (even if visible) were ignored.[95] For over 30 years, from 1877 to 1880 and from 1884 to 1911, Porfirio Díaz ruled Mexico as president with a strong hand. During this neocolonial era, Díaz "imposed strict political control, encouraged European and U.S. investment, and gave special influence to a group of positivist thinkers called Científicos."[96] By heralding in the external influences of Europe and the United States, this neocolonial moment allowed those elite Mexicans of the aristocracy and educated classes who traveled outside of Mexico to return with more liberal thoughts about sexuality, which also influenced modern-colonial conflations of fashion with masculinity.[97] After the events on November 20, 1901 (detailed below), newspaper reports capitalized and proliferated on the scandal of El Baile because many of the men were elites. Several corridos (folk songs) and illustrations transformed El Baile into popular legend and literature, and with these reports, songs, and illustrations, the infamous dance of the 41 maricones changed how Mexican masculinity and sexuality was viewed within a modernizing Mexican society.[98] However, the chismé is that there were actually 42 guests in attendance.

Ignacio de la Torre, Porfirio Díaz's son-in-law, was rumored to have attended El Baile de Los 41 Maricones, and "as the story goes, half the men were dressed as women, half as men" when the police raided the party yet only arrested the odd (not even) number of 41 men.[99] Ignacio de la Torre was rumored to have been the missing man because, supposedly, he was recognized by the police, and his identity was protected by/for Porfirio Díaz.[100] Not only did this event give rise to the number 41 becoming a symbol of Mexican male homosexuality,[101] but also, it created Mexican slang where "cuarenta y dos (number forty-two, the one who got away) refers to someone who is covertly passive (a male who is sexually receptive to other males)."[102] After immediately being jailed, these 41 Maricones were punished through a variety of humiliations.

In illustrations, the 41 were depicted as men with large mustaches in dresses, and these men were ridiculed repeatedly in newspapers over several weeks and months.[103] Further, many of these men were forced to sweep the streets in dresses, and all 41 were sent to do forced labor in the Yucatán.[104] Although some were able to pay fines to avoid the embarrassment of sweeping the streets, all were "inducted into the Twenty-fourth Battalion of the Mexican Army ... to dig ditches and clean latrines."[105] However,

> much of what we "know" comes from fictional accounts, and many presumably factual versions contradict each other .... The 41 themselves are never given the chance to speak; their history lies in the hands of critics and gossips who did not participate in or even witness what happened.[106]

Like most of history, Jotería experiences are remembered for us rather than with us. As I return again and again to this Jotería-historia, I desperately wish one of the 41 could tell me how they were treated, how they were able to survive, and what truly happened to them. What theories in the flesh were lost to us in that historical moment? What theories in the flesh are located in the borderlands narrative of chismé?

Mitos

As an illustration of mitos (myths/legends) for this book, I discuss the myth of Xochiquetzal (feathered flower of the maguey) and the scorpion and offer a brief analysis of this myth through the lens of Jotería studies. This mito is as follows:

> In the scorpion story, the [warrior] man went to the mountains to fast and, most important, refrain from any sexual activity. If he successfully maintained his vigil, the gods would give him the power to kill his enemies. Upon Xochiquetzal's successful seduction of the man, however, a warrior beheaded him and turned him into a scorpion . . . . In the tale of the scorpion we find a warning: a violation of a vow (in this case, the man's vow not to have sexual intercourse) can lead the gods to disempower you (turn you into a scorpion).[107]

Xochiquetzal, god/dess of nonprocreative sexuality and love, is an example of how there was a socially sanctioned place for nonheteronormative sexualities, intersex, and genderqueer persons prior to the Spanish conquest for Jotería.[108] Xochiquetzal was both male and female—called Xochipilli (prince of flowers) in her male form—and s/he is considered the deity of homosexuality.[109] Prior to the Spanish conquest, conceptions of male homosexuality had a place in Mexica society that did not involve the violent destruction of male homosexuals as a norm. In fact, a popular board game called Patolli, which was under the supervision of Xochipilli as a player, was played frequently in everyday life by elites and common folk alike in Mesoamerica. When a player rolled a "0," Xochipilli would "take" one of six offerings (maguey, gold, etc.), and this offering would be placed aside in a pile. Once one player had lost all six offerings, Xochipilli gifted all the offerings to the winner. Patolli had been played throughout Mesoamerica for over a millennium, and it was one of the first things outlawed by Catholic priests during the Spanish conquest and the colonial period that followed. Xochiquetzal was a principal god/dess within Aztec mytho-cosmology who served an important purpose in regulating cultural norms; in ceremonies for fertility, agriculture, and curing; and in everyday rituals.[110]

Indeed, there are no gendered pronouns in Nahuatl, and the word teotl (god) has no gender. So, the Aztec gods and goddesses, who did not live by human rules, did not follow the strict gender divisions that we now understand within the colonial-modern gender system.[111] Like most of the gods in the Aztec pantheon, s/he had a positive and negative aspect:

In Xochiquetzal's positive aspect, s/he was the deity of loving relationships and the god/dess of artistic creativity; it was said that nonreproductive love was like art—beautiful and rare. In his/her negative aspect, s/he was the deity of sexual destruction; s/he incited lust and rape, and inflicted people with venereal disease and piles.[112]

These aspects were not gendered in that the female was positive and the male was negative; rather, Xochipilli/Xochiquetzal were one dynamic being. For instance, Xochipilli, in a famous representation of the god/dess protected in the National Museum of Anthropology in Mexico City, is depicted wearing a mask with his legs crossed and happily singing while fully covered in flowers, psychotropic plants, hallucinogenic mushrooms, and animal skins.[113] The story of "The Flower and the Scorpion" has many cultural ramifications for Jotería studies and the everyday life of the ancient Mexica/Aztec.

First, there is the quotidian aspect of survival in the tale because, when/ if one was stung by a scorpion, then a curer/healer would recount this story to the afflicted man or woman, and the curer/healer would simulate or actually partake in sexual intercourse with that scorpion-stung person.[114] The curer, as Xochiquetzal, and the afflicted, as a conduit of scorpion, re-enact the ritual per-formance of the story to remind "the scorpion that, because he failed to maintain his vigil, he cannot kill this person."[115] In this case, the sex act of Xochiquetzal may have disempowered the man but offered salvation to humankind because scorpion stings were a regular and potentially dangerous everyday occurrence faced by the Mexica.[116] Second, this is not a story of chaste and puritanical sex-uality but, rather, a story of balance and a warning against excess. The Mexica believed in a spirituality that was radically interconnected with all things, so sexual acts in excess or in lack were potentially dangerous to society and the universe. A warrior who makes a vow of celibacy to maintain male potency is also maintaining balance with/in the cosmos, and to receive the blessings of the gods in warfare, he must take his vows and warrior role/duties solemnly as an act of spirituality. Although not necessarily a desired sexual act for Mexica males, homosexual acts were not understood as "sin," but rather, sex acts between men were accepted in certain ceremonies and rituals. In fact, male-male desire and sexual acts were accepted in moderation and balance, and not all same-sex inter-course was accepted the same way (i.e., being the receiver in the sex act was not as tolerated as being the inserter).[117]

In regard to Jotería studies, as a dual-gendered deity, Xochiquetzal's seduc-tion of a man offers an understanding of the place of male homosexuality in pre-conquest times. Cuiloni is a Nahautl word that "derives from 'someone/something taken,' and is clearly related to the anus, thus one taken from behind."[118] However, the literal translation behind the term is contested, and it has been speculated to mean sodomite, faggot, one who is fucked, queer, passive sodomite, or puto.[119] The cui- means "to take," and -oni is a passive modifier of a verb. So, cuiloni refers to the passive position in sodomy.[120] Further, the word tecuilonti means to "cause someone to do cuiloni" and thus refers to the "inserter" position during anal sex.[121] However, Pete Sigal notes how the sexual performance of cuiloyotl, or "sodomy, homosexuality, the act without which the cuiloni could not exist," within Nahuatl documents was viewed as deserving denigration but not the people themselves.[122] Homosexual acts were related to the gods, sacrifice, and ritual, and as a warrior/war-centric society, the Nahuas did not connect cuiloyotl to "sin" but connected the sexual act to excess.[123] As Sigal explains, cuiloni "would not reference an internalized sexual identity, but rather would specify a contextual set of sexual characteristics based upon one's actions at a given time, actions that presumably would require confession" to the Aztec goddess of excess, Tlazolteotl.[124] Although the receptive male was stigmatized, the Mexica placed an emphasis on the sexual act not the person, and as such, male same-sex acts and desire had a place within Aztec society. In other Native American spaces, neither the act nor the person were stigmatized, and like the Mexica, there was a place within society, culture, and the order of the cosmos.

Chicana feminists have often revisited and redeployed indigenous Mesoamerican myths to push back on heteropatriarchal structures within Chicano/Latino cultures. Cuentos of legendary and mythological figures, such as Coatlicue, Coyolxauhqui, Cihuacóatl, La Llorona, La Virgen de Guadalupe/Tonantzin, Tlazolteotl, and Malintzin Tenépal, record history, provide archetypes for other ways of being and thinking, push back on stereotypes, and so much more.[125] For instance, Grisel Gómez-Cano charts the historical record of the Mexica pilgrimage from Aztlán to the Mexico Basin alongside Mexica mitos of goddesses to track the slow move toward more patriarchal societal structures in Aztec society, and further, she connects these mitos through an anthropological approach to historical events and figures whose lives influenced the very creation of these goddesses and their various mitos.[126] For this project, mitos are understood as a form of sacred poetics performatively done/made by "religious actors" to "manage the often harsh and potentially overwhelming conditions they confront—the battle for survival and more, dignity, love, freedom—by deploying the most powerful weapons in their arsenal: signs, myths, rituals, narratives, and symbols."[127] The systemic erasure of myths, legends, and folk heroes and healers is a modern-colonial violence that robs Jotería of our history, culture, and religious poetics.

Mitos are narrative forms that serve "power as an ideological mechanism of social control, exploitation, and domination" and are "also effectively deployed in attempts to destabilize those very same forces by people who have access to only the bare resources that constitute conventional power."[128] However, mitos can entrap the everyday performances of culture and identity into tropes of monstrosity, so like other narrative forms, mitos have the potential to silence Jotería and reinforce dominant narratives of otherness and difference.[129] As a theory in the flesh, Luis León, a borderlands religious studies scholar, describes this social-historical ideological mechanism as a religious poetic:

> Through a strategy of performed and narrated religious discourse, tactics, and strategies, social agents change culturally derived meanings and, indeed, the order of the phenomenal world by rearranging the relationships among symbols and deftly inventing and reinventing the signification of symbols—especially those held sacred.[130]

To cope with the trauma of living in perpetual liminality due to their colonial condition, Chicanos often draw on these mitos of Mesoamerican gods and goddesses in their celebrations, art, and literary works to create worlds in the present that are more livable. How do Jotería utilize religious poetics to enact agency and resistance through the borderlands narrative of mitos?

Testimonios

Testimonios as a borderlands narrative form contain theories in the flesh in that they provide an avenue to learn from the embodied experiences of the subaltern and/or marginalized.[131] Testimonios are reflexive narratives that emerged in the context of the 1970s and liberation efforts in Latin American countries and are utilized in the fields of Latin American studies, anthropology, education, ethnic studies, humanities, women's studies, Latina/o communication studies, and psychology.[132] Testimonios are a methodological intervention, a bridge from oppression to liberation, a personal-global political act.[133] Further, testimonio is "a mode that crafts knowledge and theory through the communication of oppressive personal experiences, and it highlights the impact of the process of theorizing our own realities."[134] The testimonialista does not consider herself the sole authority on an issue, yet as a speech act, the narratives (re)told purposely speak for communal experiences against dominant discourses.[135] Specifically, testimonios are a form of collectivist discourse that create "new understandings about how marginalized communities build solidarity and respond to and resist dominant culture, laws, and policies that perpetuate inequity."[136] From this epistemology, testimonios are considered a text, video, performance, or audio that serve a political, methodological, and pedagogical purpose with a social action telos toward solidarity from the reader/witness.[137]

For example, Holling examines femicidal violence in Ciudad Juarez by utilizing testimonios as a method of social science research. She argues for a rhetorical/cultural understanding of testimonios that examine how language is used, identifies rhetorical function(s), theorizes appeals created, and analyzes the political critique conveyed.[138] Additionally, Rigoberta Menchú, an indigenous Guatemalan woman, received the Nobel Peace Prize in 1992 for her testimonio in the book *I, Rigoberta Menchú: An Indian Woman in Guatemala*, which brought to light the plight and violence experienced by Mesoamerican indigenous peoples.[139] Delgado explores Menchú's testimonio as a form of collectivist discourse to argue for more (inter)cultural nuances to rhetorical criticism.[140] Furthering this work, Avant-Mier and Hasian explore and analyze the controversies that erupted in response to Menchú's testimonio, principally by scholar David Stoll, to defend the heuristic value of testimonios to communication studies research.[141] In particular, Avant-Mier and Hasian identify four key discursive functions: (1) a sense of autobiographical truth, (2) a sense of solidarity and potentiality for alliance-building, (3) a supply of discursive materials for historical remembrances, and (4) a counter-hegemonic device.[142] Whether rejected, accepted, or critiqued, testimonios generate a collectivist discourse that functions to blur "the traditional boundaries that exist between fact and fiction, material truths and social truths, and the acts of recording and witnessing."[143] Yet, it is important to take a borderlands lens to narrative theory because "*testimonios* provide frameworks to illustrate how we claim our space in unwelcoming places."[144] Testimonios allow a researcher an opportunity to see how borderlands narratives are constitutive to larger master narratives, how Jotería testimonialistas survive atrocities, and how the process of witnessing narratives allows for revival, healing, and possibility.[145]

Consejos

Consejos or cultural sayings/advice contain intricate relationships with control and dominance, so Jotería deconstructions of these taken-for-granted sayings expose these relations and reconstruct theories in the flesh from these embodied experiences in the borderlands. The deconstruction of common or taken-for-granted sayings that are aimed at silencing "wild tongues" exposes the tradition of silence disciplined into the minds and bodies of (LGBTQ) Chicanas/os.[146] In the cultural saying, " 'No te dejes' ('Don't let them do that to you' or 'fight back')"[147] offered by Martínez, he breaks his own silence surrounding incest and embodied cultural-patriarchal impulses to theorize "why some queer Latino youth may not 'fight back' when faced with homophobic violence, and what the seeming inaction might tell us."[148] By postponing a response in the moment of homophobic violence, Martínez explains that Jotería "postpone falling into dominant scripts and repertoires and they postpone practicing masculinity in misogynist and homophobic terms."[149] In this book, consejos are sometimes explicitly offered theories in the flesh meant for and directly to other Jotería, such as when the author shares affirmations or collected oral history interviews.

Although perhaps an everyday narrative act of advice, consejos are historical and political, because as numerous (LGBTQ) Chicanas and Chicanos in the academy have critiqued, academia continues to function as a White supremacist, capitalistic, cisheteropatriarchal structure of power that marginalizes (queer) people of color. For instance, reflecting on his experiences of graduate school, Daniel Enrique Pérez shares this consejo:

> I understand that many of the opportunities that I was given for advancing as a graduate student and getting scholarships, fellowships, and teaching gigs happened because I just happened to be hanging around the department a whole lot.[150]

In this narrative, Pérez offers insights into what he did with his body, where he strategically placed it, and the potentiality for success if this performance is mimicked by other LGBTQ Chicanas/os. Or, as he explains, "when you are hanging around the department so much and a faculty member gets information about a scholarship or fellowship, they are much more likely to share it with you or encourage you to apply for it."[151] The consejos collected and remembered in this book offer explicit theories in the flesh meant to be deployed by other Jotería to carve out spaces to survive and possibly thrive.

Decolonizing Communication Studies

Jotería studies is a decolonial political project that challenges homonormativity, modernity, and social hierarchies based on racial, gendered, sexual, classed, and aged differences.[152] Challenging coloniality means making visible the powerful reduction of human beings to animals, to inferiors by nature, in a schizoid understanding of reality that dichotomized the human from nature, the human from the non-human, and thus imposes an ontology and a cosmology that, in its power and constitution, disallows all humanity, all possibility of understanding, all possibility of human communication, to dehumanized beings.[153]

By utilizing borderlands theory and its subsequent expansions and transformations, Jotería studies offers a critique of culture, history, and society that utilizes a mestiza/o consciousness to hold theories of intersectionality and discourses of postcoloniality in tension.[154] Therefore, Jotería critique often implicates and interrogates White supremacist capitalist cisheteropatriarchy as it manifests and is propagated as part of everyday life within the modern/colonial gender system.

During a recent Zoom check-in with my mother, I mentioned that I will never be able to love my stepfather because he will always be the one she chose over me. I have held onto the fear that if my own mother, who gave birth to me and raised me for nearly 18 years, could choose someone else after only knowing them a few weeks, then who would choose me? Why invest your time if your own mother abandoned you? Each real or imagined betrayal/abandonment perceived sent me into that dark place: "You are not enough. Who could ever love you?" In that moment on Zoom, I felt brave and vulnerable as I directly communicated my feelings to my mother. Later, she texts me: "Oh so that this is clear. I will choose you over him any day. Ok. Get it. Know it." Some days, I believe her and other days, I don't, but in this text message, I felt the full return of a karmic circle. Since this plática, we have made commitments to each other, and I wonder about who I am and where our relationship will go next.

Jotería history and politics are in a constant state of being and feeling in/between; therefore, (re)membering snapshots of Jotería means entering into a state that challenges the colonial/modern gender system, which has erased Jotería experience. In this book, I oftentimes identify these borderlands narratives for the reader, and other times, I leave space for the reader to identify the deployment of these narratives for themselves. For me, this book is being co-constructed the minute you decode the symbol/word "co-constructed" written on the page (or spoken through a device), so we are in this together. I want to give the reader lots of avenues into this book, but it is ultimately up to the reader to find their own way out. We make meaning together.

It is time to climb.   Look to the horizon.

They can't believe you are ascending.   stone
    temple stairs

       nothing
but my will   the community

no heart palpitating in front of my eyes will stop me
     no need to hold my arms down. I have made the choice.
       the   knife   the   fear   the   pres-
sure   over   and over

     destroy me with this challenge
     breathe in
     remember you are loved.

Notes

1. Robert Gutierrez-Perez, "Question(ing) One in the Coatlicue State: A Call for Creative Engagement in the LGBTQ Movement," *Liminalities: A Journal of Performance Studies* 11, no. 1 (2015): 1–18; Robert Gutierrez-Perez and Luis Manuel Andrade, "Queer of Color World-Making: <Marriage> in the Rhetorical Archive and the Embodied Repertoire," *Text and Performance Quarterly* 38, nos. 1–2 (2018): 1–18.
2. Robert Gutierrez-Perez, "Disruptive Ambiguities: The Potentiality of *Jotería* Critique in Communication Studies," *Kaleidoscope* 14 (2015): 94.
3. Gloria Anzaldúa, *Borderlands/La Frontera: The New Mestiza* (San Francisco: Aunt Lute Books, 2012); Fernando Delgado, "The Complexity of Mexican American Identity: A Reply to Hecht, Sedano, and Ribeau and Mirande and Tanno," *International Journal of Intercultural Relations* 18, no. 1 (1995): 77–84; Roxanne Dunbar-Ortiz, *An Indigenous Peoples' History of the United States* (Boston: Beacon Press, 2014); Luis D. León, *La Llorona's Children: Religion, Life, and Death in the U.S.-Mexican Borderlands* (Berkeley and Los Angeles: University of California Press, 2004).
4. Robert Gutierrez-Perez, "I Get It from My Mother," in *This Bridge We Call Communication: Anzaldúan Approaches to Theory, Method, and Praxis* (Lanham: Lexington Books, 2019).
5. Linda Alcoff, "The Problem of Speaking for Others," *Cultural Critique* 20 (1991): 5–32.
6. Patricia Hill Collins, *Black Feminist Thought: Knowledge, Consciousness, and the Politics of Empowerment* (New York: Routledge, 1991); Haneen Ghabra, "Disrupting

Privileged and Oppressed Spaces: Reflecting Ethically on My Arabness through Feminist Autoethnography," *Kaleidoscope: A Graduate Journal of Qualitative Communication Research* 14 (2015): 1–16; Rachel A. Griffin, "Cultivating Promise and Possibility: Black Feminist Thought as an Innovative, Interdisciplinary, and International Framework," *Departures in Critical Qualitative Research* 5, no. 3 (2016): 1–9; Chandra Talpade Mohanty, *Feminism Without Borders: Decolonizing Theory, Practicing Solidarity* (Durham and London: Duke University Press, 2003).

7. Eric E. Peterson and Kristin M. Langellier, "The Performance Turn in Narrative Studies," *Narrative Inquiry* 16, no. 1 (2006): 173–80.

8. Ibid., 175.

9. Ibid., 176.

10. Ibid., 177.

11. Ibid., 178.

12. hooks, bell, *All About Love: New Visions* (New York: HarperCollins, 2001).

13. Peterson and Langelier, "The Performance Turn," 175.

14. Gloria Anzaldúa, *The Gloria Anzaldúa Reader*, ed. AnaLouise Keating (Durham, NC: Duke University Press, 2009); James Baldwin, "My Dungeon Shook: Letter to My Nephew on the One Hundredth Anniversary of the Emancipation," *The Fire Next Time* (New York: Vintage Books, 1993).

15. Robin P. Clair et al., "Narrative Theory and Criticism: An Overview Toward Clusters and Empathy," *Review of Communication* 14, no. 1 (2014): 1–18.

16. Lynn M. Harter, "Narratives as Dialogic, Contested, and Aesthetic Performances," *Journal of Applied Communication Research* 37, no. 2 (2009): 140–50; Kurt Lindemann, "Live(s) Online: Narrative Performance, Presence, and Community in LiveJournal.com," *Text and Performance Quarterly* 25, no. 4 (2005): 354–72.

17. Horacio N. Roque Ramírez, "Recording a Queer Community: An Interview with Horacio N. Roque Ramírez," *Oral History and Communities of Color*, eds. Teresa Barnett and Chon A. Noriega (Los Angeles: UCLA Chicano Studies Research Center Press, 2013), 141.

18. Peterson and Langellier, "The Performance Turn."

19. Ibid., 174.

20. José Esteban Muñoz, *Disidentifications: Queers of Color and the Performance of Politics* (Minneapolis, MN: University of Minnesota Press, 1999), 99.

21. Peterson and Langellier, "The Performative Turn," 178.

22. Ibid., 175.

23. Richard Jones Jr. and Bernadette Marie Calafell, "Contesting Neoliberalism through Critical Pedagogy, Intersectional Reflexivity, and Personal Narrative: Queer Tales of Academia," *Journal of Homosexuality* 59, no. 7 (2012): 957–81; Peterson and Langellier, "The Performative Turn," 176.

24. Luis M. Andrade, "CAUTION: On the Many, Unpredictable Iterations of a Yellow Border Sign Ideograph and Migrant/Queer World-Making," *Text and Performance*

Quarterly 39, no. 3 (2019): 203–28; Bernadette Marie Calafell, "Disrupting the Dichotomy: 'Yo Soy Chicana /o?' in the New Latina /o South," *The Communication Review* 7, no. 2 (2004): 175–204; Dustin Bradley Goltz, "It Gets Better: Queer Futures, Critical Frustrations, and Radical Potentials," *Critical Studies in Media Communication* 30, no. 2 (2013): 135–51; Michael Hames-García, *Identity Complex: Making the Case for Multiplicity* (Minneapolis: University of Minnesota Press, 2011); Jones and Calafell, "Contesting"; Stacey K. Sowards and Richard D. Pineda, "Immigrant Narratives and Popular Culture in the United States: Border Spectacle, Unmotivated Sympathies, and Individualized Responsibilities," *Western Journal of Communication* 77, no. 1 (2013): 72–91; Kate Willink, "Economy & Pedagogy: Laboring to Learn in Camden County, North Carolina," *Communication and Critical/Cultural Studies* 5, no. 1 (2008): 64–86; Naida Zukic, "Webbing Sexual/Textual Agency in Autobiographical Narratives of Pleasure," *Text and Performance Quarterly* 28, no. 4 (2008): 396–414.

25. Jackson B. Miller, "Coyote's Tale on the Old Oregon Trail: Challenging Cultural Memory through Narrative at the Tamástslikt Cultural Institute," *Text and Performance Quarterly* 25, no. 3 (2005): 220–38; Kate Willink, Robert Gutierrez-Perez, Salma Shukri, and Lacey Stein, "Navigating with the Stars: Critical Qualitative Methodological Constellations for Critical Intercultural Communication Research," *Journal of International and Intercultural Communication* 7, no. 4 (2014): 289–316.

26. Michael Hames-García and Ernesto Javier Martínez, "Introduction: Re-membering Gay Latino Studies," *Gay Latino Studies: A Critical Reader*, eds. Michael Hames-García & Ernesto Javier Martínez (Durham, NC: Duke University, 2011), 4.

27. Peterson and Langellier, "The Performative Turn," 178.

28. Michael Hames-García, "Jotería Studies, or the Political Is Personal," *Aztlán: A Journal of Chicano Studies* 39, no. 1 (2014): 135.

29. Frederick Luis Aldama, *Brown on Brown: Chicano/a Representations of Gender, Sexuality, and Ethnicity* (Austin: University of Texas Press, 2005); George Hartley, "The Curandera of Conquest: Gloria Anzaldúa's Decolonial Remedy," *Aztlan: A Journal of Chicano Studies* 35, no. 1 (2010): 135–61; Kristin M. Langellier, "Personal Narrative, Performance, Performativity: Two or Three Things I Know for Sure," *Text and Performance Quarterly* 19, no. 2 (1999): 125–44.

30. Lisa A. Flores, "Challenging the Myth of Assimilation: A Chicana Feminist Response," International and Intercultural Communication, Annual Vol XXIII: Constituting Cultural Difference through Discourse, ed. Mary Jane Collier (Thousand Oaks, CA: Sage, 2001), 39.

31. Linda Tuhiwai Smith, *Decolonizing Methodologies: Research and Indigenous Peoples* (New York: Palgrave Macmillan, 2012), 147.

32. Alcoff, "The Problem."

33. Gloria Anzaldúa, *Interviews/Entrevistas* (New York: Routledge, 2000); John Charles Chasteen, *Born in Blood and Fire: A Concise History of Latin America* (New York: W. W. Norton & Company, 2001).

34. Alicia Arrizón, *Queering Mestizaje: Transculturation and Performance* (Ann Arbor: University of Michigan Press, 2006), 6–7.
35. Anzaldúa, *Borderlands*, 27.
36. Theresa Delgadillo, *Spiritual Mestizaje: Religion, Gender, Race, and Nation in Contemporary Chicana Narrative* (Durham, NC: Duke University Press, 2011).
37. Chasteen, *Born in Blood.*
38. Pete Sigal, *The Flower and the Scorpion: Sexuality and Ritual in Early Nahua Culture* (Durham, NC: Duke University Press, 2011), 203.
39. Stephen O. Murray, "Mexico," *The Politics of Sexuality in Latin America: A Reader on Lesbian, Gay, Bisexual, and Transgender Rights*, eds. Javier Corrales and Mario Pecheny (Pittsburgh: University of Pittsburgh Press, 2010), 62.
40. Héctor Carrillo, *The Night Is Young: Sexuality in Mexico in the Time of AIDS* (Chicago and London: University of Chicago Press, 2002); Chasteen, *Born in Blood.*
41. Arthur. P. Bochner, "Narrative's Virtues," *Qualitative Inquiry* 7, no. 2 (2001): 134.
42. Dwight Conquergood, *Cultural Struggles: Performance, Ethnography, Praxis*, ed. E. Patrick Johnson (Ann Arbor: University of Michigan Press, 2013), 75.
43. Hill Collins, *Black Feminist Thought.*
44. Devon W. Carbado et al., "Intersectionality: Mapping the Movements of a Theory," *Du Bois Review: Social Science Research on Race* 10, no. 2 (2013): 303–12.
45. Patricia Hill Collins and Sirma Bilge, *Intersectionality* (Malden, MA: Polity Press, 2016), 25.
46. Ibid., 27.
47. Ibid., 27–9
48. Shinsuke Eguchi and Bernadette Marie Calafell, "Introduction: Reorienting Queer Intercultural Communication," *Queer Intercultural Communication: The Intersectional Politics of Belonging in and across Difference*, eds. Shinsuke Eguchi and Bernadette Marie Calafell (Lanham, MA: Rowman & Littlefield, 2020), 1–16; Gust A. Yep, "Queering/Quaring/Kauering/Crippin'/Transing 'Other Bodies' Intercultural Communication," *Journal of International and Intercultural Communication* 6, no. 2 (2013): 118–26; Gust A. Yep, Fatima Zahrae Chrifi Alaoui, and Ryan M. Lescure, "Relationalities in/through Difference: Explorations in Queer Intercultural Communication," *Queer Intercultural Communication: The Intersectional Politics of Belonging In and Across Difference*, eds. Shinsuke Eguchi and Bernadette Marie Calafell (Lanham, MA: Rowman & Littlefield, 2020), 19–45.
49. John T. Warren and Deanna L. Fassett, Communication: A Critical/Cultural Introduction (Thousand Oaks, CA: Sage, 2014).
50. Dwight Conquergood, *Cultural Struggles: Performance, Ethnography, Praxis*, ed. E. Patrick Johnson (Ann Arbor, MI: University of Michigan Press, 2013); D. Soyini Madison, *Critical Ethnography: Method, Ethics, and Performance* (Thousand Oaks, CA: Sage, 2012); D. Soyini Madison, "Performing Theory/Embodied Writing," *Text and Performance Quarterly* 19 (1999): 107–24.

51. Sandy Grande, "Red Pedagogy: The Un-Methodology," *Handbook of Critical and Indigenous Methodologies*, eds. Norman K. Denzin, Yvonna S. Lincoln, & Linda Tuhiwai Smith (Thousand Oaks, CA: Sage, 2008), 233–54; Kathleen Pendleton Jiménez, "Start with the Land": Groundwork for Chicana Pedagogy," in *Chicana/Latina Education in Everyday Life: Feminista Perspectives on Pedagogy and Epistemology*, eds. Sofia A. Villenas, Francisca E. Godinez, Dolores Delgado Bernal, and C. Alejandra Elenes (Albany: State University of New York Press, 2006), 219–30.

52. Maria Lugones, "Toward a Decolonial Feminism," *Hypatia* 25, no. 4 (2010): 742.

53. Hill Collins, *Black Feminist Thought*.

54. Hill Collins and Bilge, *Intersectionality*, 9.

55. Brenda J. Allen, "Theorizing Communication and Race," *Communication Monographs* 74, no. 2 (2007): 259–64.

56. Allen, "Theorizing."

57. Mark Rupert, "Reading Gramsci in an Era of Globalising Capitalism," *Critical Review of International Social and Political Philosophy* 8, no. 4 (2005): 483–97.

58. Hill Collins and Bilge, *Intersectionality*, 7.

59. Antonio Gramsci, *The Antonio Gramsci Reader: Selected Writings 1916–1935*, ed. David Forgacs (New York: New York University Press, 2000), 424.

60. Deanna Fassett, John T. Warren, and Keith Nainby, *Communication: A Critical/Cultural Introduction* (San Diego, CA: Cognella, 2018), 262.

61. Hames-García, *Identity*; Amanda Martinez and Robert M. Gutierrez-Perez, "Are We Post-Post-Race Yet? Moving Beyond the Black-White Binary Towards a Mestiza/o Consciousness," in *The Assault on Communities of Color: Exploring the Realities of Race-Based Violence*, eds. Fasching-Varner, Hartlep, Martin, Cleveland Hayes, Mitchell, and Allen-Mitchell (Lanham, MD: Rowman and Littlefield Publishers, 2015), 49–54.

62. Luz Calvo and Catriona Rueda Esquibel, *Decolonize Your Diet* (Vancouver, BC: Arsenal Pulp Press, 2015), 22.

63. Hill Collins and Bilge, *Intersectionality*, 17.

64. Rona Tamiko Halualani, S. Lily Mendoza, and Jolanta A. Drzewiecka, "'Critical' Junctures in Intercultural Communication Studies: A Review," *Review of Communication* 9, no. 1 (2009): 17–35; Gust A. Yep, "Toward the De-Subjugation of Racially Marked Knowledges in Communication," *Southern Communication Journal* 75, no. 2 (2010): 171–75.

65. Halualani, Mendoza, and Drzewiecka, "Critical," 23.

66. Louis Althusser, *On the Reproduction of Capitalism: Ideology and Ideological State Apparatuses* (New York: Verso, 2014); Richard Delgado and Jean Stefancic, *Critical Race Theory: An Introduction* (New York: NYU Press, 2001).

67. Ernest Doring, "Growing Up Gay and Latino," *Queer in Aztlán: Chicano Male Recollections of Consciousness and Coming Out*, eds. Adelaida R. Del Castillo and Gibrán Güido (San Diego, CA: Cognella, 2014), 23.

68. Luis M. Andrade and Robert M. Gutierrez-Perez, "On the Specters of Coloniality: A Letter to Latina/o/x Students Journeying through the Educational Pipeline," *Latina/o/x Communication Studies: Theories, Methods, and Practice*, eds. Leandra H. Hernández et al. (Lanham, MD: Lexington Books, 2019), 313–31.

69. Hames-García, *Identity*, 13.

70. Shantel Martinez, "Lessons from My Battle Scars: Testimonio's Transformative Possibilities for Theory and Practice," *Latina/o/x Communication Studies: Theories, Methods, and Practice*, eds. Leandra H. Hernández et al. (Lanham, MD: Lexington Books, 2019), 360.

71. Robert Gutierrez-Perez, "Brown Fingers Ran Down," *Queer Praxis: Questions for LGBTQ Worldmaking*, eds. Dustin Bradley Goltz and Jason Zingsheim (New York, NY: Peter Lang, 2015).

72. Blindjaw, "How to Clean Your Ass Before Anal Sex," accessed October 31, 2019, https://howtocleanyourass.wordpress.com.

There are two types of cleaning when it comes to preparing oneself for anal sex: fast and full. A fast cleaning takes about 10–30 minutes and is advised for when you will be having anal sex in the next few hours whereas a full cleaning can be 30 minutes to 2 hours and is intended for long sessions, "monster dicks," fisting, and large sex toys. There are also several types of anal cleaning tools, such as the shower hose, enema bulb, fleet enema, and an enema bag. In general, depending on the type of cleaning necessary and the tool chosen, the process is as follows: (1) take the time to pass your bowels first prior to beginning your cleaning, (2) count to 5 to fill your rectum with water for a fast clean or count to 30 for a full clean. Be careful not to overfill if attempting a fast clean as you will need to undertake a full cleaning should water pass the sigmoid in the lower intestines, (3) release the water held within the anus, and (4) repeat steps 2–3 until the water comes out clear. For more details and tips, please utilize the link above to access a free illustrated guide for all genders and sexual preferences.

73. Anzaldúa, *Interviews*; Bernadette Marie Calafell, "Pro(re-)claiming Loss: A Performance Pilgrimage in Search of Malintzin Tenépal," *Text and Performance Quarterly* 25, no. 1 (2005): 43–56; Bernadette Marie Calafell, *Latina/o Communication Studies: Theorizing Performance* (New York: Peter Lang, 2007); Ilan Stavans, "The Latin Phallus," *Transition* 65 (1995): 48.

74. Octavio Paz, *The Labyrinth of Solitude: Life and Thought in Mexico* (New York: Grove Press, 1961).

75. Robert McKee Irwin, "The Famous 41: The Scandalous Birth of Modern Mexican Homosexuality," *GLQ: A Journal of Lesbian and Gay Studies* 6, no. 3 (2000): 365.

76. Matthew C. Gutmann, *The Meaning of Macho: Being a Man in Mexico City* (Berkeley and Los Angeles: University of California Press, 1996); Irwin, "The Famous 41"; Gust Yep, Fatima Zahrae Chrifi Alaoui, and Ryan M. Lescure, "Relationalities in/ through Difference: Explorations in Queer Intercultural Communication," *Queer*

Intercultural Communication: The Intersectional Politics of Belonging in and across Differences, eds. Shinsuke Eguchi and Bernadette Marie Calafell (Lanham, MD: Rowman & Littlefield, 2020), 19–45.

77. Irwin, "The Famous 41," 365.
78. Martin Nesvig, "The Complicated Terrain of Latin American Homosexuality," *Hispanic American Historical Review* 81, no. 3–4 (2001): 699.
79. Ibid., 699.
80. Ibid., 721.
81. Jennifer Ayala et al., "Fiera, Guambra, y Karichina! Transgressing the Borders of Community and Academy," *Chicana/Latina Education in Everyday Life: Feminista Perspectives on Pedagogy and Epistemology*, eds. Sofia A. Villenas et al. (Albany, NY: State University of New York Press, 2006), 261–80.
82. Francisca Godinez, "Haciendo Que Hacer: Braiding Cultural Knowledge into Educational Practices and Policies," *Chicana/Latina Education in Everyday Life: Feminista Perspectives on Pedagogy and Epistemology*, eds. Sofia A. Villenas et al. (Albany, NY: State University of New York Press, 2006), 25–38.
83. Patricia Sánchez and Lucila D. Ek, "Cultivando La Siguiente Generación: Future Directions in Chicana/Latina Feminist Pedagogies," *Journal of Latino-Latin American Studies* 5, no. 3 (2013): 181–87.
84. Bañales, "Jotería"; Antonio Duran, Roberto C. Orozco, and Sergio A. Gonzalez, "Imagining the Future of Jotería Studies as a Framework in the Field of Higher Education," *Association of Mexican American Educators Journal* 14, no. 2 (2020): 67–86; Juan Carlos González and Edwardo L. Portillos, "Teaching from a Critical Perspective / Enseñando de Una Perspectiva Crítica: Conceptualization, Reflection, and Application of Chicana/o Pedagogy," *International Journal of Critical Pedagogy* 4, no. 1 (2012): 18–34.
85. Elena Avila, *Woman Who Glows in the Dark: A Curandera Reveals Traditional Aztec Secrets of Physical and Spiritual Health* (New York: Jeremy P. Tarcher/Putnam, 1999); George Hartley, "The Curandera of Conquest: Gloria Anzaldúa's Decolonial Remedy," *Aztlán: A Journal of Chicano Studies* 35, no. 1 (2010): 135–61.
86. Bernadette M. Calafell et al., "Conclusion: The Futures of Latina/o/x Communication Studies: A Plática with Senior Scholars," *Latina/o/x Communication Studies: Theories, Methods, and Practice*, eds. Leandra H. Hernández et al. (Lanham, MA: Lexington Books, 2019), 371–92.
87. Roberto Rodriguez, "Chile Relleno," *Queer in Aztlán: Chicano Male Recollections of Consciousness and Coming Out*, eds. Adelaida R. Del Castillo and Gibrán Güido (San Diego, CA: Cognella, 2014), 65.
88. Ernesto Javier Martínez, *On Making Sense: Queer Race Narratives of Intelligibility* (Stanford, CA: Stanford University Press, 2013), 14.
89. Martínez, *On Making Sense*, 14.
90. Moreman, "Rethinking," 1.

91. Martínez, *On Making Sense*, 14.
92. Ibid., 14.
93. Ibid., 14.
94. Ibid., 14.
95. Irwin, "The Famous 41."
96. Chasteen, *Born in Blood and Fire*, 328.
97. Carrillo, *The Night Is Young*; Gutierrez-Perez, "Brown Fingers."
98. Robert McKee Irwin, *Mexican Masculinities* (Minneapolis: University of Minnesota Press, 2003).
99. Carrillo, *The Night Is Young*, 18.
100. Ibid.
101. Irwin, *Mexican*.
102. Murray, "Mexico," 63.
103. Irwin, *Mexican*.
104. Carrillo, *The Night Is Young*; Murray, "Mexico."
105. Murray, "Mexico," 63.
106. Irwin, "The Famous 41," 357.
107. Sigal, *The Flower*, 8–9.
108. Murray, "Mexico"; Sigal, *The Flower*.
109. Murray, "Mexico."
110. David Carrasco, *The Aztecs: A Very Short Introduction* (Oxford and New York: Oxford University Press, 2012); Sigal, *The Flower*.
111. Hames-García, *Identity*; Hames-García, "Jotería"; Sigal, *The Flower*.
112. Murrary, "Mexico," 61.
113. Mark Cartwright, "Xochipilli," *Ancient History Encyclopedia*, September 6, 2013, https://www.ancient.eu/Xochipilli/.
114. Sigal, *The Flower*.
115. Ibid., 8.
116. Ibid.
117. Ibid.
118. Ibid., 193.
119. Ibid.
120. Ibid.
121. Ibid., 193.
122. Ibid., 177–93.
123. Ibid., 197.
124. Ibid., 197.
125. Norma Alarcón, "Anzaldúan Textualities: A Hermeneutic of the Self and the Coyolxauhqui Imperative," *El Mundo Zurdo 3: Selected Works from the 2012 Meeting of the Society for the Study of Gloria Anzaldúa*, eds. Larissa M. Mercado-López, Sonia Saldívar-Hull, and Antonia Castañeda (San Francisco: Aunt Lute

Books, 2013), 189–208; Anzaldúa, *Borderlands*; Arrizón, *Queering*; Calafell, *Latina/o Communication*; Sarah Amira de la Garza, *María Speaks: Journeys into the Mysteries of the Mother in My Life as a Chicana* (New York: Peter Lang, 2004); Judith Flores Carmona, "Cutting Out Their Tongues: Mujeres' Testimonios and the Malintzin Researcher," *Journal of Latino-Latin American Studies* 6, no. 2 (2014): 113–24; Teresita Garza, "The Rhetorical Legacy of Coyolxauhqui: (Re) collecting and (Re)membering Voice," *Latina/o Discourse in Vernacular Spaces: Somos de Una Voz?*, eds. Michelle A. Holling and Bernadette Marie Calafell (Blue Ridge Summit, PA: Lexington Books, 2011), 31–56; Gloria González-López, "Conocimiento and Healing: Academic Wounds, Survival, and Tenure," *Bridging: How Gloria Anzaldúa's Life and Work Transformed Our Own*, eds. AnaLouise Keating and Gloria González-López (Austin: University of Texas Press, 2011), 91–100; Jessica Heredia, "My Path of Conocimiento: How Graduate School Transformed Me into a Nepantlera," *Bridging: How Gloria Anzaldúa's Life and Work Transformed Our Own*, eds. AnaLouise Keating and Gloria González-López (Austin: University of Texas Press, 2011), 39–44; Irene Lara, "Daughter of Coatlicue: An Interview with Gloria Anzaldúa," *EntreMundos/AmongWorld: New Perspectives on Gloria Anzaldúa*, ed. AnaLouis Keating (New York: Palgrave Macmillan, 2005), 41–55.

126. Grisel Gómez-Cano, *The Return of Coatlicue: Goddesses and Warladies in Mexican Folklore* (Bloomington, IN: Xlibria, 2010).

127. León, *La Llorona*, 5.

128. Ibid.

129. Bernadette Marie Calafell, *Monstrosity, Performance, and Race in Contemporary Culture* (New York: Peter Lang, 2015).

130. León, *La Llorona*, 4.

131. Dolores Delgado Bernal, Rebeca Burciaga, and Judith Flores Carmona, "Chicana/Latina Testimonios: Mapping the Methodological, Pedagogical, and Political," *Equity & Excellence in Education* 45, no. 3 (2012): 363–72.

132. Lindsay Pérez Huber, "Disrupting Apartheid of Knowledge: Testimonio as Methodology in Latina/o Critical Race Research in Education," *International Journal of Qualitative Studies in Education* 22, no. 6 (2009): 639–54; Martinez, "Lessons."

133. Nivea Castaneda, "Using Testimonios to Untame Our Silent Tongues: Exploring our Experiences of Child Sexual Abuse through an Anzaldúan Perspective," *This Bridge We Call Communication: Anzaldúan Approaches to Theory, Method, and Praxis*, eds. Leandra Hinojosa Hernández and Robert Gutierrez-Perez (Lanham, MD: Lexington Books, 2019), 3–16; Martinez, "Lessons"; Manuel Alejandro Pérez, "Testimonio as a Queer Puente for Healing," *This Bridge We Call Communication: Anzaldúan Approaches to Theory, Method, and Praxis*, eds. Leandra Hinojosa Hernández and Robert Gutierrez-Perez (Lanham, MD: Lexington Books, 2019),

17–26; Linda T. M. Scholz, "Hablando Por (Nos)Otros, Speaking for Ourselves: Exploring the Possibilities of 'Speaking Por' Family and Pueblo in Bolivian Testimonio 'Si Me Permiten Hablar,'" *Latina/o Discourse in Vernacular Spaces: Somos de Una Voz?*, eds. Michelle A. Holling and Bernadette Marie Calafell (Blue Ridge Summit, PA: Lexington Books, 2011), 203–22.

134. Castaneda, "Using Testimonios," 5.

135. Delgado Bernal et al., "Chicana/Latina"; Scholz, "Hablando."

136. Delgado Bernal et al., "Chicana/Latina," 363.

137. Delgado Bernal et al., "Chicana/Latina"; Michelle A. Holling, " 'So My Name Is Alma, and I Am the Sister of'. . . : A Feminicidio Testimonio of Violence and Violent Identifications," *Women's Studies in Communication* 37, no. 3 (2014): 313–38; Kathryn Blackmer Reyes and Julia E. Curry Rodríguez, "Testimonio: Origins, Terms, and Resources," *Equity & Excellence in Education* 45, no. 3 (2012): 525–38.

138. Holling, "So My Name," 317.

139. Rigoberta Menchú, *I, Rigoberta Menchú: An Indian Woman in Guatemala*, ed. E. Burgos-Debray, trans. A. Wright (London: Verso, 1984).

140. Fernando Delgado, "Rigoberta Menchú and Testimonial Discourse: Collectivist Rhetoric and Rhetorical Criticism," *World Communication* 28, no. 1 (1999): 17–29.

141. Roberto Avant-Mier and Marouf A. Hasian, "Communicating 'Truth': Testimonio, Vernacular Voices, and The Rigoberta Menchú Controversy," *The Communication Review* 11, no. 4 (2008): 323–45.

142. Ibid., 330.

143. Ibid., 330–31.

144. Martinez, "Lessons," 359.

145. Castaneda, "Using Testimonios," 13; Pérez, "Testimonio."

146. Anzaldúa, *Borderlands;* Castaneda, "Using Testimonios."

147. Ernesto Javier Martínez, "¿Con Quién, Dónde, y Por Qué Te Dejas?: Reflections on Joto Passivity," *Aztlán: A Journal of Chicano Studies* 39, no. 1 (2014): 240.

148. Ibid., 237.

149. Ibid., 243.

150. Daniel Enrique Pérez, "Out in the Field: Mariposas and Chicana/o Studies," *Queer in Aztlán: Chicano Male Recollections of Consciousness and Coming Out*, eds. Adelaida R. Del Castillo and Gibrán Güido, (San Diego, CA: Cognella, 2014), 283.

151. Ibid., 283.

152. Bañales, "Jotería."

153. Lugones, "Toward a Decolonial," 751.

154. Anzaldúa, *Borderlands;* Bañales, "Jotería"; Vincent D. Cervantes, "Traces of Transgressive Traditions Shifting Liberation Theologies through Jotería Studies," *Aztlán: A Journal of Chicano Studies* 39, no. 1 (2014): 195–206; Gutierrez-Perez,

"Disruptive"; Hames-García, "Jotería Studies"; AnaLouise Keating, ed., *EntreMundos/AmongWorlds: New Perspectives on Gloria Anzaldúa* (New York: Palgrave Macmillan, 2005); Horacio N. Roque Ramírez, "Gay Latino Histories/ Dying to Be Remembered: AIDS Obituaries, Public Memory, and the Queer Latino Archive," *Beyond El Barrio: Everyday Life in Latina/o America*, eds. Gina M. Pérez, Frank A. Guridy, and Adrian Burgos Jr. (New York: NYU Press, 2010), 103–28.

2

"I (Will) Always Watch You"—Remembering Loss, Spirituality, and Cultural Inheritance

Fear.
Realized
when you didn't know who I was,
but I know you knew that it was me.
You leaned into my hand
smoothing your hair
outlined baby-skinned cheek
It did something having us there,
right?

Fear.
when you did see me
through the fog
the pain
the call to come home
to say

"I (will) always watch you"

In the title of this book chapter and in the poem above that I wrote for my mater-nal grandfather's eulogy, I used parentheses to set off the word "will" in order to highlight the way American Sign Language (ASL) is untranslatable when translated into English. You see, when my grandfather was dying, he was coming in and out of consciousness because of the pain medication and the pain itself. It was scary how normalized his shouts of agony became over those three to four days when I was visiting him for the last time in hospice care; it was on the last night of my visit that he finally recognized me. It is a moment I will never forget because he immediately gave me three signs: (1) placing the symbol for the letter "i" on his chest, (2) pointing his index finger up to the ceiling and drawing a tight circle ("always"), and (3) turning his fingers into a "peace" symbol but then pushing these fingers toward me as if watching me = "I always watch you."

As mestizos, we come from multiple backgrounds of race, ethnicity, gender, sexuality, and (dis)ability, so in order to understand spirituality, we must be reflexive and remember our multiple, interconnected selves to remain whole in a world that wants us fractured and on the fringes. Spirituality is about deep interconnectivity, knowledge, and healing.[1] Many scholars have written about hybridity[2] and mestizaje[3] and have focused on what it means to be brown,[4] working class,[5] queer of color,[6] and/or on the margins of the academy.[7] So as a queer Chicano, what right do I have to center the life of a cisgendered White male?

All I can say is that he loved me. He was not perfect. He purposely missed my wedding to a gay Mexican-American male, and members of his family wrote angry emails to me during the Proposition 8 vote that placed my queer marriage up for public debate. However, his blood runs through my veins, and in many ways, I am him. His deaf friends testified that he was always a positive person who loved to laugh and joke (like me), he was a direct communicator (like me), and he was always so reliable (am I like that?). Looking in the mirror, I see our ears, our smile, and our body type, and so, I cannot and I will not cut out my grandfather from my mestizaje. He is already gone, and I desperately want to hold on to the only parts of him I have left. I must remain whole even if my heart is bleeding and soaking in so much loss and pain. Is this queer Chicana/o spirituality? I know that I have to write about queer spirituality because without connection without spirit/soul where else can one turn to in moments of trauma to find release and healing.

> Fear.
> Of what I might see
> or not see
> what I might remember
> what I might forget
> forever.

Will I lose the memory of that time
. . . you put me on your lap and together we drove your truck
. . . you yelled at me every time I walked in front of the TV
. . . the smell of VO5
. . . the golf range with mini-clubs created by you from your old ones
Will these memories be enough?

When I was born
you signed to me

"I Love You"

I worked hard
to interpret
to translate
images of hands
features of passionate face
nonverbal messages
woven into a language
Trying to return your gesture
of love

I could only get out

"Milk"

The witnesses laugh and cry at this poem about my first word, or who knows, because I look back down at my eulogy notes. Who knows who is out there laughing and who is out there crying? I can't risk anything but the dramatic pause that is created by cutting off eye contact because it is a real bodily response. It is here. He is gone. As the eldest grandson, I was chosen to remember my maternal grandfather at his burial ceremony, and as the last speaker, I held the final words (signs) that these witnesses would experience before the final prayers were uttered. Like Bryant Keith Alexander, "I am standing in the silence of family and I realize that they expect me to resurrect my [grand]father with words. To make conscious and not only awaken in them the memory of who he was, but to color memory with a tone of civility establishing an impulse of kind remembrance that will linger for a lifetime. And I must oblige."[8] Yet, right now and on this page:

I will miss feeling his warmth. His laugh . . . . We never felt alone or ashamed of who we were because he taught us to rely on each other and to be honest with each other always. Even now speaking up here alone, I am proud . . . because he made us special, and through him we are connected to each other always. However, I feel lost.

In the act of remembering loss of spirit and cultural inheritance, I have weaved throughout this book chapter the text from my grandfather's eulogy and observed ethnographic moments and personal experiences to make meaning from this traumatizing event in my life. Although I have tried to follow the method of autobiographical performance and performative writing in the *doing* of this chapter, I have not yet completed my work because I have only begun to "touch and feel" the surface of this moment of loss and spirituality.[9]

By spirituality, I am discussing vulnerability, identity, and the integration of the soul and spirit into critical thinking and crossing the boundaries of what we consider knowledge.[10] By loss, I am drawing on Anzaldúa in "Speaking Across the Divide" when she writes that "depression is a loss of spirit," and "suffering is one of the motivating forces of the creative impulse."[11] I feel changed, and I do not know exactly how to begin remembering acts of fathering and notions of raced masculinity, "and like many, I feel that I may have slept through most of my childhood, taking the everydayness of family life as a given."[12] By focusing on social scientific methodology, I argue that autobiographical performance and performative writing are the best choices for undertaking this scholarly investigation into lived experience and cultures of grief. I have not finished grieving, and as I look at the picture of my grandfather with my grandmother placed next to my computer screen (see Figure 2.1), I do not know how to start or end this chapter. Should I leave it incomplete, like I feel, or do I try to share more about the emptiness in my heart?

Figure 2.1: Grandmother and grandfather of the author prior to a high school dance.
Source: Author

I want to write about loss of spirit and the cultural inheritance of those who have fathered me, but the words are not coming out right in syntax and grammar because "I have to inhabit the body [to] discover its sensitivity and intelligence."[13] In part, I am thickly describing an ethnographic scene from my grandfather's funeral, and as a qualitative design, I am in a position of power. I quote John T. Warren to discuss the modern-colonial power dynamics inherent in ethnography: "Ethnography, by its conceptual design, is about entering, penetrating, breaking into the other in order to get what one wants. The site—that ethnographic other—is the land of plenty. It is there to be taken, to be consumed, to be tamed."[14] As queer Chicanas/os/xs, our bodies exist because of generations of mestizaje and crossing the boundaries of gender, sexuality, and spirituality, so by focusing on issues of loss and cultural inheritance from the loss of my White grandfather, I critically remember to make meaning and reflect on spirituality for Jotería. First, I define autobiographical performance and performative writing as a reflexive methodology that is a vulnerable, political, and particular act that implicates the reader and larger cultural systems. Next, I thicken this methodological approach of reflexivity and (re)membering utilizing a (queer) women of color epistemology to make a methodological intervention into the ethnographic gaze and further analyze the cultural performance of the eulogy, masculinity, and fathering. Finally, I argue that the clashes and conflicts in/between our multiple, intersecting cultural inheritances implicate queer Xicanas/os and Chicanas/os as active agents in their cultural practices, and Jotería spirituality is created from the very experiences of loss and cultural inheritance that make each of us so unique and special.

(Re)membering Loss and Spirituality through Autobiographical Performance

Autobiographical performance often means putting your body on the line in ways that leaves the writer feeling vulnerable and exposed. For example, my grandfather became deaf at a young age because of an illness during childhood, and, therefore, he and the family he created existed within a culture of (dis)ability and bilingualism. At his funeral, many of his deaf friends from childhood offered "signs" of love. By signs, I am referring to the embodied nature of ASL and as the only hearing/speaking eulogist, my performance was bilingual. In the opening poem of this chapter and in my eulogy, I signed "I Love You" with my two middle fingers down and my pinkie, index finger, and thumb of my right hand prone and shaking left and right to the racing beat of my heart. That was my first childhood memory of my grandfather, and I remember being incapable of holding back tears and choking sobs when I shared that sign of love to the witnesses gathered at the funeral. However, having to write in the past tense about a man that I truly cherished does not allow me the privilege of forgetting about power dynamics.

Michael Hames-García and Ernesto Javier Martínez, two Joteria scholars, write about the critical act of remembering as a tactic for LGBTQ Latinxs to resist histories of violence.[15] Further, remembering is a vulnerable act because you must delve into your flaws and privileges for all to see, and it is risky when you break silences around cultural taboos enforced by powerful ideologies.[16] Remembering my ancestor becomes a commitment to "listening to an inner order," and by allowing this labor to manifest "through the artist's body and into the body of the work," we share the workload and build connections to worlds and spaces that feed our collective souls.[17] Our spiritual practices as Jotería emerge out of our deep and personal investigations into the very bodies and locations we inhabit. What does it mean to be a queer Chicano writing about the death of a

White grandfather? Alexander writes that "reflexivity is an act of political self-awareness,"[18] so remembering requires critical attention to power and privilege. In undertaking any research project, one must be aware of the politics of one's methodological choices.[19]

Remembering through autobiographical performance is a commitment to writing performatively from a space of particularity. Keith Berry and John T. Warren explain that "an experience is always spatiotemporally rooted in (or informed by) given locations (physical, emotional, thoughtful context), subject to divergent meanings, and is necessarily subject to change over time as reflection (and further reflection) changes what happened more and more."[20] For instance, my grandfather was half-English and half-Dutch and immigrated to California from the states of Alabama and Arkansas with his family as a young child, yet I am half-Mexican, a quarter African-American, and a quarter of my grandfather. This intermingling of bloodlines makes me a mestizo, yet it cannot be lost that a deaf White man marrying and having children with a hard of hearing Mexican woman during the 1950s and 1960s was a very political act. There are rumors and whispers of the racist oppressions and microaggressions endured by both of my grandparents from their family and from society for their interracial coupling. I often hear stories from my aunts that my grandfather's father never believed his son was deaf. Until his death, he believed that my grandfather was faking his (dis)ability, and there were rumors that his family back in Arkansas had ties to the Ku Klux Klan. As I learn more about my grandfather and our cultural heritage from family and friends and as time begins to separate me from the emotions of this final ritual, the particularities of my cultural heritage embodied in history transforms this autobiographical performance into a political and embodied act of resistance.

Recently, I was signing with my maternal grandmother, and she was telling me the story of how she got married. When I became an assistant professor of culture and communication at the University of Nevada, Reno, my grandmother was very proud of me, and to show how connected we are to Reno, she mentioned how Reno is where my grandfather took her to get married. She signed the story with facial expressions and flourishes that made it clear that this was a funny story. She remembered how he had asked her if she had ever been to Reno before, and she had told him that she had never been there. As an adventurous woman, she was excited to go with him to visit Nevada and see the sights. At the time, my aunt was already born, but she was not my grandfather's biological daughter. According to my grandmother, she was a catch, and she had many deaf and hearing men who wanted to marry her. My grandma made a face that moved from pantomimed shock to confusion as she explains that, when they arrived at

Reno, my grandfather had parked in front of a church and said he would be right back. The faces she made were to show how she was feeling as she waited and waited and waited for him to return to the car. When he did return to the car, he brought her into the church and told her that they were going to get married. My grandmother laughs but betrays a bit of exasperation. As a critical scholar, it doesn't miss my eye (as she is signing to me) or my ears that she was pressured and then forced into marriage with my grandfather.

In remembering autobiographical performance and performative writing, I define and focus on reflexivity and how it is a vulnerable act, how it is an act of political self-awareness, how it comes from a space of particularity, and how it implicates others.[21] In fact, reflexivity is always a vulnerable act "because the process exposes that which is always concealed in scholarly research and particularly in ethnographic research."[22] When I remember my grandfather and the act of delivering his eulogy, I cannot help but feel an ache deep inside me that leaks out my eyes like a dam on the verge of breaking. During a Día de los Muertos altar ceremony, I confessed to my colleagues that my grandfather taught me how to be a man. Although I love my father, he never knew his father. Like in a telenovela, he and his three brothers were never told the names of their various fathers. To this day, I know that the absence of a father is why my own father is more of a friend than a father figure. Raúl Coronado advocates for more queer Chicano scholarship that shares secrets and argues that "it is time for men to explore how we have become the men that we are, how our relationships with men in our family have shaped and formed our sense of masculinity, how our sexual and emotional desires impact and are shaped by other aspects of our identity."[23] This act of remembering is about dealing with a deep loss, but it is also about race, gender, sexuality, (dis)ability, and the politics of research methodology. It is finally time to explore how I became the (cisgender) man I am.

(Re)membering Queer Cultural Inheritances through Acts of Fathering

Today, while walking on the treadmill, I witnessed a moment between a father and son that triggered memories of my own father. You see, the father was yelling at his son through the guise of teaching/learning about how to bench lift. It was an informal and violently verbal lesson on: "How to Be a Man."[24] While the son in the gym learned how to turn his pain, hurt, and betrayal inward into an outward display of silence with hard and blank facial features, I, in my memories, turned outward by crying openly during team sports and athletics. I was an embarrassment to my father. He was a former high school football player who, with all his former high school friends, still annually attends "The Big Bone" game held between the San José High Academy Bulldogs and the Abraham Lincoln High School Lions. As I've written elsewhere, "To *feel* this body, the reader must be open to and actively search for the emotions that framed the work for the writer,"[25] so here's the chismé. My father and I just ended a fight in which we did not speak to each other for nearly three months. It was the longest we have ever not spoken to each other.

And right now, I am stuck somewhere "in-between" searching for an answer to a question—do I want to remember *that* history? Hames-García and Martínez explain remembering as an active and resistive act that draws tactics of resistance into the present by examining the history of conflict and coalition that has been "dis-membered by a history of ideological violence."[26] As a decolonial move to resist the marginalization of queer of color experiences, everyday acts of fathering, as embodied through my relationship with my White grandfather and Black and Mexican bi-racial father, connects our experiences of masculinity to intersectional structures of power. As a project dedicated to "not just what colonization was about but what being dehumanized meant for our own cultural practices,"[27] I have to connect this narrative to the historical and political moment where my body is located.

Between wanting to buy a Trump piñata every time I shop at my local mercado to being afraid of being mass shot while watching a movie or going to Walmart with my husband, I am somewhere in between two or five worlds, yet I am cognizant of other worlds grappling with the record numbers of transgender women of color who have been murdered and/or silenced this past year.[28] With so much on the line, I don't know if I am the best messenger to demand that our community measure its successes by the "safety and well-being of our most vulnerable community members."[29] What is it about remembering that makes me shift into academic quotes and defining of terms rather than embodied emotional responses to colonial trauma? It is like I am hiding underneath a security blanket woven by academic training, societal expectations, and knowledge of "big words." Linda Tuhiwai Smith explains remembering as "connecting bodies with place and experience, and, importantly, people's responses to that pain."[30] I know that remembering our queer cultural inheritances is key to our continued resistance to those forces that would have us silenced at any cost, yet I can't stop performing the "cisgender man avoiding his feelings" as I remember the father figures in my life. The fear of truly showing myself and my family to you is a learned behavior that I must cast aside here and now, but I have never been taught how to cope with emotional pain in a healthy way. Perhaps, it starts by telling a story.

When I came out of the closet during my undergraduate years, I told my cousin and brother first—but at different times—because we have literally grown up together since birth. If I had them, then I knew I would be okay. Next, I told my father. We were in his Ford red truck, and he had just picked me up from my fraternity house at San José State University. We were in good spirits because we were about to pick up the rest of my brothers and sister to do something, or we were about to get something to eat. Either way, it felt right, so I told him: "Dad, I think I am bisexual." Although my understandings of queer desire and belongings have changed since that moment of queering, I remember the music moved onward in the background as time slowed down and made each breath important. Always a quick man, he told me about how it was perfectly fine to be attracted to lots of different types of people. He said, "I've dreamt of men before." I was stunned. In my coming out narrative, he chose to love and comfort me by being vulnerable. He queered himself for me.

However, for those three months of anger, I resisted speaking with my Dad because I was upset with his continuing issues of physically abusing the people he loves. Receiving that FaceTime call from my youngest brother and seeing the marks on his shoulder and neck brought back memories on my own body with its own marks. For instance, like the time you lifted me up the wall by my neck and I peed myself, or like those angry trips home yelling at me in the front seat of your truck after baseball games where I embarrassed you. Is this capacity for violence within me as well? So, I admit it. I confronted him head on. I spit the bile that had been sitting in my esophagus for years into that telephone. When I hung up, I used one of the most powerful tools at my disposal, and I called family members for hours describing every detail of the event and sharing all the chismé. Over those three months, the gossip spread, judgments reverberated, and I have suffered without him in my life. I catch him in the mirror when I make *that* face or when I "go too far" with one of my jokes. I can't escape him.

How is our queerness handed down? Not only in public memory but also in those everyday moments of connection in place and experience. I am my father's son. I catch him when I slur a bit when I am thinking too quickly or when I get passionate and yell (even when I don't think I am yelling). As a queer person of color, I see his sense of humor, bad eating habits, love of weightlifting, and my understanding of mestizaje reflected in my everyday acts of being. My husband tells me: "You're just like your father." What are these queer cultural inheritances?

Are they queer because I do them or because he does? Like Anzaldúa, I feel disorientation, confusion, and dislocation coming from entering that push-pull sway state of nepantla, which means in-between space in Nahuatl. I've been here before.

When I was in the third grade, I fell off the slide and ended up with a huge blood clot in my right cheek. The clot enlarged my cheek to cartoon size for several months as my body slowly cleared out the dead blood vessels. My mom was so angry because no one had called my parents from school to tell them about my injury. Of course, I still had to play baseball and stand in the outfield hoping nothing important would fly my way. For me, baseball was just a series of running in and out of the bullpen and hours of ostracization leading up to and after the "big game." I hated it. Walking up to the batter's box, I saw my Dad and Mom in the stands cheering, and they were smiling and waving at me. My Dad yells out, "You can do it, Rabbit!" It was his new nickname for me because of my swollen cheek and big front teeth. Of course, I didn't achieve much with that bat and that ball, but this is the memory that returns when I rub the scars on my cheek in the mirror. When he is feeling silly or in a good mood, he still calls me Rabbit. How can I dismember our relationship when he is written all over my body?

Remembering acts of fathering is a complex task because human beings are not flat characters in an essay. In confronting large power structures, I conceptualize these relations as interlocking, so White supremacy is connected to capitalism yet intertwined with patriarchy, heteronormativity, cissexism, and more.[31] In remembering my Dad, I refuse to let him become another stereotypical angry man of color because I have to believe that there is hope for us. I have to believe that—by witnessing the struggles of women of color[32] and working as feminists to empower women and to address critical issues—men can be part of the solution. Listening, reflexivity, and critical literacy can be powerfully active tools that can help those with privilege participate in struggles for social justice. However, this is not about absolution or easy fixes or dismembering past violences and injustices as if power differentials no longer exist. Remembering is often painful, but ultimately, it is an act that serves the purpose of addressing trauma as a way of sharing and healing with and for the community.

When I finally decided to call my Dad to reconcile, he had responded quicker than I was expecting to the missed call and voicemail I had left him earlier that morning. I didn't respond to him for days because I wasn't as ready to face him like I had thought. My husband had told me what a big deal it was that I had confronted him three months earlier: "Who else would have done that Robert?

You are the oldest. You're the next head of the family." I'm hearing this echo in my head as I answer the phone ringing in my hand. He wants to tell his side of the story. I listen. I tell him that, after some deep reflection, I was sorry for the things I said to him, but I was not sorry for pointing out how he pushes away the people he loves the most when he is the most in pain. I knew why the conflict had happened, but I was disappointed in him for not handling it as a mature and caring older man. He opened up about his mother's recent death; he felt responsible because he was the one who had to make the ultimate decision that led to her having surgery rather than an intense drug regimen. She died because of that surgery. He carries that burden everyday. I told him why and how much I love him. He told me that he loves me too. My father never had a father. I forget that he is learning how to be a man with me too.

(Re)membering Performative Writing and Queer (Women) of Color Epistemologies

Autobiographical performance implicates others in the telling of narratives through emotion and the breaking of silences. For example, I want to share how my male cousins hugged after the end of the burial ceremony for my grandfather, but how do I show-not-tell about this embrace? When my male cousin walked over to his older brother to comfort him with a hug, it was a significant moment in their relationship, and I want to tell you the chismé—but what is at stake? Should I explain how the older cousin's adopted father comforted both his sons in that moment too? How do I break the silence surrounding masculine performances of loss without laying out their dirty laundry for all to see? We cannot forget that telling narratives of emotion and breaking silences connect us to others in sometimes unpredictable ways. Aimee Carrillo Rowe terms this accountability to each other as a "politics of relation" and explains that we come to our queer Chicana/o and Xicana/o identities "through the relational choices and investments" that we make and "continue to make."[33] Within autobiographical performance and performative writing, we are challenged to do scholarship that is vulnerable, politically self-aware, and from a particular space yet capable of implicating others.

Calafell discusses the methodology of performative writing as a framework to engage communicative interactions and events that can account for and tap into the realm of the affective.[34] As a project that aims to locate theories in the flesh for GBTQ Chicanos/Xicanos, performative writing as an aesthetic method of inquiry opens borders, removes disciplinary walls, and stands on shifting sands "to let the culture dictate the language and the rules of its existence."[35] Theories in the flesh "emerge out of an interlocutors lived reality and experiences struggling to feed themselves and their families, to cover their heads with a roof, or to avoid/survive physical, emotional, mental and/or spiritual violence."[36] For example, Calafell has utilized performative writing as a method to honor the experiences of Chicanas/os throughout her scholarship, and utilizing her work as a muse to guide me through my own performative writing process,[37] I also acknowledge how performative writing is evocative, metonymic, subjective, nervous, citational, and consequential.[38] By viewing the reader as a co-performer in the production of the text, the performative writer invites dialogue, loose ends, and multiple audiences.

Given that this chapter is interested in loss, performative writing understands how, in the eulogy for my grandfather, I had to address his absence ("My grandfather wouldn't have wanted us to be sad or afraid because I know he would never leave us by ourselves"). As a deaf man, it was not lost on me that in death "he is listening to our voices for the first time right now, and I do not want my voice to crack." This is because "I want him to know every word of love, admiration, and respect. He needs to hear that he was our treasure and that every moment with him was a precious gift," and I cannot do the work of honoring my cultural heritage by placing borders on knowledge. Chicana feminist approaches encourage the use of autobiographical voice and share my commitment to transdisciplinary methodology, such as in the organization, in the structure of writing, and in the stylistic blending of genres.[39] For instance, this book chapter moves from communication studies to performance studies to poetry to theory to eulogy text back to queer of color scholarship and autobiographical performance. This act of transgression is not without risks, as charges of vanity or narcissim are often leveled against scholars of color who embrace personal voice and personal experience.[40] However, our work as queer Chicanas/os and Xicanas/os has always been risky,[41] and for the right to remember my own grandfather, I, like my queer ancestors before me, choose to dwell in the borderlands—and dare to thrive in the cracks. Anzaldúa notes how "the goal of spirituality is to transform one's life,"[42] and if I want to heal from the trauma of this loss, then I must trust that "creativity sets off an alchemical process that transforms adversity and difficulties into works of art."[43] Spirituality, for Jotería, are acts in everyday life and not simply words.[44] As a writer/artist, "I have to trust this process. I have to serve the forces/spirits interacting through me that govern the work. I have to allow the spirits to surface."[45] I resist through my writing not only because I am Chicano but also because I was raised by a deaf grandfather who faced a society that was not created for him to be successful.

Performative writing is a method of inquiry that is social scientific in nature; yet, utilizing a performance approach, this embodied method focuses on both materiality and mobility as a critical researcher investigates a culture, ideology, theory, image, or encounter.[46] Sharing personal narratives and ethnographic notes from the eulogy of my grandfather creates a scene with characters, plotlines, and scenery that when woven together creates an autobiographical performance; yet, performative writing allows one to utilize art and aesthetics to connect scholarship and activism to critique how a communicative event or scene was done.[47] Elsewhere, I have written about how "in critical performative writing, those who do not reflexively locate their place in hierarchies of power or who attempt to transcend the pain of their own shame and guilt about privilege by taking over 'other' ('exotic' or 'ethnic') subjectivities are not doing the work of emancipation."[48] As a queer Chicano, I cannot wait for approval or acceptance of how my writing should look and feel like from an academy-dominated, patrolled, and skewed by historically privileged bodies. When conducting research with and to Jotería communities, culture, and identity, performative writing that is aligned with Chicana feminist thought must inhabit "a proactive space that does not seek approval, acceptance, or intellectual legitimacy from exterior sources and domains" because historically, the narratives and experiences of Jotería have been marginalized, ignored, or violently silenced.[49]

In this chapter, I have connected everyday acts of fathering with intersectional power structures through the act of remembering as a decolonial praxis for resistance. As nonheteronormative mestizas/os with gender and sexuality performances that challenge the binary thinking and Western assumptions underlying normalized reality, our acts of remembering are political because these narratives are consciously constructed to push back on dominant scriptings of how things should or can be. Remembering these acts of fathering means that I have had to grapple with why and how my hand always moves to the throat during violent confrontations. It has meant putting all my dirty laundry out there for you (the reader) to touch and feel. It has meant grappling with the collective shadows of our community and the very real ways we inherit our values, beliefs, and norms about masculinity from our fathers.

It is because of my investments in (queer) Chicana theorizing and the fathering practices in my life that I chose to write this book chapter sin vergüenza (without shame). Encouraging one to "speak secrets"[50] and to make meaning from silence(s) is a form of spiritual labor that addresses the contentious and painful negotiations of communicative space within culture, society, and the self. For instance, when I was child, my father never told me he loved me unless he was drunk or partying; yet now, he calls me only to tell me he loves me. This took years of labor where I had to communicate my feelings to him and vulnerably wait for his response. Over time, silence at my disclosure of affection turned to a hesitant affirmation turned to a normalized expectation within our relationship. Things can change because communication creates reality. At my grandfather's funeral on that hot day in February (Valentine's Day), I stood in Fresno, California to bury a man that I love who had filled the void left by my father's lack (see Figure 2.2). Probably hearing me for the first time, my last words at my grandfather's funeral still make me cry:

> We are who we are because of you. We love you so much. Although I feel loss and fear, I choose to be brave like he was. I choose to embrace life and family like him. I choose to continue to trust his last words to me because he was always reliable. Our rock. Please keep watching over us because we still need you.

Figure 2.2: The author as a baby with his grandfather. Source: Author

Notes

1. Gloria González-López, "Conocimiento and Healing: Academic Wounds, Survival, and Tenure," in *Bridging: How Gloria Anzaldúa's Life and Work Transformed Our Own*, eds. Analouise Keating and Gloria González-López (Austin: University of Texas Press, 2011), 91–100.

2. Cherríe Moraga, *Loving in the War Years: Lo Que Nunca Paso por Sus Labios* (Cambridge, MA: South End Press, 2000); Shane T. Moreman, "Memoir as Performance: Strategies of Hybrid Ethnic Identity," *Text & Performance Quarterly* 29, no. 4 (2009): 350–70; Shane Moreman, "Qualitative Interviews of Racial Fluctuations: The 'How' of Latina/o-White Hybrid Identity," *Communication Theory* 21, no. 2 (2011): 197–216.

3. Gloria Anzaldúa, *Borderlands/La Frontera: The New Mestiza* (San Francisco: Aunt Lute Books, 1987).

4. Jonathan Xavier Inda, "Performativity, Materiality, and the Racial Body," *Latino Studies Journal* 11, no. 3 (1996): 74–99.

5. Curtis Márez, "Brown: The Politics of Working-Class Chicano Style," *Social Text* 48 (1996): 109–32.

6. E. Patrick Johnson, " 'Quare' Studies, or (Almost) Everything I Know About Queer Studies I Learned from my Grandmother," *Text and Performance Quarterly* 21, no. 1 (2001): 1–25; E. Patrick Johnson, "Queer Theory," in *The Cambridge Companion to Performance Studies*, ed. T. C. Davis (Cambridge, MA: Cambridge University, 2008): 166–81; Shane Moreman and Dawn Marie McIntosh, "Brown Scriptings and Rescriptings: A Critical Performance Ethnography of Latina Drag Queens," *Communication & Critical/Cultural Studies* 7, no. 2 (2010): 115–35; Jose E. Muñoz, *Disidentifications: Queers of Color and the Performance of Politics* (Minneapolis: University of Minnesota, 1999).

7. Bernadette M. Calafell and Shane T. Moreman, "Envisioning an Academic Readership: Latina/o Performativities Per the Form of Publication," *Text and Performance Quarterly* 29, no. 2 (2009): 123–30; Fernando Delgado, "Reflections on Being/Performing Latino Identity in the Academy," *Text and Performance Quarterly* 29, no. 2 (2009): 149–64.

8. Bryant Keith Alexander, "Standing in the Wake: A Critical Auto/Ethnographic Exercise on Reflexivity in Three Movements," *Cultural Studies <=> Critical Methodologies* 11, no. 2 (2011): 102.

9. Robert Gutierrez-Perez, "Warren-ting a 'Dinner Party': *Nepantla* as a Space In/Between," *Liminalities: A Journal of Performance Studies* 8, no. 5 (2012): 195–206.

10. Suzanne Bost, "Hurting, Believing, and Changing the World: My Faith in Gloria Anzaldúa," in *Bridging: How Gloria Anzaldúa's Life and Work Transformed Our Own*, eds. Analouise Keating and Gloria González-López (Austin: University of Texas Press, 2011), 191–96.

11. Gloria Anzaldúa, *The Gloria Anzaldúa Reader*, ed. AnaLouis Keating (Durham, NC: Duke University Press, 2009), 291–92.
12. Alexander, "Standing in the Wake," 101.
13. Anzaldúa, *Reader*, 292.
14. John T. Warren, *Performing Purity: Whiteness, Pedagogy, and the Reconstitution of Power* (New York: Peter Lang, 2003), 141–42.
15. Michael Hames-García and Ernesto Javier Martínez, "Introduction: Re-membering Gay Latino Studies," in *Gay Latino Studies: A Critical Reader*, eds. Michael Hames-García and Ernesto Javier Martínez (Durham, NC: Duke University, 2011), 2.
16. Ernesto J. Martínez, "¿Con Quién, Dónde, y Por Qué Te Dejas?: Reflections on Joto Passivity," *Aztlán: A Journal of Chicano Studies* 39, no. 1 (2014): 237–46.
17. Anzaldúa, *Reader*, 291.
18. Alexander, "Standing in the Wake," 105.
19. Kate Willink, Robert Gutierrez-Perez, Salma Shukri, and Lacey Stein, "Navigating with the Stars: Critical Qualitative Methodological Constellations for Critical Intercultural Communication Research," *Journal of International and Intercultural Communication* 7, no. 4 (2014): 289–316.
20. Keith Berry and John T. Warren, "Cultural Studies and the Politics of Representation: Experience ↔ Subjectivity ↔ Research," *Cultural Studies ↔ Critical Methodologies* 9, no. 5 (2009): 601.
21. Alexander, "Standing in the Wake."
22. Ibid., 105.
23. Raúl Coronado, "Bringing it Back Home: Desire, Jotos, and Men," *The Chicana/o Cultural Studies Reader*, ed. A. Chabram-Dernersesian (New York: Routledge, 2006), 239.
24. Robert McKee Irwin, *Mexican Masculinitie* (Minneapolis: University of Minnesota Press, 2003).
25. Gutierrez-Perez, "Warren-ting a 'Dinner Party,'" 199.
26. Hames-García and Martínez, "Introduction: Re-membering Gay Latino Studies," 4.
27. Linda Tuhiwai Smith, *Decolonizing Methodologies: Research and Indigenous Peoples* (New York: Palgrave Macmillan, 2012), 147.
28. Francisco J. Galarte, "On Trans* Chican@ S," *Aztlán: A Journal of Chicano Studies* 39, no. 1 (2014): 229–36.
29. Amanda Martinez and Robert M. Gutierrez-Perez, "Are We Post-Post-Race Yet? Moving Beyond the Black-White Binary Towards a Mestiza/o Consciousness," in *The Assault on Communities of Color: Exploring the Realities of Race-Based Violence*, eds. Fasching-Varner, Hartlep, Martin, Cleveland Hayes, Mitchell, and Allen-Mitchell (Lanham, MD: Rowman and Littlefield Publishers, 2015), 52.
30. Tuhiwai Smith, *Decolonizing*, 147.

31. Martinez and Gutierrez-Perez, "Are We Post."

32. Cherríe Moraga and Gloria Anzaldúa, eds., *This Bridge Called My Back: Writings by Radical Women of Color* (New York: Kitchen Table, 1983).

33. Aimee Carrillo Rowe, "Subject to Power—Feminism Without Victims," *Women's Studies in Communication* 32, no. 1 (2009): 27.

34. Bernadette Marie Calafell, "Love, Loss, and Immigration: Performative Reverberations between a Great-Grandmother and Great-Granddaughter," in *Border Rhetorics: Citizenship and Identity on the US-Mexico Frontier,* ed. D. Robert DeChaine (Tuscaloosa: University of Alabama Press, 2012), 155.

35. Kate Willink, Robert Gutierrez-Perez, Salma Shukri, and Lacey Stein, "Navigating with the Stars: Critical Qualitative Methodological Constellations for Critical Intercultural Communication Research," *Journal of International and Intercultural Communication* 7, no. 4 (2014): 303.

36. Ibid., 307.

37. Bernadette Marie Calafell, *Latina/o Communication Studies: Theorizing Performance* (New York: Peter Lang); Bernadette Marie Calafell, "Mentoring and Love: An Open Letter," *Cultural Studies <=> Critical Methodologies* 7, no. 4 (2007): 425–41; Bernadette Marie Calafell, *Monstrosity, Performance, and Race in Contemporary Culture* (New York: Peter Lang, 2015).

38. Della Pollock, "Performing Writing," in *The Ends of Performance*, ed. Peggy Phelan and Jill Lane (New York: New York University Press, 1998): 73–103.

39. Karen M. Davalos, "Sin Vergüenza: Chicana Feminist Theorizing," *Feminist Studies* 34, nos. 1/2 (2008): 153.

40. Bernadette M. Calafell and Shane T. Moreman, "Envisioning an Academic Readership: Latina/o Performativities Per the Form of Publication," *Text and Performance Quarterly* 29, no. 2 (2009): 124–25.

41. Cherríe Moraga, *A Xicana Codex of Changing Consciousness: Writings, 2000–2010* (Durham, NC: Duke University Press, 2011)

42. Anzaldúa, *Reader*, 289.

43. Ibid., 292.

44. Analouise Keating and Gloria González-López, "Building Bridges, Transforming Loss, Shaping New Dialogues: Anzaldúan Studies for the Twenty-First Century," in *Bridging: How Gloria Anzaldúa's Life and Work Transformed Our Own*, eds. Analouise Keating and Gloria González-López (Austin: University of Texas Press, 2011), 1–16.

45. Anzaldúa, *Reader*, 291.

46. Robert Gutierrez-Perez, "Theories in the Flesh and Flights of the Imagination: Embracing the Soul and Spirit of Critical Performative Writing in Communication Research," *Women's Studies in Communication* 41, no. 4 (2019): 407.

47. Robert Gutierrez-Perez, "Bridging Performances of Auto/ethnography and Queer Bodies of Color to Advocacy and Civic Engagement," *QED: A Journal of GLBTQ Worldmaking* 4, no. 1 (2017): 148–56.

48. Gutierrez-Perez, "Theories in the Flesh," 410.

49. Davalos, "Sin Vergüenza," 155.

50. Ibid., 154.

3

Haunting Breath—A Testimonio (Talkback) of Desire and Belonging

Lately, I (Rob's brother) have fallen victim to a new spell. Well, I'll be honest. I've always been in its grip—white-knuckle tight since I could record the world through these eyes—thinking a lot about people I wish were near me and thinking of people who are near me. I am deathly afraid to be around those I care about. My dad gave me a plastic egg with a Walgreens gift card in it the other day. He had it delivered to me via my sister because I think he's afraid to talk to me. Sometimes, after not speaking with him for months, he will send me a text apologizing for "not being there when I was young." I don't know what to say because, if anything, his presence was over abundant. It's not what he didn't do but what he did do. It haunts me.

Am I spitting into the wind or am I just spitting wind? I see him run from all that he cares about. I can see it in his brow when he wants to be comforting. He knows the impression he has left and will leave. He knows the weight of his words and his body, but he can't for the life of him walk from the darkness. I can see his hurt. He likes to hold onto it. How do you break a spell so strong that it's passed through blood? One night this summer, I'm going to dig a hole in the middle of the East Hills, and I'm going to bury these thoughts of me. Bury the sounds of hushing to counteract this spell.

I'm always pleading with myself to make sure people know how much I care. It's usually not enough. I think I spend the majority of all social situations by myself in a corner pretending I'm in a very important text conversation when I'm really just opening and closing apps. I try my hardest to break this cycle, but to unlearn things is a constant struggle. It is a struggle I think you never actually "win." Every now and again you pass through a cloud, and it's too foggy to see the steps ahead. So you go with what you know and not what you should. I know I need to do more, but my ability to reciprocate is muffled by all the thoughts of possible vulnerability and emotional recklessness. What is the root of this fear of proximity? This fear of closeness?

When I think of closeness, I think of apology. I think you show empathy and care when you've fucked up. I visited my cousin on a road trip once. We grew up together in the same house at times and experienced endless oceans of bullshit. He moved away from San José a few years back, bought some land in Northern California with his wife, and is about 5 or more hours from any family member. I would get texts from him telling me to stop by when I'm on tour with my band and see his chickens, so I decided to take the opportunity when I was passing through. He came out with his new baby and the largest smile on his face. I didn't realize how much I missed him until I saw that grin. I do a lot of separating from my family. I guess I am always trying to prove to myself that I am *not* the same. It's a mistake, I think. There are bits of them that I want to keep. I don't want to lose myself or all their histories in the process of belonging somewhere. I am a mound of loosely tucked-away memories and perseverances, and I am one of my cousin's closest and longest friends.

When I arrived at his house for the visit, he immediately wanted to show us every corner of his property and a video on punk music in the third world that he had saved on his DVR for two years waiting to show me! But not before making a round of mixed drinks for everyone and showing us holes in the wall where he had punched drunk but hadn't gotten around to fixing yet. He used to protect me a lot when we were kids. He'd stop the trains from crushing me in their path when I could not hear the horns approaching. He's only about four years older than me, but as a kid, that's a gap wide enough to feel like worlds apart. Then and now, I admire how he could slice his heart so thin and give everyone in the room a piece. That's something not all people possess.

As the night progressed, I noticed his spirit slouch as everyone's eyes got heavy enough to shut. He kept me up wanting to talk more. I could see his conversation trailing away from happy and tiptoeing back around to feelings hidden deep away within him. In my mind, he was the same as me. He had separated himself from the family and finally got away. I was happy for him! He had a baby, got married, has a house and farm with animals, and he was busy and happy. I was giggling at a story he was telling about my dad and my uncles when it flipped a switch in him. He was overtaken with emotion and loosened by the booze. He didn't get away from his past at all. It followed him through the serpentine roads and peaking mountains all the way out into the middle of the woods. Its roots dug way down in him. With everyone asleep, he began to cry and get angry. He said, "ITS FUCKED UP WHAT THEY DID TO US! THAT'S NOT RIGHT!" He brought up an assortment of fucked up things our family/extended family had done. I have spent years trying to "unlearn" and move past these things, but this fucked me up. I began to think that maybe I am not unlearning; I'm just hiding away pretending these things no longer exist. Lying in the sun, they wait in the blades of grass.

Something he brought up ruined me for months after my visit. I remembered this one night during the summer that my mom, brother, and I were at home. I think this was around the final time my parents had separated, so we were all alone. I remember looking into the entertainment system glass window half open and seeing my reflection and realizing that it wasn't me; it was my dad. He had come in, and he was emotionless but present. I've seen statues with more emotion. My mom was scared, and I was confused. He was upset about something, but I couldn't tell what it was because he could not for the life of him express it in any way other than misplaced anger and sadness. He had stolen a gun from another cousin and headed over drunk. I could smell it on his breath. He placed the gun barrel against his chest and was trying as hard as he could to just push it all the way through. He asked my mom to forgive him for something that had happened. Or maybe it was just to forgive him for being alive? She cried, and he looked to my brother and I. Essentially, he was asking us to choose between him or my mom: "If I have nothing, then I will be nothing." This is proximity or closeness. He was so close to us that he was willing to die. He wanted us to choose if he should die. Intense feelings of love can cloud your mind and cause a kind of spiritual susto, and if you can't process it, it can be the most painful thing on earth. Eventually, he put down the gun, the cops came, and he went to jail—again.

No matter what you do, it lingers. These stains on your mind or these spiritual shocks haunt us. I think about this within the relationships I hold with people and how hard it is to make myself available emotionally to them. You know it's not enough to speak of pain. It's just a stone tossed at a fortress made up of steel—a test of strength. You need to go further and stand in front of the structure and be willing to destroy it. Go ahead! Test its density. You know that relationship between the mass of the substance and how much space it takes up. Walking down this pathway will feel like your eyes are closed and hands are reaching out, fingertips tracing shapes on the walls, listening for familiar sounds. Focus on the feelings and the clashes between them. You will find in this process a duality that is often hidden away from Black and Brown men. To feel that haunting breath of belonging and desiring masculinity is a hard thing to confront and shake from, and you will need to understand that. It's a revelation to become aware of a scale tipped to one end. I recognize that more and more; (re) visiting the pain gives me some perspective.

Testimonio Talkback

There is something special about this testimonio that goes beyond the immense power of narrative to create knowledge, resist dominant scripts, and transform spaces and places. As an openly queer Chicano cisgendered male, I (Robert) am drawn to the queerness of your performances of social anxiety and depression throughout this testimonio, which are issues of ability that are often obfuscated by dominant renderings of queer theory and Latino culture in academia and popular culture. Yet, to be frank, I feel implicated by this narrative in ways that go beyond the simple fact that I am your brother. I can touch and feel the circuitries of gender scriptings moving through yours, our cousin's, and our father's everyday lives, and as such, I am invited to understand notions of masculinity and fatherhood beyond platitudes and abstract theory. For example, I sat with this narrative for weeks, and just like our father and cousin, I have been avoiding you and my feelings. How and where did we learn this strategy? Although I have experienced episodes with our cousin similar to yours, I genuinely do not remember the shocking moment of our father threatening to murder himself if he couldn't be a part of our lives. In many ways, forgetting has been my defense mechanism for many of the "assortment of fucked up things" in my life. What does it mean that you are my only link to this memory? What does it mean that I need you to know/remember me? I can't believe that you have been carrying the burden of these memories for me for so long.

Over the years, we have drifted apart as we have taken separate paths to resist and survive a world embedded in histories and politics of oppression and power. I have missed you dearly. In fact, part of writing this piece is about (re)connecting with you beyond the dominant scripts of masculinity that have locked us in perpetual separation. I just can't seem to move past the surface to touch your spirit. Another part of writing this piece with you is to "show" not "tell" how to empower voices that exist outside academic circles. Testimonio is a method for bringing the knowledge, experiences, and histories of folks on the margins of society to the forefront of dialogue in ways that allow you to hear their subaltern voices. Testimonios are those purposefully political narratives that we encounter that demand that the researcher or listener move out of the way and allow the speaker to tell their own truth. In fact, this "talkback" is not about validating or explaining your "theories in the flesh," but it is about honestly grappling with what you have brought to the table. I am transformed after reading and helping you edit this testimonio in ways that have left me walking around my apartment like a ghost daydreaming about gender, culture, and power. Like a cool breath on the back of the neck, I am haunted by the knowledge that my desire for and belonging to the cult of masculinity has many implications beyond each of us.

You Call Me Monster[1]

Entering the academy
you noticed me
   but you didn't say hi
even with collared shirt and tie
you see a lion
   too proudly shaking his mane
baring his teeth
licking his lips
to feed
on you

Misunderstood
I transform and further   conform
cold-blooded
sharp-fanged
slithering into your mind
squeezing your imagination   to feel
my skin scab
my phallic body writhe
out of the husk

You prefer me naked, don't you?

Brown skin
vulnerable to your lick

Brown skin
oppressed by your desire

Brown skin
to colonize
to pillage
to mark

Other

Do you see why
I had to learn to grow wings?
Why I soar to higher places?
Why I hide in the cracks?

I'm gathering data
about what lies ahead
about what you left behind
about what you can't see

right in front of you

Fragmented
constantly moving
because your voice
sends me galloping
to the fringes
because this game
pushes all of my selves out
because standing on earthquakes
shifts feet to hooves
shifts head to horns
shifts my humanity
to charge
at your face

In and out
of shadows
of shit   you don't want to see
you call me monster,
mestizo, mixed-blood, mongrel,
at-risk, marginalized, queer
problem.

You call *me* monster
but being all these things
is the only way I can   be.

Note

1. Influenced by my first time attending the El Mundo Zurdo Gloria Anzaldúa conference, I was (re)filled with inspiration, hope, and passion for activism, philosophy, and pedagogy. Within weeks, I attended the 99th Annual National Communication Association conference to partake in a pre-conference entitled "Word of Mouth" with renowned independent performance artist Tim Miller. With Gloria Anzaldúa and the pressures of graduate school heavy on my mind, I decided to utilize this performance space to process feelings of isolation and trauma that unfortunately are often the norm for queer people of color in academia. This poem is an edited version of this staged performance.

4

Embracing Nepantla to Survive Intersectional Traumas of Higher Education

As a mestizo teacher within higher education spaces, I remain slippery like a fish so I can swim against the current and into and through moments of liminality in a way that allows students to experiment with course concepts and critical thinking. A liminal space (or a nepantla space) is marked by feelings of disorientation, fragmentation, confusion, or being torn apart. In these spaces, I operate as a nepantlera—a special type of mediator who, because of their particular position in multiple worlds (e.g., sexual, political, racial, etc.), helps others enter and exit nepantla spaces.[1] However, you cannot be torn apart and enter nepantla without a challenge, and you cannot place yourself back together and leave nepantla without material and/or performative changes to your engagement with the world. Oftentimes through interactions, students and teachers experience anger, fear, frustration, shame, or guilt. Bridges are burned, rebuilt, and then burned again. Why do people think that healing is easy? Utilizing Moraga and Anzaldúa's theory of the flesh, this book chapter argues that healing is not painless and that, by embracing nepantla, queer of color educators and students hold possibilities for surviving and thriving within higher education spaces.

Embracing Nepantla

Nepantla is the Nahuatl word for "in-between space,"[2] and for Anzaldúa, nepantla had multiple meanings: a liminal space, a transitional period, a creative act, a process in the (re)construction of identity, a metaphor for forbidden knowledges, perspectives on reality or alternative ways of thinking, and a function of the mind.[3] As a liminal space, nepantla, like la mestiza, is a crossroads[4] betwixt and between temporal, spatial, cultural, mental, emotional, and spiritual worlds and perspectives.[5] These "places of ambiguity, of change, where you're in nepantla, in a liminal, in-between space—you can go either way," and it is in this place that you are "trying to make sense, trying to organize and make meaning out of all the pieces and come up with a different identity, labels, terms" for yourself and others who share your various interconnected cultures.[6] For instance, I am undertaking this book chapter as a creative act to understand the most recent trauma I experienced within the academy. As a project that utilizes critical self-reflection to (re)construct my identity as a queer Chicanx male, I am diving into intersectionality, queer of color theory, and nepantla to explore forbidden knowledge, perspectives on reality, and/or alternative ways of thinking in order to transform into an identity that will allow me greater freedom within academic spaces and beyond. As an in-between space in the healing process of changing identities, nepantla implicates us all in relation to the intersectional structures of power and privilege that we co-create together through communicative practices.

Nepantla is an epistemological step in the "path of conocimiento" that we each embody in our experiences of everyday, mundane life. The path of conocimiento is "an epistemology that tries to encompass all the dimensions of life both inner—mental, emotional, instinctive, imaginal, spiritual, bodily realms—and outer—social, political, lived experiences."[7] It is a coming together of opposites, of inner and outer, of contradictions, and of self. The path of conocimiento "sharpens critical consciousness, restores connections within the self severed by oppressive ideologues and leads to a more profound appreciation of both the ineffable and one's present relations."[8] Further, the path of conocimiento, which Anzaldúa considered to be an overarching theory of consciousness, is a continual, cyclical, epistemic inquiry that requires braving the passage or crossing through nepantla over and over again.[9] It is not a linear activity, but it is a painful process where you "have to destroy, tear down, in order to put together and rebuild."[10] As a reoccurring stage in between a process, nepantla feels like something when embodied by the flesh. It is a performance felt in the body that we express when we utilize communication in the social construction of reality.

In nepantla, you often feel disoriented, fragmented, and confused. It is disorienting because nepantla "involves being torn from security"[11]and "being in a constant state of displacement—an uncomfortable, even alarming feeling."[12] This discomfort or choque is a reaction: "individual and collective self-conceptions and worldviews are *shattered* as apparently fixed categories—whether based on gender, ethnicity/'race,' sexuality, religion, or some combination of these categories and often others as well—are destabilized and slowly stripped away."[13] The apprehension surrounding change or the "fear of being different"[14] causes us to "fragment the self, revealing what we think might be acceptable to others and keeping the subversive, unacceptable side hidden."[15] With your various values, beliefs, and norms now scattered and ripped apart, "you're confused, you don't know who you are,"[16] and "it's hard to come to terms with change and new ideas if they make us doubt and distrust our sense of self."[17] For example, Anzaldúa herself discusses feelings within nepantla in reaction to the New York terrorist bombings on September 11, 2001. "Wounded, I fell in shock, cold and clammy. The moment fragmented me, dissociating me from myself. Arresting every vital organ within me, it would not release me."[18] She felt nepantla in/with her body. Given the inevitability of experiencing nepantla in higher education, the identity process within the path of conocimiento, and the pain and *choque* of this in/between space, this book chapter advocates for queer people of color and their allies to embrace nepantla in order to survive and thrive in higher education spaces.

Moving down the path of conocimiento in academia often feels like crawling over miles and miles of broken glass. Since my high school graduation in 2000, I have moved slowly but surely through higher education spaces. Beginning in community college and transferring to a state-funded four-year university through a master's program at this same state-funded school, I lay resting in a puddle. Exhausted, gastric fluid and blood metaphorically leaked between my first and second year as a doctoral student. When I first started drafting this book chapter in 2017, I felt neither here nor there because I thought this suffering would be over by this point in my journey to the Ph.D., but I fear that the disorientation, fatigue, and dizziness will never end. Will my mestizo and queer ways of being ever be accepted? Will my identity as a scholar ever begin? Only by braving nepantla can we transform our identities; so, having faith in the writing process can be a frightening spiritual journey. A journey into the soul. Wincing, I move my right hand to hold in my intestines as I use my left to pull my carcass a few centimeters further. The effort adds more length and girth to the bloody trail. I freeze. Petrified. Something knows that I need to let my blood congeal to let the scab form, but the hissing and rattling behind me makes me afraid to look back. I am afraid of what I might see—in me.

In Nepantla or How to Read This Essay

Through the method of autobiographical performance and performative writing, I am attempting to create a space in/between the writer and the reader that facilitates the process of transforming identities found within the nepantla state—this is both our stories and not. By autobiographical performance, I draw on the epistemology of Latina/o studies, Chicana/o and Xicana/o studies, performance studies, and queer theory. Utilizing autobiographical writing is a common method in many Chicana feminist and queer women of color work,[19] as well as queer men of color scholarship.[20] However, the method of autobiographical performance is committed to reflexivity as a vulnerable act, as political self-awareness, as from a space of particularity, and as a tool to implicate others.[21] Additionally, autobiographical performance from a queer and/or Chicana/o and Xicana/o studies epistemology is not only about utilizing autobiographical voice, but it also asks the writer to utilize a transdisciplinary method in the organization, structure of writing, and style of the work.[22] There is a move by these works and this method to speak secrets or break silences,[23] so in this book chapter, I utilize autobiographical performance to give voice to my secret or silenced experiences in nepantla at the intersection of race, gender, and sexuality due to traumas experienced within higher education spaces.

Drawing from this same epistemology, this book chapter utilizes performative writing as a method to create this nepantla aesthetic in order to theorize within the space in/between the writer and the reader. Performative writing is defined as a method that involves the reader in the co-construction of knowledge within the uncertain, provisional, and normative practice of reading and writing,[24] and it feels anxious in the body as it crosses "various stories, theories, texts, intertexts, and spheres of practice, unable to settle into a clear linear course, neither willing nor able to stop moving, restless, transient and transitive, traversing spatial and temporal borders."[25] For instance, this book chapter draws on personal narratives created from experiences within higher education spaces. However, it also utilizes poetry created during and after these traumas, and it weaves in weekly writing assignments for a graduate-level course alongside scholarly research on race, gender, and sexuality. Oftentimes in the archiving of culture, an autobiographical performer must break the normative constructions of grammar, syntax, and style to capture the complexity and fluidity of the culture under analysis. For example, Anzaldúa, in *Borderlands/La Frontera: The New Mestiza*, breaks up her critiques and analysis of culture and identity with poetry, personal narrative, academic scholarship, and historical accounts of mythological figures: "I jerk the reader around by also code-switching in genre: mixing genres, crossing genres from poetry to essay to narrative to a little bit of analysis and theory."[26] This book chapter utilizes a similar method to embody the act of writing as a disorienting, fragmenting, and confusing state that both the writer and the reader must navigate.

It is hard to find/write a book chapter in nepantla because it is somewhere in/between. Yes, between you and me. But also, in between *these* words on *this* page. ¿Tú sabés?

> I use the word *nepantla* to theorize liminality and to talk about those who facilitate passages between worlds, whom I've named nepantleras. I associate nepantla with states of mind that question old ideas and beliefs, acquire new perspectives, change worldviews, and shift from one world to another.[27]

Nepantla is a state of consciousness like a pile of body parts (i.e., arm on top of leg on top of tongue), and it is hard to write a book chapter in nepantla because you have to remember your past to imagine a different future. For example, my right leg doesn't need to return to my right hip bone; I like it better as an arm. I've replaced my toes with fingers, and it works just fine now—maybe even better. I'm okay with wearing my heart beating on my sleeve or with having teeth for fingernails. I just need to put myself back together; it is an imperative. "The Coyolxauhqui imperative is an ongoing process of making and unmaking. There is never any resolution, just the process of healing,"[28] and this "orientation to chaos opens us to the fractal and rhizomatic knowledges that are (re)iterated through embodied engagement and not only through linear and hierarchical arguments."[29] Nepantla is an in/between space or a crossroads at the intersection of multiple interconnected worlds, and if we (the writer and the reader) are to survive and thrive in higher education spaces, then we must brave this transformative space together.

Specifically, I did not write this book chapter in the "normal" way in terms of my own personal preference and in terms of the structured, linear, Western way of constructing an essay. I did not begin at the introduction, move to the method then the analysis, and land like a gymnast on the conclusion with my hands held perfectly balanced in the air. I started in the middle. I started by arranging my poetry like bones to create an affective structure that I later secured by ripping apart my weekly writing assignments and placing them around the poetry like sinew. Next, I wrote the essay titled "Ripping the Scabs/Letting the Wounds Bleed" to confront my own performances of masculinity in the classroom. I embraced the pain of knowing that I may never fully heal from the process that disciplined my gender into my body. It hurt learning that we will always have to shout against the wind in order to be allies to each other, so I wrote this method section to help the reader and myself understand my theories of the flesh. With newfound direction, I slithered into the essay titled "Lost Somewhere In/Between" because I wanted to speak directly to my fellow queer Latinos. However, I found that I was indeed in nepantla and returned to the beginning to construct a literature review on this powerful Anzaldúan theory. In the end, I found myself resisting ending this essay. I avoided the conclusion. I sat with this manuscript for weeks as I reviewed my journal entries written throughout the summer and desperately searched for my identity. Who am I? What am I? As a nepantlera, I have embraced that I am not normal, that I am a borderlands dweller, that I will never fit in. Is this how I thrive?

As a performative writing method, I am trying to spin-in-place to make myself and the reader dizzy and disoriented. As we dance our disorienting dance, the roads blur into each other and create images and metaphors that may replace and heal the old and dead metaphors that continue to harm our bodies, minds, and spirits.[30] It is my hope that the writer and the reader can discover those non-man-made paths out of this in-between space together to make a new face or identity to engage the world.[31] However, healing is not painless, and we need to be willing to "rip out the stitches, expose the multi-layered 'inner faces,' attempt to confront and oust the internalized oppression embedded in them, and remake anew both inner and outer faces."[32] In higher education spaces, queer and/or people of color can expect to experience moments of trauma that will thrust them into that painful and transformative state of nepantla. Are you ready? Are you willing to enter nepantla with me?

Mr. Big Stuff
You think you are bad
because you're on top
of your
self
mountainously
walking around

privileged

everyone owes you
knows you
wants your
admiring strut
your "good works"

Mr. Big Stuff

Who do you think you are?
asking me
to encapsulate over 30 years
of humanity
in 10 seconds
invading
ignoring
my requests
for space.

"Brotha,
you gonna have to be okay with that"
You didn't even look up from your cellphone

Mr. Big Stuff

Who do you think you are?
my savior
on a white horse
making promises you can't keep
apologies for bureaucracy
capitalistic necessities
that erased
my voice

I'm happy you asked for me
building bridges are important
but not after this
not before dialogue
and definitely not
when you are struggling
in the thick of public
humiliation.

That's karma.

You see the world
works out ugly
the world is made to bring down
Big Stuff
shaking her belly
blowing her truth
rolling fluid from her pools
of dripping deep
creaming all over
your skyscrapers

mr. big stuff
there is hope for change
but I think
We are
too much for you
too here
too right now.
"You're gonna have to find another
to dance on command."

Ripping Off the Scabs/Letting the Wounds Bleed

In the poem above, I experienced a moment caused by two other men (one African-American and the other White) at a conference that threw me into nepantla. Like most, I avoid picking at the scabs of the wounds that I inflict on others or that have been inflicted upon me. However, Anzaldúa, in *Borderlands/La Frontera: The New Mestiza*, asks us to dive into the pain, face our shadow beasts, dwell in the Coatlicue state, and work through the darkness.[33] I must face the fact that I maintain male privilege too. If the trauma itself has not already ripped the hardened flesh open, bleeding, and oozing yellow puss, then in nepantla, you must pick and scratch until it does. This wound called male privilege never heals fully and is marked not only on my body but on many other bodies as well. Like when I raise my hand in graduate-level classrooms to follow the established decorum of who speaks and who does not, I pick at the scab as the straight male of color jumps into the conversation—taking his space, voicing his concerns, setting the battlefield for the conversation that follows. I feel the throbbing red heat surrounding the opening of past wounds as the queer White woman pushes back on the flow of things. Throughout my educational career as a student and teacher, I always felt misunderstood or silenced, and I thought that here and now in this graduate classroom that I would finally be heard. So, I break decorum, rip the scab, and speak my queer man of color truth: "Where are the queer people of color in this analysis?!" Blood runs down my arm as I realize that as a queer man of color my only means to be heard often manifests by exercising my male privilege.

Utilizing male privilege as a tool to push back in higher education spaces is embodied in some very specific communication tactics. Moreman discusses how male students in a particular class created a coalition that led to hurtful slanders ("That you're a fag") meant to take power away from the instructor during conversations on sexuality and gender.[34] In this example, the male students used language to assert themselves, to challenge the instructor in power, and perhaps to defend their loss of personal status due to the feminist and queer coursework. Further, these male students used nonverbal communication through vocal inflection and volume to increase their strength and dominate the space. Men often use proxemics to accord themselves larger territories and use touch to invade the spaces of those deemed not powerful so as to direct them, to assert power, or to express sexual interest.[35]

Although Latino masculinities navigate through and against these prevailing masculinities maintained by a dominant White U.S. culture,[36] manliness in Latino culture is often connected to sexual and physical power, fearlessness, and the ability to withstand or seek out pain.[37] Additionally, Michelle Holling, a rhetorician and intercultural communication scholar, analyzed and critiqued the television show *Resurrection Blvd.* to discuss Chicano masculinity as maintaining nationalistic tendencies, hypermasculinity, and heteronormativity. For Chicanos, these male privileges can create dysfunctional spaces (e.g., spousal abuse and misogynistic machismo) that reinforce patriarchal systems of dominance, violence, and authoritarianism.[38] Even fatherhood can become a patriarchal dysfunction when one takes the protector role too far, and the individual will and power of the child is negated.[39] Exercising male privilege often reinforces the oppressive power structure of the academy and patriarchy.

Given these ruminations on male privilege, patriarchy, and masculinity, how can I reconcile the contradiction of breaking the silence on queer men of color voices and using my male privilege to get my voice heard in academic settings? The problem with defining masculinity within a gender binary that places femininity as a polar opposite is that these critiques often create an us versus them binary that denies the socially constructed nature of identity. If gender is "an identity instituted through a *stylized repetition of acts*,"[40] then a gendered identity is not a stable category but a processual facade constructed through embodied performances and performatives disciplined into the body and continuously repeated in specific temporal, historical, and political spaces. Further, Jonathan Xavier Inda's writing on Judith Butler notes that

> "woman" absolutely does not refer to a pre-constituted body. It is, instead, a name that retroactively constitutes and naturalizes the bodies to which it refers. "Woman" thus works performatively to constitute the gendered body itself rather than merely mirroring a body that already exists out there in the world.[41]

In other words, whether we self-identify as a man or a woman, we each deny the complexity of gender in the moment of naming, and in that denial, we each forget to be reflexive about the privileges inherent to the false assumptions surrounding a stable gendered identity. This is cisprivilege.

It is too simple to point at an Other and label masculinity as the end-all definition of oppression, and additionally, it denies and often blinds us to the privilege that any cissexual and/or cisgendered position holds. What privileges are (re)created in any act of disciplining others? Julia R. Johnson, in the *Journal of International and Intercultural Communication*, explains:

> If one's sex identity matches her/his morphology, the s/he is cissexual. If one's gender identity aligns with sex morphology, s/he is said to be cisgender. These definitions emphasize that sex and gender are most frequently identified in relationship to a stable and socially binding center when, in fact, the categories of sex and gender are constructed and performed.[42]

Some forms of cissexual and cisgendered privilege ("cis-" means on the same side as) manifests as: never having one's government-issue identification questioned or having medical care denied on the basis of sex and gender; not being asked what one's genitals look like; and not being refused or having to experience physical, mental, and spiritual violence when accessing sex-segregated spaces, such as bathrooms, homeless shelters, prisons, and domestic violence centers.[43] Relying on static identity formations or a gender binary of masculine and feminine reinforces and recreates violence.

Let me be clear, I am not denying the very real ramifications of gender performances of masculinity; however, I am seeking a more contextual and intersectional way to reconcile the processual nature of gender identity and my own lack of voice within academic spaces. Power is fluid and complex. It often moves through, with, and in/between multiple intersections, so whether on this side or that side of the canyon, we need to be careful about pointing fingers because oftentimes "calling out" acts like a mirror sending both bodies into nepantla together. As Anzaldúa writes, "There is another quality to the mirror and that is the act of seeing. Seeing and being seen. Subject and object, I and she."[44] It is time to acknowledge that there is an unexamined connection to privilege inherent to calling out, and each of us is responsible for the power relations involved in the act of speaking up. If calling out is from a place of love, are you prepared to journey with and help mediate the path through nepantla?

BETRAYAL

Two people stand on opposite sides of a canyon
One queer
One normal
Both need each other
to define
the canyon
the world
themselves
At first
each began the work
chopping wood
sketching architectural designs
shouting encouragement
each envisioning
one day
they could speak
without shouting

"I'm tired,"
one yells. Drinking
heavily
exhausted
from eating too many
tamales.
"Can you build alone for just one day?"

The Other
knows

Its pile of wood is smaller
Trees don't grow as abundantly

Water must be conserved
on this side of the canyon.
Days turn to years to lifetimes
Thirsty, it asks for help
and the other critiques:
"How can I start my side
when your side is
so unstable,
so ugly,
so lacking.
Did you not see my design?
It was perfect for me."

"But, here there is no stability
here we had to learn
to face
constant wind
to stand
on shifting sand
to live
without"

"That sounds problematic"
shooting
flaming
arrows

"Please listen!"
the half-bridge afire

"How?
There are no bridges
to cross the canyon!"

This is normal.

Lost Somewhere In/Between

Queer theory is typically understood as any person or group that "resist[s] or elide[s] categorization, to disavow binaries (that is, gay versus straight, black versus white) and to proffer potentially productive modes of resistance against hegemonic structures of power."[45] For example, "A poor, fifty-year-old, African American female rugby player from the southern United States might be considered 'queer,' . . . because each of the adjectives that describe her do not comport with the traditional ideas of who plays rugby."[46] However, queer theory is often critiqued as being too big of an umbrella—one that ignores race and class and, thus, ignores people of color. As a "big umbrella" theory for LGBTQ people, queer theory has the potential to be co-opted by dominant structures.[47] This has led scholars to create new lines of research that take race, class, gender, and the body seriously as important intersections of sexuality, such as in Quare theory[48] and Joto studies,[49] or that considers transnational womanist approaches to understanding how these Quare intersections operate at the local and transnational levels, such as Kauer theory.[50] However, as a queer and as a mestizo, I am lost somewhere in/between these multiple and overlapping theoretical lenses for sexuality studies.

As a queer teacher and student, I am always hesitant to reveal my sexual orientation because I fear that any label might leave parts of my identity at the classroom door. As John T. Warren and Nicholas Zoffel discuss, bisexuality is a liminal space that thrives in ambiguity and contains the privilege of passing. For instance, Warren and Scott William Gust discuss how claiming his bisexuality in the classroom at times requires "proof, the membership card that grants entry" because he is married to a woman and has two kids, and how his bisexual identity sometimes allows him "the luxury of being granted permission to be who/what I claim I am."[51] On the reverse, my claims to queer are scrutinized, evaluated, and in need of proof because I am married to a gay Mexican-American man. As one of the 18,000 couples married before the passage of Proposition 8, my partner and I have many critical concerns over the marriage equality movement, but when we found each other, we found a bond worth all the resistance in the world. However, does this mean that I must give up my sexual orientation identity?

Although popular media, the law, and the White homonormative establishment insist that we were all "born this way" or sexual identities are static, scholarly research by queer theorists and intercultural communication studies acknowledge that sexuality, like all identity categories, is fluid.[52] For example, I am often conflicted on whether I am bisexual or gay because of my long-term relationship and marital status with another man. However, in graduate school, I remember a particularly stressful moment in our relationship when I began developing feelings for another woman and man simultaneously. Does being with a woman prove my bisexuality? Does it make me straight? If I allowed another man to enter my body, does this back-to-back male sexual encounter solidify my identity as gay? The conflict arises because my body has knowledge of feeling multiple-gendered flesh and has inner desires that must be acknowledged, but my outer face must grapple with static considerations of identity that limit who and what I can say and do. Am I bisexual because of my desire or am I gay because of my sexual performances? As a mestizo in an LGBTQ culture dominated by White men and women, I am lost in/between multiple conflicting cultural assumptions about queer Chicano/Xicano sexuality. A queer Chicano position, because of the history and politics between the United States and Mexico, experiences a cultural dualism that is burdened with gendered and conflicting assumptions about homosexuality. These conflicting assumptions are a complex and fluid terrain to navigate for the borderlands dweller seeking companionship, physical affection, or friendship within LGBTQ spaces because of the homonormative centering on the needs and desires of White bodies.

For example, I am at a local gay bar after an academic conference with some colleagues looking for companionship, physical affection, or friendship. The night is young and full of possibilities, yet I am noticing that no one is approaching me. As a cisgendered and queer male, I perform my masculinity in forms that are often aligned with popular conceptions of manhood. Given the complexities of Latino masculinity and sexuality, I am caught in/between the opposing categories of macho and maricon.[53] If asked, my sexual preference is best identified as versatile, yet within Latinidad, gay male identity is understood as "pasivo" (passive or the penetrated) or "activo" (active or the penetrator). In a study conducted with 294 Latino gay men in New York City, it was found that perceptions of masculinity in a partner determined the sexual role performed:

> When the partner is perceived as more macho, more aggressive, taller, endowed with a bigger penis, darker, more handsome, more respondents report they are more likely to take the receptive role in oral and anal sex. Conversely, when the partner is perceived as more effeminate, less aggressive, shorter, with a smaller penis, lighter skin colour, or less handsome, more respondents are more likely to take the inserter role in oral and anal sex.[54]

In other words, my cisgendered, queer male performance and dark *mestizo* body make it necessary for me to be the instigator of communication within this space of the gay bar because of cultural assumptions surrounding my performance of gender, but it is more than a gendered understanding of my body.

As a dark-skinned *mestizo* male within LGBTQ spaces, Whiteness plays a role in this and other experiences of the gay bar. Warren defines Whiteness as a privilege enjoyed simply because one appears White,[55] and as a privilege, Peggy McIntosh writes that Whiteness functions as "an invisible weightless knapsack of special provisions, maps, passports, codebooks, visas, clothes, tools, and blank checks"[56] that "I can count on cashing in each day, but about which I was 'meant' to remain oblivious."[57] For Latinos, Whiteness stereotypes Brown male bodies as the "Latin Lover" or the heterosexual, affectively excessive, and hypersexualized "Latin Papi."[58] In LGBTQ spaces, these stereotypes mirror the dominant heterosexual culture and refract into social scripts that drain queer Latino bodies of their subjectivity. They become objects for the enjoyment and desires of White bodies, or as Lawrence La Fountain-Stokes writes the "main interest in Latino culture often seems to be to find a fuckable boy toy."[59] Anzaldúa questions this aspect of the dominant White LGBTQ culture:

> Do they want us to be like them? Do they want us to hide the parts of ourselves that make them uneasy, i.e., our color, class, and racial identities? If we were to ask white lesbians to leave their whiteness at home, they would be shocked, having assumed that they have de-conditioned the negative aspects of being white out of themselves by virtue of being feminist or lesbian. But I see that whiteness bleeds through all the baggage they port around with them and that it even seeps into their bones.[60]

As I stand in a gay bar post-conference alone, I am suddenly hyper-aware of the racial, gendered, and sexual politics of this space, and again, I am thrust into nepantla because even my LGBTQ community was not created for me to just be me. This is normal.

"See How You Are?"

Is this what it means to "move up?"

to make you proud
letting go
with an elongated "o"
family and friends
that are too ghetto
with a capital "G"

See how you are?
Getting rid of people who "hold you back"
from rubbed concrete
grating
viscerally
shredding your face.
What if I love

tasting blood
and giggling
when I spit it back
into your mouth?

I dare you.
Is it possible to remain sane
on quests for gold
and indoctrination?
What treasure do you abandon?
What stories do you piss on and leave
for some other asshole to swallow?

I find myself lost
making lists
(not on paper)
but in mental surges
zapping serotonin to brain endings
grilling fatty tissue
smoldering naked
flesh

It hurt to add your name
to the right side
of my brain.
The creative side
drowning in emotion
that I cannot bring with me
east.

Weeping for my lost loves list
each drop
like echoes of river
roiling down limestone
underground caverns
spreading wide circles
on the surface of a lake.

Always alone
even with you.

Alone.

I hate my left brain list
filled with people to impress,

people I pretend I want to be
even though I see
that they are just pretending
their spiderwebs are no less fragile
even if spun with lost ancestors
stolen silver and fame
our names will never be in stone.

So I obsess over my list
sending you from one brain ending
to another
hoping I can keep you
always
somewhere
in-between

Either way
you
can't
have
me

Either way
neither of us is free
Is it sad to hear the truth?
small "t"
we
can never
be.

Concluding: A Nepantlera in the Academy

It is a miscalculation to believe that healing is not about pain or that it is solely a pleasant experience. In the realm of the body, a broken ankle in a cast does not end the lack of mobility or speed up the rate in which bone, muscle, and sinew repair at a cellular level. Yet, this temporary (dis)ability repositions the subject in a new world with new constitutions of privilege and power. For example, I never realized how inaccessible my multi-cultural and diversity-focused university was until I tried to move around campus, go up stairs, or try to sit in a desk with crutches. This may be a superficial experience, but nevertheless, I received dehumanizing stares coupled with quick avoidances of eye contact. I've never *felt* like *that*. Healing is not painless. These wounds are deep, and yes, I feel angry, afraid, frustrated, ashamed, and guilty. However, it is not my calling to diagnose your illness for you or to painlessly do the work of transformation for you. As a nepantlera, I am charged with healing old and dead metaphors, so I must brave nepantla and endure the pain of transforming again and again in and out of multiple worlds.

A nepantlera is defined as a mediator of in-between spaces,[61] and as a mediator, nepantleras "help us mediate these transitions, help us make the crossings, and guide us through the transformation process."[62] Embracing nepantla means that you consciously choose to occupy the liminal realities between worlds, including the contradictory stances and shifting sands of this space, to perform the role of a supreme border crosser,[63] and this act of moving toward rather than acting to avoid "implies a willingness to confront darkness and declare oneself its creature."[64] Embracing the role of a nepantlera shifts the queer person of color from a survival state to a state of thriving because "this act, risking the personal, political, and the spiritual . . . [is] where the visionary meets the pragmatist and a spiritual activism combines with deliberate actions and physical pain to transform material realities."[65] Spiritual activism is at the core of Anzaldúan theories of nepantla and conocimiento, and spiritual activism is a continual, cyclical, epistemic form of inquiry that empowers by sharpening critical consciousness and by restoring connections within the self that have been ripped to shreds by oppressive ideologies.[66] As Koshy explains, "to inhabit complexity and liminality effectively; to risk disidentification, as a conscious step towards establishing new common ground with others; to live in the space between margin and center, complicating rather than essentializing these so-called 'oppositional positions' " makes one "fearless, open, sensitive, and vulnerable."[67] Although embracing nepantla as a nepantlera is empowering and a necessity for some of us, I do not want to downplay the risks that this positionality holds in the realms of the physical, the mental, the emotional, or the spiritual.

There are several risks to embodying the positionality of a nepantlera (whether by choice or by nature) that deserve careful consideration and critique. In the academy, there are several risks to working against the current, and given the very real effects of trauma held by this position, I quote at length Kavitha Koshy writing in the edited anthology *Bridging: How Gloria Anzaldúa's Life and Work Transformed Our Own*:

Nepantleras who risk subverting traditional identity categories realize that those who resist change might also resist them. By rejecting labels and yet finding nonbinary ways of identifying, nepantleras are "threats" to the dominant/accepted ways of existence. What was once considered home, too, can become unsafe and dangerous. In fact, nepantleras who question the existence of categories/homes rather than take comfort in them run the risk of being ostracized or driven out. Exposing the falsities and fears within categories can be dangerous, for we jolt those who share/claim this space out of their own complacency.[68]

In my own experience, I have felt both the overt and subtle forces of the academy trying to push me out of the conversation. Oftentimes, this type of ostracizing occurs when I question the socially constructed nature of "professionalism" in academic spaces that dictates collegiality and hierarchal distance between faculty, between students, and between faculty and students.

There are times when I must hold my tongue, chew and swallow my rage, and construct a blank and subservient face in order to survive. For example, I am always shocked by how quickly and unreflexively my words and actions are perceived in their most extreme forms, so a simple question concerning method transforms into a threatening and scathing critique of another's personal and professional identity. In a matter of moments, a mythos is created around my body as aggressive, silencing, and hurtful, which simultaneously ignores how these academic spaces are surveilled, disciplined, and enact violence onto my nepantlera positionality. Given how quickly I become the angry queer man of color, direct dialogue with me is avoided, so my name, words, and actions become the subject of chismé and the preferred topic within "White bonding," which is a concept used to describe the ways in which White bodies use communication amongst other White bodies to (re)inscribe White privilege by discussing, and, therefore, othering bodies that are not in the space. As queer people of color, we need to be ready for these risks, and by embracing the trauma, we know that these risks will tear us apart. We know that we will transform. As Koshy writes, "occupying in-between spaces requires consciously giving up safe spaces and power; that is, we are consciously risking the reality of the bridge."[69] Are you ready to stand between the canyon?

I think I am ready to face her. My clothes are stiff from the dried blood and urine, so I think I can start moving again. A diamond minefield of glass. I am ready to face my male privilege, my lack of safe spaces, and the risks of being a nepantlera in the academy. I can no longer avoid her/my face, and I *am* scared to see the worst parts of my/self. I am afraid of what you may think of me (loss) and my ugliness (fear) because after this I cannot be beautiful, yet it can no longer be stopped. She is too powerful. Lifting my throbbing head with her/my nail, I do it—I look behind me. Who are those people navigating this field along with me? Their wounds are like mine; their struggles are like mine; and there is something familiar about them. Is that my queer student from last semester back there? Over there, is that my nephew? Are they using my trail like a bloody map? Are they navigating this academic terrain by following my experiences and traumas? It is here that I realize I cannot stop moving. I cannot fall victim to mind traps, exhaustion, cynicism, or nihilism. Embracing nepantla means accepting that we are part of a larger struggle, and in order to survive, we must thrive in the pain because we are creating bridges for others to follow. In this book chapter, I have enfleshed meaning to the liminal state of nepantla to help others dwell in the body knowledge that the healing process of changing identities in relation to the intersectional structures of power and privilege is not a painless process.

> Pull.
> One more inch.
>
> Reach.
> One more goal.
>
> Bleed.
> One more scrape on your knees.
>
> They are coming. They are with you. One more time.
> Embrace nepantla.

Notes

1. Gloria Anzaldúa, *The Gloria Anzaldúa Reader*, ed. AnaLouise Keating (Durham, NC: Duke University Press, 2009).
2. Ibid., 322; Karina L. Céspedes, "A Call to Action: Spiritual Activism ... An Inevitable Unfolding," in *Bridging: How Gloria Anzaldúa's Life and Work Transformed Our Own*, eds. AnaLouis Keating and Gloria González-López (Austin: University of Texas Press, 2011), 79; Keating 143; Kavitha Koshy, "Feels Like 'Carving Bone': (Re)creating the Activist-Self, (Re)Articulating Transnational Journeys, while Sifting through Anzaldúan Thought," in *Bridging: How Gloria Anzaldúa's Life and Work Transformed Our Own*, eds. AnaLouis Keating and Gloria González-López (Austin: University of Texas Press, 2011), 200; Vilandrich 35.
3. Gloria Anzaldúa, *Interviews/Entrevistas*, ed. AnaLouise Keating (New York: Routledge, 2000), 176; Keating in Anzaldúa, *Interviews* 5.
4. Ibid., 279.

5. Anzaldúa, *Reader*, 322.

6. Anzaldúa, *Interviews*, 168.

7. Ibid., 177.

8. Theresa Delgadillo, *Spiritual Mestizaje: Religion, Gender, Race, and Nation in Contemporary Chicana Narrative* (Durham, NC: Duke University Press, 2011), 9.

9. Delgadillo, *Spiritual Mestizaje*, 9.

10. Anzaldúa, *Interviews*, 226.

11. María DeGuzmán, " 'Darkness, My Night': The Philosophical Challenge of Gloria Anzaldúa's Aesthetic of the Shadow," *Bridging: How Gloria Anzaldúa's Life and Work Transformed Our Own*, eds. AnaLouis Keating and Gloria González-López (Austin: University of Texas Press, 2011), 216.

12. Anzaldúa, *Reader*, 243.

13. Keating, "Risking the Vision," 143.

14. Anzaldúa, *Interviews*, 264.

15. Koshy, "Feels Like 'Carving Bone,' " 202.

16. Anzaldúa, *Interviews*, 239.

17. Ibid., 279.

18. Anzaldúa, *Reader*, 303.

19. Ibid.; Gabriela F. Arrendondo, Aida Hurtado, Norma Klahn, Olga Nájera-Ramírez, and Patricia Zavella, eds., "Introduction" in *Chicana Feminisms: A Critical Reader* (Durham, NC: Duke University Press, 2003), 1–18.; Bernadette Marie Calafell, "The Future of Feminist Scholarship: Beyond the Politics of Inclusion," *Women's Studies in Communication* 37, no. 3 (September 2, 2014): 266–70; Karen M. Davalos, "Sin Vergüenza: Chicana Feminist Theorizing," *Feminist Studies* 34, no. 1/2 (2008): 151–71; Sarah Amira De la Garza, *María Speaks: Journeys into the Mysteries of the Mother in My Life as a Chicana* (New York: Peter Lang), 2004; Perlita R. Dicochea, "Chicana Critical Rhetoric," *Frontiers* 25, no. 1 (2004): 77–92; Moraga.

20. Bryant Keith Alexander, "Standing in the Wake: A Critical Auto/Ethnographic Exercise on Reflexivity in Three Movements," *Cultural Studies <=> Critical Methodologies* 11, no. 2 (2011): 98–107; Raúl Coronado, "Bringing It Back Home: Desire, Jotos, and Men," in *The Chicana/o Cultural Studies Reader*, ed. A. Chabram-Dernersesian (New York: Routledge, 2006), 233–40; Robert Gutierrez-Perez, "Performance and Everyday Life, or a Latina/o/x in Intercultural Communication," *Journal of Intercultural Communication Research* (September 29, 2020): 1–9; Hames-García and Ernesto Javier Martínez, "Introduction: Re-membering Gay Latino Studies," in *Gay Latino Studies: A Critical Reader*, eds. M. Hames-García and E. J. Martínez (Durham, NC: Duke University Press, 2011); Shane T. Moreman and Persona Non Grata, "Learning from and Mentoring the Undocumented AB540 Student: Hearing an Unheard Voice," *Text and Performance Quarterly* 31, no. 3 (July 2011): 303–20; Daniel Enrique Pérez, "Out in the Field: Mariposas and Chicana/

o Studies," *Queer in Aztlán: Chicano Male Recollections of Consciousness and Coming Out*, eds. Adelaida R. Del Castillo and Gibrán Güido (San Diego: Cognella, 2014), 277–292.

21. Alexander, "Standing in the Wake," 101.

22. Davalos, "Sin Vergüenza," 153.

23. Anzaldúa, *Reader*, 132–34; Davalos, "Sin Vergüenza," 154.

24. Della Pollock, "Performative Writing," in *The Ends of Performance*, ed. Peggy Phelan and J. Dolan (New York, NY: New York University Press, 1998), 95.

25. Ibid., 90–91.

26. Anzaldúa, *Reader*, 189–90.

27. Ibid., 248.

28. Ibid., 312.

29. Amy K. Kilgard, "Chaos as Praxis: Or, Troubling Performance Pedagogy: Or, You Are Now," *Text and Performance Quarterly* 31, no. 3 (2011): 220.

30. Anzaldúa, *Reader*, 121–23.

31. Ibid., 124–25.

32. Ibid., 125.

33. Anzaldúa, *Borderlands*, 63–73.

34. Shane T. Moreman, "Rethinking Dwight Conquergood: Toward an Unstated Cultural Politics," *Liminalities: A Journal of Performance Studies* 5, no. 5 (2009): 9.

35. Julia. T. Wood, *Gendered Lives: Communication, Gender, and Culture* (Boston: Wadsworth, 2009).

36. Michelle A. Holling, "El Simpático Boxer: Underpinning Chicano Masculinity with a Rhetoric of Familia in Resurrection Blvd," *Western Journal of Communication* 70, no. 2 (July 2006): 91–114.

37. Fernando P. Delgado, "Golden, but Not Brown: Oscar De La Hoya and the Complications of Culture, Manhood, and Boxing," *International Journal of the History of Sport* 22 (2005): 204.

38. Fernando P. Delgado, "All Along the Border: Kid Frost and the Performance of Brown Masculinity," *Text and Performance Quarterly* 20 (2000): 395; Delgado, "Golden," 197.

39. De la Garza, *María Speaks*, 6.

40. Judith Butler, "Performative Acts and Gender Constitution: An Essay in Phenomenology and Feminist Theory," *Theatre Journal* 40, no. 4 (1988): 519.

41. Jonathan Xavier Inda, "Performativity, Materiality, and the Racial Body," *Latino Studies Journal* 11, no. 3 (1996): 75.

42. Julia R. Johnson, "Cisgender Privilege, Intersectionality, and the Criminalization of CeCe McDonald: Why Intercultural Communication Needs Transgender Studies," *Journal of International and Intercultural Communication* 6, no. 2 (2013): 138.

43. Johnson, "Cisgender Privilege," 138.

44. Anzaldúa, *Borderlands*, 64.

45. E. Patrick Johnson, "Queer theory," in *The Cambridge Companion to Performance Studies*, ed. T. C. Davis (Cambridge, MA: Cambridge University, 2008), 166.

46. Johnson, "Queer," 166.

47. E. Patrick Johnson, " 'Quare' Studies, or (Almost) Everything I Know About Queer Studies I Learned from my Grandmother," *Text and Performance Quarterly* 21, no. 1 (2001): 2–6; Moreman, "Rethinking," 10.

48. Johnson, " 'Quare' Studies."

49. Moreman, "Rethinking."

50. Wenshu Lee, "Kauering Queer Theory: My Autocritography and a Race-Conscious, Womanist, Transnational Turn," in *Queer Theory and Communication: From Disciplining Queers to Queering the Discipline(s)*, eds. Gust A. Yep, Karen E. Lovaas, and J. P. Elia (Binghamton: Harrington Park Press, 2003), 147–70.

51. Scott William Gust and John T. Warren, "Naming Our Sexual and Sexualized Bodies in the Classroom: And the Important Stuff That Comes After the Colon," *Qualitative Inquiry* 14, no. 1 (2008): 117–18.

52. Gust A. Yep, "Toward Thick(er) Intersectionalities: Theorizing, Researching, and Activating the Complexities of Communication and Identities," in *Globalizing Intercultural Communication,* eds. Kathryn Sorrells and Sachi Sekimoto (Thousand Oaks, CA: Sage, 2016), 85–94; Gust A. Yep, "The Violence of Heteronormativity in Communication Studies: Notes on Injury, Healing, and Queer World-Making," *Journal of Homosexuality* 45, no. 2–4 (2003): 11–59.

53. Pérez, 142.

54. Alex Carballo-Diéguez, Curtis Dolezal, Luis Nieves, Francisco Díaz, Carlos Decena, and Ivan Balan, "Looking for a Tall, Dark, Macho Man . . . Sexual-role Behaviour Variations in Latino Gay and Bisexual Men," *Culture, Health & Sexuality* 6, no. 2 (2004): 163.

55. John T. Warren, *Performing Purity: Whiteness, Pedagogy, and the Reconstitution of Power* (New York: Peter Lang, 2003), 185–86.

56. Peggy McIntosh, "White Privilege: Unpacking the Invisible Knapsack," in *Reconstructing Gender: A Multicultural Anthology*, 5th ed., ed. Estelle Disch (Boston: University of Massachusetts, 2009), 79.

57. Ibid., 78.

58. Moreman, "Rethinking," 4; Bernadette Marie Calafell and Shane Moreman, "Iterative Hesitancies and Latinidad: The Reverberances of Raciality," in Handbook of Critical Intercultural Communication, ed. Rona Halualani and Thomas Nakayama (Malden, MA: Wiley-Blackwell, 2010), 400–416.

59. Lawrence La Fountain-Stokes, "Gay shame, Latina- and Latino-style: A Critique of White Queer Performativity," in *Gay Latino Studies: A Critical Reader*, eds. Michael Hames-García and Ernesto J. Martínez (Durham, NC: Duke University, 2011), 56.

60. Anzaldúa, *Reader*, 152.

61. Ibid., 317.

62. Ibid., 310.

63. Koshy, Feels Like "Carving Bone," 200.

64. María DeGuzmán, " 'Darkness, My Night': The Philosophical Challenge of Gloria Anzaldúa's Aesthetic of the Shadow," in *Bridging: How Gloria Anzaldúa's Life and Work Transformed Our Own*, eds. AnaLouis Keating and Gloria González-López (Austin: University of Texas Press, 2011), 216.

65. Koshy, "Feels Like 'Carving Bone,' " 200.

66. Delgadillo, *Spiritual Mestizaje*, 9.

67. Koshy, "Feels Like 'Carving Bone,' " 203.

68. Ibid., 201.

69. Ibid., 203.

Part Two:

Narrating and Staging Theories and Methods of Resistance

Unbecoming the Poem[1]

I put my life in your hands
loving in the war years like Moraga
choosing flowers and petals over Xiuhcoatl
flaming like   rubbing sticks together
a spark, a dream, a kiss
a release

Aye! Here come los conquistadores
con todos colores   flags waving
together in their tragic nostalgia
can't believe that
can't be   with her
losing heart
being pushed off buildings
hiding in the shadows

All around me!

"We gotta get away"
playing on repeat

I need a journey to find our power
somewhere in the mountains

searching for Coatlicue   the mother
place of beginnings and endings
state of deep knowledge
a soulful mourning in the layers
depression, pain, tremors
she won't protect me
quaking   moving   transforming
giving me   what I need, not what I want
always connecting   connecting
connecting

Why can't we connect?
micro aggressions in the department meeting
gatekeeping ideas and norms
investing in Whiteness and imagined pasts
heteronormativity oozing out of every cell wall
classed values built into the bricks
myths of meritocracy rusted red
ingrained and spackled with your ego

Sigh

Such an old story
Anzaldúa says gente
Listen to your Jotería
De las otras
Dancing while bullets are flying
No warning for these shots
No DJ announcement
Texting final farewells in bathroom stalls
Reaching for your husband's hand
Watching your mother die in front of you,
So you can get away
cantos   de adios
bailando   con las sombras
But where do we go from here and now?

We are   canvassing
throwing shadows like everyday oppressors
Painting a cruel Rorschach test
I see the joy you take in looking at yourself
all over my body   constructing
a bizarre star in your porno

a face to ruin with your sea of men
a hole with your name on it
a thing to claim
mine

Sizing up our gente
I'd say we are surviving
not thriving
we are reacting
and acting too civil
forgetting our mission
We, the first climate change activists
knowing our place in the cosmos
embracing difference in movement
harmony in unknown ordered chaos
balance in chance
understandings organically grown

We   are not   in charge

In this sixth Sun,
let's choose the center   not stability
let's choose grounding   not nostalgia
let's choose multiplicity
inclusive excellence
Muñoz's utópico on the horizon
a new home place a la bell hooks
a definition of love that moves like a verb
never a noun, never a tool of abuse or neglect
an old language of care and affection
still alive and being retold
an unbecoming with commitment
a flower and song of mutual recognition
a poem of hate and fear undone
a truth revealed in and between the cracks
con mucho respecto
openly, honest communication
we   need   you

Note

1. Previously published in Border-Lines XI, 2019, 160–63.

5

Performance Auto/ Ethnography—The Disruptive Ambiguities of Disidentification at "Latina Drag Night"

How are you processing
what you see?
I am
inside
outside
a part
apart
from the very real ramifications
of performing female
tucking my junk
padding my behind
squeezing into a dress
too small
to fit all the possibilities
of gender
of sexuality

How am I processing what I see?
I am feeling
the community
tasting what I have always tasted

licking every ashtray
smelling tequila and cologne
trying to hear voices
that move over
under
in/between
without orders
without borders
to simply
be

Latina Drag Night as Context

In the opening poem, I contextualize this ethnographic report within a specific personal/political moment or feeling because there is a need within queer theory and LGBTQ studies to understand the ways in which race, gender, class, and sexuality work intersectionally in the process of identity construction and cultural production. Shane Moreman discusses this need for more intersectional understandings of LGBTQ Latina/o identity and culture:

> My Latino + gay + male positionalities cannot be exclusively isolated; however, for the majority of the academy, the impossible isolations of joto are unrecognizable. Additionally, joto's inseparabilities are not well-recognized in an academy that still tries to cleanly isolate out gender and race and sexuality from one another.[1]

Further, there is an urgency to this work because the number of transgender Chicana and Latina women has steadily risen over the past five years.[2] By offering a thick description of "Latina Drag Night" at an LGBTQ Latina/o nightclub in the Rocky Mountain region of the United States, this book chapter examines the inseparability of race, gender, class, and sexuality in the construction of gay Latino spaces and places.

By spaces, I am referring to the material culture of the ethnographic site (i.e., the architecture, the beer bottles, the colors, the layout), and by places, I am interested in the performances and performativities that create meaning out of the space. In other words, what transforms this material culture into something more than things in a particular time and location? This ethnographic research report focuses on the context of Drag Night at El Potrero Night Club. El Potrero translates literally as the little corral, but through its many definitional uses, hypermasculinity or machismo is an implied innuendo. Translations like the pasture, the cattle ranch, the playground, or the stud farm indicate a particular type of man is welcome here. As a space and place co-constructed by and for gay Latinos, I was interested in the following: (1) How do LGBTQ Latinos perform homeplace in spaces where they are the majority? (2) How does LGBTQ Latino culture performatively manifest? In essence, I am interested in how these drag performers not only mirror or reflect the larger LGBTQ Latino culture but also how they are producers of this very same marginalized culture.

On one level, this research report is concerned with performances of LGBTQ Latinos in spaces where they are the majority, and on another level, this report is interested in performativities of machismo and the maintenance of patriarchy in LGBTQ Latino places. By performance, I am discussing the *doing* of culture and identity as it is produced and reproduced through a process of mimesis, poiesis, and kinesis.[3] For example, there are rules for how to interact with the drag performers. If you wish to tip the performer, then you respectfully stand or sit with your arm extended with the dollar bill held out lengthwise like a long finger to the performer. She will make her way to you when there is a break in the choreography or when it fits in with what she is already doing near you, but those who are outsiders often break this rule of decorum. By mimicking this performance of tipping, I was able to gain a particular amount of access to this culture, and yet, others through their movement choices broke and remade the space into a particularly violent place that marked their poetics as "outside" the norm. This process of mimesis, kinesis, and poiesis are tied to performativity as well.[4]

By performativity, I am discussing how the doing of culture and identity is *done.* For example, the Latina drag queen costume changes not only from night to night but also from performance to performance by the same performer. Wigs are always a part of the look and can be blond, brunette, red, black, or some combination; while I noticed that long hair is the most common and expected, there are shorter styles from time to time. It is rare to see a drag queen in pants because short provocative skirts are the norm at El Potrero. However, if pants are worn, then they are usually a stretchy material that holds tight to the form of the buttocks (very form-fitting jeans will also be worn). Showing skin is important to the costuming, so the drag performer shows lots of leg, reveals a deep plunge in the back, boosts cleavage out of her costume, or shows off her toned midriff. The costumes themselves are very different and hard to bring under a basic theme; however, the metaphor of the peacock is appropriate here. The performativity of these costume choices is meant to not only accentuate feminine curves and lines but is also meant to gain and hold attention, so there are often multiple or unique color schemes or sequins or unusual cuts. The shoes are always heeled or heeled boots, and the footwear is meticulously coordinated with the costume, hair, and accessories. The poetic choices done to mimic the popular Latino imagination of "woman" moves the space in a particular direction and constructs a place that affirms the identity and culture of the performer and the audience.

In "Brown Scriptings and Rescriptings: A Critical Performance Ethnography of Latina Drag Queens," Shane Moreman and Dawn Marie McIntosh discuss the complex mestizaje (mixedness/mixing) performances of Latina drag queens as they counter and critique dominant social norms.[5] Moreman and McIntosh write:

> Moving between Spanish and English, across differing racialities and among a range of celebrity portrayals, the Latina drag queens' social locations are complicated because the political and material realities of one location (e.g., gender or race) cannot be separated from the other (e.g., sexuality or nationality).[6]

This durable, gendered, and raced connection to sexuality and nationality is not only part of the Latino drag and transgender community, but it is also intimately connected to how gay Latino cultural places are performatively accomplished. These "disruptive ambiguities" challenge "the racial/ethnic norms ascribed to Latinas/os," and this "ambiguous discursive and embodied disruption is potentially decolonizing."[7] Therefore, this performance auto/ethnography describes the performances and performativity of interlocutors within Drag Night as a rich field site to study Jotería cultural production and power dynamics.

In this book chapter, I discuss field observations at El Potrero to narratively highlight the performativity of the space and the patrons and to interrogate how performances of gay Latinos accomplish a homeplace for marginalized identities. Additionally, by utilizing a Four Seasons approach to ethnography,[8] I am not only honoring my own epistemological concerns (i.e., ethics of research), but as a method that questions and transgresses the borders between the researcher and the field site, my positionality as a gay cisgender Latino male is also taken into account alongside my fieldwork. El Potrero is a place created and maintained for me by other LGBTQ Latinxs, and the fact that my positionality is intimately connected to the data means that I need a method of research that moves fluidly between the ethnographic to the autoethnographic (and vice versa). All findings in this ethnography implicate my own identity and cultural location. By archiving gay Latino cultural spaces, I hope to honor my community, gain a greater understanding of my own culture and identity, and provide a unique perspective to understanding intersectional performances and performativities. In the following, I interrogate the performances of race, gender, class, and sexuality in a gay Latino night club to critically understand how the audience and performers of the Latina Drag Show employ disindentificatory politics with the material space to performatively accomplish a gay Latino cultural community.

The Four Seasons of Performance Auto/Ethnography

Throughout my participant observation, I utilized the Four Seasons of Ethnography method as conceptualized by Sarah Amira de la Garza.[9] This method is a creation-centered, cyclical, ontological approach to ethnography that deploys ethnographic methods based on a different understanding of time. By shifting ontologically, I am challenging the guiding ideals of ethnographic field studies by engaging the world from a decolonizing and indigenous politic.[10] For instance, the Four Seasons of Spring, Summer, Fall, and Winter are utilized as metaphors to explicate this method of ethnography, and in this methods section, I move through three of the four seasons to discuss how I undertook this research project.

Spring

The Spring of ethnography "is that time during which the ethnographer must prepare for what is ahead."[11] When I first began exploring issues of gay Latino identity and culture in the Spring of this ethnographic project, I was (and still am) very interested in feeling more comfortable in my own queer, Latino body. The metaphors for the Spring of ethnography are preparation, purification, tilling the soil, vision/vigil, and childhood,[12] and it is a time to assess your biases, strengths, and weaknesses.[13] During this time, it is essential that you be honest about your motivations, and even if they are embarrassing, you must undertake this stage of the process because "if you don't know what your reasons are, you aren't ready" for fieldwork.[14] Unlike in positivist research, biases are not necessarily problematic because "they are part of your subjectivity, and they provide insight into the unique perspective that you will provide in your ethnography."[15] Generally speaking, the Spring is a type of pre-ethnography that is, in fact, a gradual entry into the field.[16]

During the Spring of my research, I utilized personal journaling for three months to face the fact that I have erected borders between myself and my Jotería community throughout my life. For example, I have avoided learning the Spanish language and interacting within Spanish-speaking communities, and only within the last decade as a scholar have I begun the focused work of remembering my culture, language, and identity. Additionally, if I am being honest, I also began this project on gay Latino identity and culture because I was looking for a homeplace in a new city as a recently (at the time) accepted student in a communication studies doctoral program. As a marginalized person, I often must negotiate the self in regard to the other in White-dominated, heteronormative, and patriarchal contexts, such as the academy. In my everyday life, I tactically maneuver intercultural communication interactions through code switching and passing as an essential skill for my survival as centuries of colonial impulses are thrown onto my body.[17] These disruptive ambiguities challenge the dominant cultural norm, beliefs, and values of a space through everyday performances of identity and disidentification.[18] Like a stone in a river, the currents of earned and unearned privilege began over time to wear down on my unique angles and curved my identity into just another pebble in the riverbed. Worn down, isolated, and feeling a deep emptiness, I needed to reconnect with my community. I began this project because I longed to be with others who identified similarly to me. I needed a place to be me in all my Brown gay glory. A place to succeed *and* fail. In many ways, I needed *my* culture to help me remember and (re)construct my identity as a gay Latino.

Summer

> Just as with seasons, one wakes to the summer of ethnography gradually. It is an emergent progression from one fluid state to another. Suddenly one day you realize that you are in the midst of fieldwork proper; you are no longer preparing.[19]

The Summer of ethnography is metaphorically a season of growth, labor, community-building, work, and youth, and its basic nature is intensity, attention to details and nurturing, testing the limits of all dimensions, and rules being semi-learned or form is beginning to emerge.[20] The nature of the Summer is "intensity, requires nourishment 'rain,' attention to details and nurturing, testing of limits on all dimensions, rebellion, conflict, 'heat.'"[21] For instance, during one night of observation at El Potrero, an African-American cisgender man who self-identified as straight was shoving his dollar bills into the costumes of the performers, and later, when he tried to dance with them after the show, he would grab their butts or grind on their bodies with his crotch. These breaks in decorum were met with an ostracizing of this patron. The girls wouldn't go to get his tips; they would leave the dance floor and go to the patio where their circle of friends would literally use their bodies as a physical barrier between the performer and this patron. As a social justice-minded scholar, I felt the heat of the summer in this moment because I felt like I should have intervened; although I would later decide to join the ostracizing of this patron, I struggled internally over whether I should continue observing or participate in this moment of Summer. As Dwight Conquergood writes, "Refusal to take a moral stand is itself a powerful statement of one's moral position,"[22] and in this moment, I realized that whether I acted or not I was still a part of and apart from this community.

Of all the natural cycles, the summer season is a time of rebellion, conflict, and "heat."[23] The intensity of ethnographic fieldwork generates a heat in the form of working through mental, emotional, and spiritual fatigue or weariness, and in some field sites, literal heat exhaustion.[24] As González explains:

> This is what true immersion fieldwork is like. That is what is so frightening and threatening about it. It is during the summer that one is most apt to want to cry, "I wanna go home!" but not out of culture shock. Rather, like in a ceremony, because heat makes one quickly realize what is really involved.[25]

González cautions that culture shock, establishing intimate relationships, resisting bracketing, forgetting that observation and participation are not separate, and exhaustion are all risks that will challenge a Four Seasons ethnographer in the Summer season.[26] The "Summer is a time of intense realizations,"[27] and a Four Seasons ethnographer must remain diligent and focused during this important season. In my fieldwork, I focused exclusively on the weekly Drag Night show from the opening of the club to its closing every Wednesday night. I maintained participant-observation field notes at El Potrero for a total of 64 hours, including the transcribing of data in the form of poetry, pictures, and videos of the drag performances.

Fall

Fall is a time of harvesting, release, celebration, and adulthood, and its basic nature is community celebration, winding down, breaking away from the field site, self-knowledge, and feasting.[28] Autumn is "the cool down; it is exhilarating and intoxicating to reach a sense of completion that is dangerously misleading. The year is not over, but it feels as if the work is."[29] The Fall of ethnography is a time of "reaping what was sowed."[30] This is the time when the researcher must begin chronicling his/her experiences into categories,[31] yet this is a tentative process. The researcher must be willing and open to redefine these categories as he/she continues moving from theory to data and from data to theory. This is not "being 'wishy-washy' or noncommittal; it is the ability to believe something wholeheartedly without being attached to it."[32] Additionally, this is the season in which decisions on perspectives for analysis must be undertaken.[33]

In this chapter, I have decided to focus on the performativities of machismo, and by utilizing performative writing as a method, I am attempting to create a manuscript that *feels* like the culture under analysis. Given the complex intersections of race, gender, class, and sexuality, I am attempting to show not tell this culture, a decision that emerged from a process of continued journaling after my fieldwork ended. For three months, I wrote about my fieldwork; I tried to understand how I fit into this culture, how I became different after experiencing the heat of Summer, and how my own experiences of gay Latino continued despite my separation from this field site. Autumn "is the time to harvest. And this is a harvest from within the human instrument,"[34] so I delved deep into myself to create a manuscript that moved fluidly from ethnographic, thick description to autoethnographic performative writing and back.

Additionally, it is during this time that I realized how machismo was moving through the space in terms of clothing/fashion and how even the drag performers in their breakage of the "impersonation game"[35] performed machismo during these momentary ruptures in the drag performance. Specifically, there are three types of dress that are in line with the cultural standards typically expressed by Latinos. For men, they dressed in three basic aesthetic forms: (1) Vaquero, (2) New Millennial, or (3) Homeboy (see Figure 5.1). Often, you can tell who is an outsider because he does not fit into one of these themes. The Vaquero is clothed in a Mexican cowboy-style dress; he often wears a cowboy hat (with the bill folded close to the head on the right and left), a belt with a large metal belt buckle (the designs on the buckle are different and often intricate), pointy tipped leather boots, tight jeans, and a Western shirt (typically plaid but sometimes a basic color). The New Millennial is clothed in a younger generation style of clothing that may be considered more fashion forward. For instance, tight printed T-shirts or V-necks (with or without buttons) and tight pants of various colors are typical. The shoes are either expensive European/American-style boots or sneakers. I've often seen these New Millennials wearing scarfs, afghans, elaborate belts, and designer clothing (Guess, Express, etc.). Finally, the Homeboy is garbed in a flat-billed hat with a sports team, and these hats are usually color coordinated with their shoes or belt. Their pants are baggy and dark blue or black, and their shirts are often larger than necessary. The shirts are long or short-sleeved and are often screen printed with a brand name, clever saying, or evocative image. Women are typically very fashionably dressed in skirts or dresses with high heels and in expertly applied make-up. However, there are some women who prefer a masculine gender identity, so their clothing is often in the style of the Homeboy described above.

During the Fall of ethnography, I made decisions about what to prioritize from my field data. Ultimately, I decided to follow the guiding ideals of the Four Seasons of Ethnography as an approach to auto/ethnography and performative writing in order to flesh out and connect my field data to larger conversations on race, gender, class, and sexuality.

Figure 5.1: Dance floor of El Potrero with patrons dancing and wearing the three aesthetic forms. Source: Author

Setting the Stage: El Potrero as a Space

Inner: Ba-Bump. Nervously clutching the wheel driving to my site. Ba-Bump. Searching for a radio station that slows the pumping of my blood through arteries, capillaries, and heart chambers. Ba-Bump.

Outer: Entering the space, I greet the bartender and her mother. They tell me what a great show it will be tonight. They ask me how school is going. They invite me to a different night. The stage is different. Tonight, it has a small red couch on the highest level shrouded in sheer red fabric that changes with the lights from vivid blood orange to violet-red to a sickly inviting greenish hue. The stage is set for another Latina drag show.

As a space, El Potrero is a vast nightclub with many rooms, nooks, and crannies to explore and experience. There are five major spaces: entryway/bathrooms, cocktail/bar area, stage/dance floor, patio, and the second floor. As one enters the space, there are black brick walls on either side that are covered in flyers of upcoming and past drag shows, Miss Transsexual contests, special promotions, and/or dance nights. To the right are the bathrooms, to the left is a staircase to the second floor and a walkway that leads to the stage/dance floor, and straight ahead is the cocktail/bar area. This cocktail/bar area is the only bar open for Drag Night, and the room features a long bar top with no chairs, several tall cocktail tables with approximately four to five chairs each (see Figure 5.2), and a long cocktail table alongside the railing that frames the stage/dance floor with several stools for people to sit and watch the show.

Figure 5.2: El Potrero bar top with patrons under neon pink lighting. Source: Author

The stage/dance floor is a kaleidoscope of colors as lights change, turn off then on, move, and shake to the rhythm of the music. The DJ booth, which shares a wall with the entryway, is the most visible from this stage/dance area, and there are more cocktail tables with tall chairs on the other side of the railing directly on the periphery of the dance floor. The stage is the main focal point of this area, and directly to the left of the stage (when facing it), there are four glass double doors that lead out to the patio area. One of the four double doors serves as the backstage entrance, and this door is blocked partially from view by a red and white curtain on the patio that allows for some privacy for the performers to get ready prior to the show. The rest of the patio is furnished with square outdoor plastic tables and chairs for patrons, and there is a railing surrounding the patio with a single door that leads out to one of the two parking lots. The second floor is typically closed during Drag Nights, but there is a second dance floor, a third bar, two gender-neutral bathrooms, and a VIP area upstairs. As a space, where communication can take place at El Potrero is restricted because of the volume of the music. Although people do talk at their cocktail tables, along the cocktail railing, and while dancing with each other, it is on the patio and in the bathrooms that most interactions take place as people can actually hear each other and exchange dialogue.

Stage

The stage is an important part of the material culture at El Potrero and during Drag Night (see Figure 5.3). There is an entrance behind the stage that comes from a cordoned-off area of the patio where the drag performers prepare their costumes and provide feedback on their looks and/or emotional state. As the performer enters the stage from the top-most level, it is a grand entrance in which the intricately decorated mirrored design with two disco balls combines with the body/costume to create a climactic moment. The stage is different every week, but to the left and right of the center backdrop are more intricately decorated mirrors catching the lights, and the lights move and change colors and switch to the rhythm of the very, very loud music. The music moves fluidly from Spanish to English or both simultaneously. As the performer moves from the top level down to the dance floor level, she must go down six steps with the final four being covered by a red carpet; she is a queen making her grand entrance. Sometimes, there are different fabrics hanging from the ceiling to the stage. If sheer, then there is an effect of mystique. If glittered or oblique, then there is a feeling of a grand burlesque theatre. Sometimes, there is furniture that matches the fabric that the performer will seductive sprawl out on, contort on, or bend over on. With the enormous number and variance of lights in every section of the space and the large flat-screen televisions and projectors on every inch of the nightclub, there is something unsaid to be said about the performativity and affect of the Latina drag queen performance.

Figure 5.3: The stage at El Potrero prior to the Latina drag show. Source: Author

Bar

The bar and the bar products are an essential part of the culture. Although there are some domestic drafts available, the bar otherwise sells only Mexican beer, and, therefore, there are always tons and tons of limes cut up for the preparation of this particular type of beverage. Additionally, there are small Coronita bottles on every cocktail table and bar top throughout the entire nightclub, and these bottles are filled with salt, again, for the preparation of Mexican beer. Tequila is consumed after every drag show by each of the performers, and if someone is celebrating a birthday, then the drag hostess will take a shot with the birthday person. This tequila is provided for free by the establishment. On Drag Nights, only one of the three bars is open for the purchase of liquor, and the owner of El Potrero is the only person allowed to operate the register. Every Wednesday night is a two-for-one drink special on all drinks.

El Potrero as a Place of Machismo

Inside, I am nervous because I want to get it right. I want to respect the people who have welcomed me into this space, and I am beginning to make friends. It has been so lonely here in Denver. In this program, I am the only out gay Latino, and I often feel overly surveilled, overly burdened, and insufficiently understood. Here, I am part of this space. It was made for me, and there are too few places for queer Latinos to simply be. I do not want to lose this place because I need it; I need to feel normal from time to time.

Outside, the show begins, the music is loud, and the lights are hypnotic. It feels like being inside a kaleidoscope of illusions, and this Latina drag hostess is the master of espejismo. She is perfectly in sync with the words of the song, and she masterfully moves from English to Spanish and those rare spaces in between language. She rolls her body, seduces the crowd, jumps, splits, winks, and changes costumes. Without realizing it, I am clapping, laughing, caught up in the trance, and yes, I am handing out my hard-earned dollars to this performer. I smile when she says thank you with a long, lingering pull of the money from my hand. It is like poetry.

The music blares out Cumbia, Banda, Hip-Hop, Reggaeton, Pop, Corrido, y mas. The lights are dancing red, green, blue, and bleed into the patchwork of Brown bodies. Brown bodies wearing backwards hats, baggy jeans, leggings, wigs, makeup, cowboy boots and dancing in the shifting points of orange, yellow, purple glow. The space is too big for the crowd gathered for Drag Night at El Potrero, and the night is too late for a Wednesday. But the community is here to support their Queens. Royalty crowned with blond, brunette, long, short, red or black hair that flips when they flip their carefully made-up faces to laugh, flirt, drink, or turn back to look at me. Walking across the dance floor, I feel like I am in heaven as the fog machine spouts out a cloud, and like an angel, I am floating along with the crowd out of the double doors to the patio. To the right, there are red-and-white curtains blocking the backstage area where the performers prepare, and sometimes the wind blows or a friend wishes a girl "Good luck," and I see a hint of skin, a taste of leg, or maybe, a wry smile knowing that I am watching.[36]

In my surveillance, I become self-conscious because this space is made for my consumption, my safety, my dark and closely positioned melanin, but it is also not for me. It is for men who tuck their pinches vergas between their legs, put on high heels, and walk confidently into the women's restroom to pee, as well as the men and women who love them. It is a place where a community gathers to honor their culture, and a place where transgender Latinas/os can explore desire, friendship, laughter, and yes, a moment in life without feeling the cutting edge of the knife pressed against their neck. The performances are important, and like others in this place, I happily and respectfully hold out my dollar bills to show my appreciation. When they walk down the stage swishing their hips to the music, I cheer; when they kick, twirl, bend over, wink, I call out for more. However, *he* is here too, and I can see the need to fight, to dominate, to colonize hidden just beneath the surface. In a blink of an eye, the glass can break, the wind can change, and the veil can reveal that this is still a male cisgendered place. We must be careful.

I am using the restroom at the urinal at the far left of six porcelain installations, and a man comes next to me to urinate. Why? We are the only ones in the restroom. I feel his eyes before I feel his left hand rubbing my newly shaven head. He says, "I like it." I say, "Thanks" and laugh nervously; "Can you stop touching me please?" He doesn't. As a loud nightclub, the least ideal places to communicate become epicenters of performances of desire. Out on the patio, on a different night, another man in head-to-toe Denver Broncos gear introduces himself to me as straight, but later, he pursues each of the drag performers on the dance floor. After a too-bold ass grab or a too-close crotch rub, these performers smile, push back, and leave him to dance alone as they rejoin their friends on the patio. Is he really straight? I've seen him here for several weeks. *He* is sitting near the DJ booth behind the long bar tables surrounding the dance floor. *He* watches in the shadows. *He* doesn't hold out his money and wait for the performer to grab the cash—*he* shoves it in their pants, their plunging necklines, or the lower regions of their backless dresses. These men drink too much and shout crude jokes; they try to center the space on them. In fact, it took me several weeks to realize that by observing the space alone rather than with friends—I looked like *him*. Arriving and watching alone marks you as an outsider. Whether straight or gay, this space can quickly become a bar brawl between Drag Queens or a possessive, invasive rub of a head or ass by a predator. Is this what I desire as a gay Latino?

Yes, it is a place where you can explore parts of your identity beyond your usefulness to the White, homonormative establishment that enjoys the mainstream and advocates for assimilation. Here Brown bodies are the norm, and the

White men are the minority. Here, you will find cowboy hats mixed with sideways baseball hats and fashionable scarves tied cutely around the neck. Here, you drink shots of tequila for your birthday and Mexican beer with lime and salt in a bucket of ice. Here, there is an opportunity to dance with the dark-skinned man of your dreams to Cumbia, Banda, Hip-Hop, or Reggaeton. You are free to pull him close (like hipbone to hipbone) and float and sway around the dance floor. If you're lucky, his eyes might lock onto yours, his hairy arms might support your weight, his balance might shift, and you might let yourself fall backwards for just a moment to dip—and this is normal! It is not a spectacle for your grandmother or primos (cousins); it is not a masturbatory dream for a White male in a White-dominated gay space. It is a chance to explore the Spanish language and a Latino history as it creates a place for a different type of male dominance made queer.

Each night at El Potrero is different because each night is for a different segment of the local Latino community in Denver. On Wednesday nights, this is a space for the transgender Latinx and/or the Latina drag performer and his/her allies. The stage for the performance transforms each week, and the show is shared by and alternates between two drag queen hostesses: Mariah Spanic and Kianna Sexton. Each woman is the head of a drag family and has "daughters" who share their last names. It seems like there is a long history of Latina drag queens performing in Denver, and I have only begun to scratch the surface of this place and this culture. I wonder if anyone else knows about these women? If I mention their names to other gay people in the Denver area, will they look at me just as puzzled as when I tell them there is a gay Latino nightclub in Denver? This is a special place. A hidden place right in front of your eyes. Don't blink.

Bending but Not Breaking Queer

Outer: The show is over. The patio is full of Brown bodies interacting with Brown bodies. Most gay. Some queer. Most male. Some women. Some performing women. Do I introduce myself? Do I stay sitting at this cocktail table?

Inner: I want to be a part of this community. I want to follow my gut and talk to that handsome man with the vaquero hat, the pointy-tipped boots, and that big silver belt buckle. I want to tell that drag queen that I love her pants, that she is beautiful, that if I wasn't married . . . but is that the right thing to say? Aren't I already a part of this place? Can I really be objective?

I know that holding the contradictions inherent to a queer ontology and male domination is indicative of the particularities of gay Latino culture, so in this chapter, I have focused on the moments of rupture between these two worlds as a way of knowing how identity is constructed and maintained in spaces where LGBTQ Latinos are the majority. Although I feel safe in the space, there is a shadow that lurks just below the surface at El Potrero. As a male-dominated place, there are moments where men attempt to dominate other men or where men take their sexual advances too far. Holding this contradiction between machismo and queerness is part of gay Latino culture and identity. I know El Potrero is a Latino space because of the material cultural artifacts throughout the nightclub. The Coronita salt shakers are on every table. The music moves between Spanish and English. The patrons are majority Latino, and the colors/lights are bright and vibrant like in the straight Latino discotheques. In order to locate the queer cultural layer, it is necessary to observe and participate with the bodies interacting in the space. If it wasn't for the men dancing with other men or the Latina Drag Show, then one would take the space to be a "normal" Latino nightclub. What is it about this intersection of race, gender, class, and sexuality that needs to feel "normal?"

There is a much stronger connection to "normal" Latino culture in this space than the connection to the "normal" in White-dominated queer spaces. By analyzing field observations and reflecting critically on my own subjectivity at El Potrero, Latina drag performers and Latina/o audience members utilize Muñoz's politics of disidentification to subvert heteronormativity yet maintain patriarchy as a social organizer.[37] In White-dominated queer spaces, it is common to see rainbow flags on the walls and male pornography and nude photography playing on screens. Yet, in this space, the material culture is being disidentified with to create a homeplace for Jotería. Given the marginalization and oppression Jotería survive within their communities and families, this Jotería homeplace mimics the material culture of the dominant Latina/o culture, and through an embodied breaking/making, Jotería disrupt through a politics of ambiguity to make (not fake) a livable space—a resistive act of queer of color worldmaking. Latina drag performers create a unique LGBTQ Latina/o community, yet they also reflect back larger structures of gay Latino identity and culture. As a male-dominated space, El Potrero nightclub provides a safe location for the Latina/o transgender and drag community, but this safety is tentative and based on rules created by and for male consumption and desire. As a Latino-dominated space, El Potrero offers a rare opportunity to interrogate the homonormativity of LGBTQ culture and, additionally, the maintenance of patriarchal ways of being as a critical component to understanding the values, beliefs, and norms of gay Latino culture and identity.

In the end, I may only be looking for a way to hold myself accountable for my own desire and creation of machismo within this Jotería homeplace. There are few public spaces for gay Latinos to fully express their intersectional identities, and further, there are few places where these interlocutors can interact, flirt, and co-construct a culture for and by them. In the White-dominated, male, middle-upper class, and straight academy, my body is constantly disciplined to mimic and feed the needs of the privileged. I must dress in a tie, arrive on time, sit up straight, be gay but not too gay, maintain "professionalism" at all costs, and never ever question the system. At times, I am okay with restraining the ways my gender is enacted in these spaces because I politically, morally, and ethically do not want to oppress women or marginalize them within the academy. Yet, this "holding back" across the lines of race, gender, class, and sexuality takes a toll on my body. I feel alien. I feel never enough. Over time, I begin to lose my identity and forget my culture, which causes physical, mental, and spiritual fatigue or illness. El Potrero is an imperfect homeplace for gay Latinos, and yet, I cannot fully commit myself to my own critique. I liked being watched. I liked being touched. I liked watching, touching, and showing off my manhood. What does this mean for my community? How can I hold myself and others accountable when this is the only place we have? Being a gay Latino means holding contradictions and living in ambiguity. At least I am not alone anymore.

Winter: The Interdependence of All Things

If "winter will be the time of writing and publishing, of sharing one's work publicly"[38] then reflection is a key aspect of the Four Seasons method of ethnography. Discussing and working with the writer and reader through the Spring, Summer, and Fall is important because "all three seasons ultimately prepare for winter."[39] The metaphors for Winter are incubation, hibernation, retreat, waiting, solitude, and elder.[40] In my time of reflection, I harvested the data from my field site, and it was during this time that I realized that, whether I am in my field site or in my university classroom, I am connected to this culture. González writes that the researcher must build an awareness that he/she is not separate from all things, and it is here that "one realizes that all experience is part of the whole process."[41] Following this line of thought, I can continue this research on the elevator, on the bus, or in my living room because taking a holistic, creation-centered approach to research acknowledges the interdependence of all things and the arbitrary nature of boundaries.

Drawing on a methodological epistemology advocated for by queer people of color scholarship within communication studies and culture studies,[42] I am opening myself up to the experience of Latina Drag Night and implicating my own body, values, and beliefs into this (auto)ethnographic study to hold myself accountable for my own performances of machismo and cisgender privilege. In many ways, El Potrero has become a homeplace for me, and I am just as responsible for the performativities of machismo as my subject(s) of study. I come to this space and stay in this place because some part of me likes the violence, the aggression, and yes, the performances of desire, such as male gaze and objectification. However, I cannot forget to acknowledge the acts of care, affection, respect, mutual recognition, commitment and open and honest communication that I have co-witnessed in this space and place.[43] Queer people of color are not often afforded a space where two men (or two women) can kiss and hold hands to show love in a friendship or in a romantic relationship.[44] It was beautiful to be able to dance with my Mexican-American husband to our favorite songs or to hear him joyously exclaim after his first visit: "I love it here!" Although El Potrero has created a safe space for queerness, the space and place does not resist but rather reinforces the worst parts of patriarchy. Like Kathryn Hobson, I want more from performances of drag and my LGBTQ community, and in attempting to loosen the Western, Eurocentric research gaze, I aim to make a critical intervention that argues for an intersectional, cyclical, and creation-centered approach to social justice.[45] Let us research in the spaces in/between theory and praxis. Let us dream of a more inclusive life. Let us be the world we want to live in.

Notes

1. Shane T. Moreman, "Rethinking Dwight Conquergood: Toward an Unstated Cultural Politics," *Liminalities: A Journal of Performance Studies* 5, no. 5 (2009): 5.
2. Francisco J. Galarte, "On Trans* Chican@s," *Aztlán: A Journal of Chicano Studies* 39, no. 1 (2014): 229–36.
3. Dwight Conquergood, *Cultural Struggles: Performance, Ethnography, Praxis*, ed. E. Patrick Johnson (Ann Arbor: University of Michigan Press, 2013).
4. Ibid.
5. Shane Moreman and Dawn Marie McIntosh, "Brown Scriptings and Rescriptings: A Critical Performance Ethnography of Latina Drag Queens," *Communication & Critical/Cultural Studies* 7, no. 2 (2010): 115–35.
6. Moreman and McIntosh, "Brown Scriptings and Rescriptings," 116.

7. Robert Gutierrez-Perez, "Disruptive Ambiguities: The Potentiality of Jotería Critique in Communication Studies," *Kaleidoscope: A Graduate Journal of Qualitative Communication Research* 14 (2015): 92.

8. María Cristina González, "The Four Seasons of Ethnography: A Creation-Centered Ontology for Ethnography," *International Journal of Intercultural Relations* 24, no. 5 (2000): 623–650.

9. González, "Four Seasons"; S. Lily Mendoza, "Doing 'Indigenous' Ethnography as a Cultural Outsider: Lessons from the Four Seasons," *Journal of International and Intercultural Communication* 9, no. 2 (2016): 140–60; Margret Jane Pitts, "Practicing the Four Seasons of Ethnography Methodology While Searching for Identity in Mexico," *Qualitative Report* 17 (2012): 1–21.

10. González, "Four Seasons"; Mendoza, "Doing 'Indigenous.'"

11. González, "Four Seasons," 637–38.

12. Ibid., 639.

13. Ibid., 638.

14. Ibid., 641.

15. Ibid., 638.

16. Ibid., 642.

17. Gutierrez-Perez, "Disruptive."

18. Ibid.

19. González, "Four Seasons," 642.

20. Ibid., 639.

21. Ibid., 639.

22. Conquergood, *Cultural.*

23. González, "Four Seasons," 639.

24. Ibid., 642.

25. Ibid., 642.

26. Ibid., 639.

27. Ibid., 642.

28. Ibid., 640.

29. Ibid., 644.

30. Ibid., 640.

31. Ibid., 645.

32. Ibid., 645.

33. Ibid., 644.

34. Ibid., 644.

35. Kerry O. Ferris, "Ain't Nothing Like the Real Thing, Baby: Framing Celebrity Impersonator Performances," *Text and Performance Quarterly* 30, no. 1 (2010): 60–80.

36. In a recent check back with the field, a solid barrier has now been erected to provide more privacy and safety for the performers.

37. José Esteban Muñoz, *Disidentifications: Queers of Color and the Performance of Politics* (Minneapolis, MN: University of Minneapolis Press, 1999).

38. González, "Four Seasons," 644.

39. Ibid., 645.

40. Ibid., 640.

41. Ibid., 633.

42. Bryant Keith Alexander, "Standing in the Wake: A Critical Auto/Ethnographic Exercise on Reflexivity in Three Movements," *Cultural Studies <=> Critical Methodologies* 11, no. 2 (2011): 98–107; Gloria Anzaldúa, *Light in the Dark/Luz en lo Oscuro: Rewriting Identity, Spirituality, Reality* (Durham, NC: Duke University Press, 2015); Bernadette Marie Calafell, "Rhetorics of Possibility: Challenging the Textual Bias of Rhetoric through the Theory of the Flesh," in *Rhetorica in Motion: Feminist Rhetorical Methods and Methodologies*, ed. E. Schell and K. Rawson (Pittsburgh, PA: University of Pittsburgh Press, 2010), 104–17; Gust A. Yep, "Queering/Quaring/Kauering/Crippin'/Transing 'Other Bodies' in Intercultural Communication," *Journal of International and Intercultural Communication* 6, no. 2 (May 2013): 118–26, https://doi.org/10.1080/17513057.2013.777087.

43. bell hooks, *All about Love: New Visions* (New York, NY: HarperCollins, 2001).

44. Robert Gutierrez-Perez, "Performance and Everyday Life, or a Latina/o/x in Intercultural Communication," *Journal of Intercultural Communication Research* 49, no. 5 (2020): 433–41. Robert Gutierrez-Perez, "A Return to El Mundo Zurdo: Anzaldúan Approaches to Queer of Color Worldmaking and the Violence of Intersectional Heteronormativity," *Women's Studies in Communication* 43, no. 4 (2020): 384–399.

45. Kathryn Hobson, "Performative Tensions in Female Drag Performances," *Kaleidoscope: A Graduate Journal of Qualitative Communication Research* 12, no. 1 (2013): 35–51.

6

The Four Seasons of Oral History Performance, or Theories from the Fringes of Aztlán

Search your heart. This is very important, and is perhaps the most important aspect of preparations. *Why* are you doing this? ... Be honest about your motives, even if they are embarrassing. —González, "Four Seasons"[1]

I'm scared to go home. I'm terrified that I won't fit in. That to my friends and family, I would be unrecognizable—a monster even to them. After posting about lumbersexuality[2] on social media for weeks, talking about it with my colleagues and friends all over Denver, and sharing my lumbersexuality research with my students in an amazing class lesson, my joke about lumbersexuality with one of my closest friends back home in California absolutely fell flat. In fact, she and the rest of our friends and family thought I was calling her a lesbian and interpreted my confused attempts to explain the joke as mocking and belittling her gender and sexuality. As the first in our friend circle to get pregnant, everyone felt an (un)natural need to leap to her defense with raised voices, aggressive body posturing, and a strange use of height as the taller ones glared down at me. It was tense. First, to learn that lesbianism is perceived as an insult to these people I called friends was a heteronormative violence, and further, she knew nothing about my latest most-talked-about personal/professional interest. That misunderstanding destroyed and/or injured several bridges to others in that space, and they were never repaired. I won't soon forget how they jumped in with their not-so-subtle disciplining of gender and sexual norms. How scary to not belong anywhere!

Oral History Performance (OHP) is a method that takes its "impetus from formal or informal oral history interviews"[3] and materializes these historical narratives in a "live representation as both a form (a container) and a means (a catalyst) for social action."[4] OHP interviewing views the narrative event unfolding between teller and told as a performance that contains "linguistic, paralinguistic, kinesic, proxemic, artifactual, and olfactory dimensions."[5] This remembering of past and present events often enfolds in a "poetic rendering and linguisting layering" between the telling and the told.[6] As a performance, oral history interviewing is embodied in intersectional meanings and contextual relationships of power. Indeed, it is the inherent value of gathering the teller's symbol system and their own phenomenological theories of what it means/meant to experience the historical event that makes oral history interviewing a provocative methodological tool.[7] Additionally, it is what the teller remembers and values as she/he tells his/her historical subjectivity that is under analysis within this method. It is between the telling and the told where theories in the flesh are narrated.

The Four Seasons approach is an ontological shift to social science research that draws on a cyclical, creation-centered understanding (conocimiento) of world events and history. The Four Seasons of Oral History Performance (FSOHP) does (and does not) introduce new methods to those utilized in performance (auto)ethnography, rhetorical criticism, and oral history performance because, as an ontological shift, it is an embodied act that challenges the way we write about communities on the peripheries. Yes, I precisely deployed a variety of familiar methods within the FSOHP, such as the taking of fieldnotes, personal journaling, and in-depth interviewing,[8] but I have also drawn upon performance methods, such as (border) arte as meditation, poetic transcription, and performative writing aesthetics, to allow historical narratives of GBTQ Chicanos to dictate their own rules of inquiry and presentation. Utilizing these various methods, I came to the following four conocimientos: a belief and value in natural cycles, radical interconnectedness, preparedness, and the discipline of harmony/balance. The following sections outline these four understandings or conocimientos that guided me during the research process and the writing of this chapter. Each of the conocimientos learned here are rooted on the guiding ideals developed by and grounded in communication by Amira de la Garza. As a methodology, each *conocimiento* is *intimately* connected to each other, as are each of the Four Seasons, and the FSOHP is guided by four conocimientos that demand a rigorous ethic geared toward reflexivity, cultural and queer conceptual nuances, and decolonial approaches to research and everyday life.

Conocimiento #1: Natural Cycles

Movement through natural cycles is the heart and center of the Four Seasons approach and is "rooted in the belief that all natural experience is ordered in cycles, which are then reflected in the processes and experiences of all living beings."[9] For example, in the Spring of my oral history performance (OHP), I struggled like a seed underground breaking its shell, reaching tendrils downward into the dark. Diligently, I pushed gravel, dirt, and filth out of my way in a desperate search for minerals, nourishment, and the cool, crisp taste of water. To illustrate this alternative movement through time and space, my Spring did not take three months like in the Western calendar, but rather, it took eight months to complete as I prepared physically, mentally, emotionally, and spiritually for this FSOHP project. There is an aspect of "appropriateness" within the natural cycles of the Four Seasons that does not rely on any academic "fixed point of experiential demarcation."[10] I, the researcher, had to reach particular inner/outer or personal/political conocimientos before I could move into the next season. At times this growth was frightening and at other times transformative. In each season, this circular and natural orientation toward time, space, and the spirit required a different kind of movement through everyday life—it was a humbling process.

Conocimiento #2: Radical Interconnectedness

> Creation-centered cultures share a close relationship with nature, and with the
> yearly cycles that govern life. Spiritual and social rituals reflect those cycles,
> respecting the interdependence between all things —González, "Four Seasons"[11]

As de la Garza describes in the epigraph, a creation-centered approach understands that there is a radical interconnectedness to all things. This *conocimiento* is rooted in an awareness that there is an "arbitrary nature [to the] boundaries that we construct for ourselves in our social experience."[12] For instance, in the Summer of my OHP, I reached out to the highly cultivated "gatekeepers" who I developed a relationship with during my Spring, and when I felt lost after few potential co-witnesses emerged from those coveted gatekeepers, I was chastised by a fellow gay Latino scholar and colleague: "Why haven't you put your call on Facebook?" In my quest to hold onto "rigid disciplinary and academic dictates of what 'counts' as a source of knowledge or information,"[13] I, as a gay Chicano, never considered asking my own Chicano/Latino/Mestizo family or gay/bisexual/trans*/queer/questioning friends for help. Here I am, an insider/outsider connected to my community and a dedicated advocate for those on the peripheries, and I never once considered how "research is [an] intimate, organic and interdependent" process.[14] Why did I put up a wall between me and my community? As a spiritual experience of knowing and being, radical interconnectedness is an onto-epistemological shift "to expand perception; to become conscious, even in sleep; to become aware of the interconnections between all things by attaining a grand perspective."[15] By centering oneself in this *conocimiento,* one navigates everyday life with a spiritual awareness that disrupts and/or bridges dualistic thinking and transgresses the colonial/modern borders between us/them, body/mind, and man/nature.

Conocimiento #3: Preparedness

With an awareness of radical interconnectedness and natural cycles, there is an element of preparedness or an understanding that "one simply can not enter into that for which he or she is not prepared appropriately."[16] This element emerged in the Spring of my OHP when I found myself avoiding the IRB application process. I was self-sabotaging my project by taking on guest lectures for colleagues' classrooms, sitting in on an excellent course, volunteering for two organizations, and so much more. One morning, an affirmation came to me during my meditation/personal journaling—it clicked. I knew how I was going to do this project. Then, an immense melancholia overcame my body that had me crying in the car with my husband during a drive to our friends' brunch. I was finally ready to begin the interview process, but I had no time to do it. I had to face my shadow beast. The process of relinquishing my lectures, explaining missing classes, and removing myself from obligations that I had convinced myself were set in stone was how I moved from Spring to Summer. Sure, the extra time allowed me to finally complete the IRB process, but it was a mental and emotional *breakdown* and a subsequent realignment of my priorities that ultimately completed the Spring cycle. I was finally prepared.

Conocimiento #4: Harmony/Balance

All three conocimientos will "manifest themselves in the ultimate awareness that all forms of experience must be respected and given attention, due to their inter-dependent nature."[17] For example, in the Summer of my OHP, I was exhausted from the heat of the interviewing process. In a moment I now regret, I did not follow my own ethics regarding how transparent I would be with my project. I felt exhausted from the Summer and rushed to set an interview without send-ing the same information I sent to all my co-witnesses. In response to my lack of preparedness and my lack of awareness of interconnectedness and the cycli-cal process, the potential interviewee canceled our interview and felt exploited. Anzaldúa writes that "methods have underlying assumptions, implying theoreti-cal positions and basic premises,"[18] so "it is the *application* of the methods within a paradigm that often demonstrates the ontological positioning of the researcher [emphasis in original]."[19]

As this narrative reveals, I had fallen into what Conquergood describes as the "custodian's rip-off," which is essentially about selfishness.[20] The custodian's rip-off is a moral/ethical performative stance in which the "strong attraction toward the other coupled with extreme detachment results in acquisitiveness instead of genuine inquiry, plunder more than performance."[21] I am confessing this to you because within the FSOHP: "What you think is a flaw simply tells you what is culturally valued, not what is 'wrong with you'. They are guides that lead you in the direction of what you might need."[22] Following these four conocimientos, I moved through the Spring, Summer, Fall, and Winter of OHP being reflexive at all stages of the research process to honor the cultural and queer nuances of each interviewee and to understand my own indoctrination into colonial-modern gender systems in both personal and political forms.

Spring: Tilling the Soil

> Let me be free
> No worries or regrets
> No Saturday morning chores
> No check off that list, this list,
> and not in the good-for-nothing
> never-take-the-dog-out kind of way
>
> There is labor in stillness

There is depth
buried like a seed
en nuestra madre

Why can't you appreciate my two spirits?

Stirring, churning, bringing meaning
I want to binge watch TV in peace
I want to consume too much porn
I want to sit in silence

Neither quiet or complacent
Everyday life is a struggle, a war,
an inner battle for control

search, searching in the darkness
what it means   to be   we

A Seed Will Not Grow Without Being Planted!

In the above poem, I share my experiences of the Spring with images, metaphor, and symbols to acknowledge the myriad possibilities inherent in this season. Yet, I want to bracket the core tenants and key processes of this methodological season because the Spring has its own cycle that must be completed. (Re)performing the "stirring, churning, bringing meaning" of my Spring through poetry is an attempt to plant a seed. Like roots growing in darkness, the Spring acknowledges that "there is labor in stillness / there is depth." Let me be clear, my Spring was not easy. Every day of my eight-month Spring cycle was "a struggle, a war, an inner battle for control." It was an always and never-ending preparation that did not stop when I did or did not read, meditate, image-make, or write poetry. As de la Garza explains:

> During the spring, the human instrument is being prepared for fieldwork. This is a time for much introspection and honest observation of the self. What are your strengths and flaws? This will tell you much about your methodological preferences and choices once you are out in the field.[23]

For me, the Spring was a natural beginning to the end of a prior Winter season of this same project. In rare form, my Winter began and ended over winter break and winter quarter of my final year in graduate school. During the hectic winter celebration season, I was taking my comprehensive exams over a marathon period of three weeks that ended in a grand total of 126 pages. Entering my Winter quarter, I, with the help of my advisor, constructed a 70-page proposal and defended and passed it by the end of March. I am happy to report I passed with distinction. Yet, this doesn't *feel* like the whole story. de la Garza explains, "A seed will not grow without being planted!"[24] Like a rabbit skinny from hibernating too long, I knew it was the moment of Spring because I was exhausted and empty. To survive that prior Winter of this project, I had to give everything to those comprehensive exams and proposal. Pieces from my multiple souls were shocked out of my body to complete my writing/career/life/identity goals. I barely survived.

(Border) Arte as Meditation

> Learning how to detach one's self from things held dear, including one's ideas, was at first practiced in the spring by bracketing one's biases and limitations —González, "Four Seasons."[25]
> Border art remembers its roots—sacred and folk art are often still one and the same. —Anzaldúa, *Light*[26]

(Border) Arte as Meditation (BAM) is a method I utilized to adapt my body, mind, and soul to the Four Seasons approach. BAM is an epistemological mestizaje of Anzaldúan concepts with those of de la Garza lived through each of my limbs as I moved, performed, and communicated. "Border Arte" tries to decolonize spaces with its aesthetics and "deals with shifting identities, border crossings, and hybridism—all strategies for decolonization."[27] Whereas "Art as Mediation" is a method utilized by de la Garza to describe a practice of creating art toward the goal of reflexive engagement with the self, world, and beyond.[28] BAM is the process I utilized to remain reflexive throughout each season and to build my awareness of natural cycles and radical interconnectedness. When I was prepared to move forward, I could *feel* it. No one told me when to move on, and yet at the same time, everything told me it was time to move on.

For me, I dived into my body in the most physical way I knew how— weightlifting. Weightlifting is one of the few physical activities that my father and I could do together. I wasn't a great athlete, and it didn't help that if I messed up during a baseball game, the ride home would be filled with either verbal or physical abuse. Alongside weightlifting, I began a consistent low-impact cardio regimen (if I push too hard I get painful knots in my lower back and hip), and after spending time with de la Garza at a Summer Creative Ethnography Institute in Arizona, I consistently integrated the practice of yoga into my BAM. These practices proved useful to reduce my stress and to rebuild my body after a tough Winter. In addition, I utilized tarot and oracle card decks as anchors to my practices to help me focus my daily meditations on my personal biases, expectations, triggers, and shadow issues; some of which I have shared previously and at the end of this book.[29] In this way, activities like reading, media viewing, passive observations of relevant cultural sites, and personal journaling all became a kind of religious poetic worked through the body—a spiritual labor germinating within the practitioner.

In Figure 6.1, I share one of the many images created through BAM. Indeed, throughout the rest of this chapter, I will continue to share poetry and images created during each season of this project as both a decolonial performative writing move and a valid form of knowledge in its own right. In this particular image, I was shocked after completing Figure 6.1 because I found that the woman staring back at me *looked* like me. She/he embodied where I belonged and where I am now. I named myself Xochito, which is the male form of "Little Flower" in a kind of Nahuatl/Spanish, she/he, xe hybrid that nodded to Xochipilli (Aztec god of art, games, dance, flowers, song, and homosexuality). At the beginning of my Spring, I was in a traumatized state from the pressures of Winter, but mainly from the politics of inclusion/exclusion operating within academia. Betrayals, lies, and gossip surrounded and followed my presence into every classroom, hallway, conference, and department office because, as a queer person of color, I am not safe. Ever. My BAM practice in the Spring was a constant diving into my mental, psychic, and spiritual wounds through my navel. Xochito came to me as a gift. A mirror to finally see myself as others see me. Aren't I so queer flipping my long hair? Don't you love the sound of my elaborate shells when I move and laugh? What a shock my intersectional voice must be! Like pink lightning flashing across a tumultuous yet beautiful purple sky. La luna voyeristic in the corner lighting my dark and stormy path. What is Xochito doing in the river? Why is xe pouring water back into the stream? Is xe healing my susto (spiritual shock)? Xochito is my nagual, and Xochito is also my shadow beast. Xe's questions and yearnings manifest in anger, fear, helplessness, addictions, numbness, disillusionment, and depression and operate like a blank eye affecting all we see, so we can maintain illusions of safety and entitlement.[30]

Figure 6.1: Xochito returns to El Rio. Source: Author

The End of Spring

For Helen.

> Go for a walk
> Buy some flowers
> Move up into the new
> spirit, trusting
> open y vulnerable:

>> I blamed you for being
>> poor, second-hand food
>> a la Chingada
>> sowing seeds from different trees
>> mahogany deep

> Love, You loved.
> Volunteering, La familia,

Laughter, Afternoons
on the porch, the east wind
en su cara

Whispering, "seek silence,
seek truth, seek
within"

Stress is coming
Adventure pushing up into the horizon,
sorrow, inner transformation
don't postpone, don't forget

Love grows.

A Summer of Oral History Performance

In Figure 6.2, the moon (my guardian) looms high in the sky as Owl (wisdom through transformation) makes a presence in my BAM practice. There is flowering and pumpkins ripe for the picking, and there is light! Light is everywhere. Summer is the time to reach out to participants, perform the in-depth interviews, maintain personal journaling, continue weightlifting and yoga regularly, member-check with the community, and sustain your BAM practice.[31] My Summer season took three months to complete, and it took place between November and January. In fact, oral history interviewing took place between December 8 and December 22, 2015. The "heat" was almost unbearable.

> Until one learns to engage in conflict and stay, one does not know what members of a culture are like. —González, "Four Seasons"[32]

I am avoiding the hard work of locating the origins of my self-hate. Whose voice is telling me these lies about myself? I look in the mirror, and I hear: "Ugly. Fat. Unworthy." I hear him when interacting with people: "They hate you. You don't belong." I feel stuck in self-hatred, and I want to break free from these bad habits. In my meditation and personal journaling, I wrote down this thought: "Where does this destructive influence come from and who needs it?"

Figure 6.2: Wisdom through transformation. Source: Author

Oral History Performance as a Dialogic Performance

We cannot be subjects without dialogue, without witnessing.[33]

My first interview for this project was with a gay Chicano friend from Commerce City, Colorado. We first met in 2014 when we co-presented a workshop on LGBTQ Latinos for a local university together. As graduate students, he and I immediately connected before and during the workshop, yet after some time, we lost touch. Like all the participants, he chose his own pseudonym, and Jay met me for the interview in the community room of my apartment complex in the Uptown neighborhood of Denver. I remember it was cold in the room, and my recording had several moments where we laughed together as I tried to fix the thermostat. Afterward, I couldn't help but flirt with this intelligent, caring, and attractive human being. This time, we have stayed in dialogue long after our interview was completed because I also shared and disclosed my experiences alongside him. Although we have maintained a strong friendship across time and space, I will never forget this first interview because of the queer intimacy of this method. I didn't realize how eager I was to see my life experiences reflected in another's queer Latinx life. I belonged.

Oral history interviewing is a dialogic performance because it is a method that utilizes the strains and frictions between difference and identity to have an "intimate conversation with other people and cultures."[34] In the moment of dialogic performance with my interviewees, I remained present by paying attention to the embodied, purposeful, reciprocal, and contextual performatives of my co-witnesses.[35] As not only a form of respect, dialogic performance and dialogic performatives acknowledge the power dynamics within the researcher-narrator relationship.[36] A shift to dialogic performance acknowledges that "participant-observation does not capture the active, risky, and intimate engage-ment with Others that is the expectation of performance."[37] Johnson discusses Conquergood's understanding of performance methodology as:

> a lens for examining culture, particularly the communication practices of subal-tern groups—the power of symbols and imagination in both consolidating and contesting oppression and how cultural creativity and human agency are both inscribed and incited by domination.[38]

Further, like Madison, I believe that performance approaches to qualitative research is dangerous work, and in this chapter, I view the collected oral histories and the co-witnessing of these Jotería accounts of everyday life as making me an "*agent* of danger" who seeks to "flip the script" and to "reposition the dangerous" from the individual/community level back onto the macro system of control that sustains the "machinery of imperialism, structures of homophobia, and phal-locentric power."[39] Performance is a method as well as a theory and a form of aesthetic presentation.

Dialogic Performance as a Co-Performative Witnessing

OHP interviewing as a dialogic performance is about co-performative witnessing of an Other culture as a feeling, sensing, being, and doing witness.[40] Due to the holiday season, each interview was conducted under the shadow of upcoming family interactions and community responsibilities. This specter of Christmas loomed large during all the interviews. For example, my second interview, via Skype, was with a gay Chicano named Positivo. Positivo was completing his Ph.D. outside of Colorado, and because of his own dissertation project, he had to skip Christmas with his family in Denver that year. With Positivo, I felt an immediate connection to his story because I too was skipping Christmas that year. To set up an interview with my interviewees, I utilized a snowball method similar to E. Patrick Johnson in *Sweet Tea* in which I reached out first to local community members and friends, and from there, I was connected to each of my interviewees.[41] For three years, I served alongside my Chicanx and Latinx community as an active committee member with the La Raza Youth Leadership Program and Conference in Denver, so I turned for recruitment help to the many leaders, volunteers, made family and friends who have been kind enough to let me advocate alongside them for our various interconnected communities. Like Positivo, I am a GBTQ Chicano in academia and part of the history and politics of the Denver metro area, so we are a witness to each other's story. I can't just take his narrative and run.

Co-performative witnessing is to live in the borderlands of contested identities, to put your body on the line within an Other's soundscapes of power, and to engage in a politics of "response (ability)."[42] By recognizing that we are sharing the OHP interview time not to maintain fixed understandings of marginalization but to witness the contestations of identities and culture within history, co-performative witnessing places the researcher into the borderlands "where you speak 'with' not 'to' others."[43] Placing one's body on line with an Other is a political act that illuminates, coalesces, and engages with soundscapes of power that are hard to capture in text.[44] As Madison explains, "Soundscapes carry with them the liveness and immediacies of sounds overlaid by worlds of inter-animation and gesture."[45] To co-witness an Other's contested identity in a soundscape of power is a political act that requires "we do what Others do *with* them inside the politics of their locations, the economies of their desires and their constraints, and, most importantly, inside the materiality of their struggles and the consequences [emphasis in original]."[46] Further, co-performative witnessing is about an ethics of response (ability).

Response (ability) means that "I do not have the singular response-ability for what I witness but the responsibility of invoking a response-ability in others to what was seen, heard, learned, felt, and done in the field and through performance."[47] As my "idealized 'subjects'" and I became "ordinary people with human frailties and faults" in front of my eyes,[48] I began to feel mental, emotional, physical, and spiritual fatigue from the co-performative witnessing of their narratives of oppression, resistance, and agency. Throughout the interview process and in check backs with my interviewees, I was "intellectually, relationally, and emotionally invested in their symbol making practices and social strategies."[49] The interview guide utilized for this oral history performance project served as a fluid framework to move through issues of machismo, gender, sexuality, and history rather than a rigid questionnaire. Further, each interview lasted between 1 to 2.5 hours, and check backs (one to two depending on the interviewee) were conducted in the media form most convenient for the interviewee (Skype, email, text, or Facebook Messenger). As such, I felt surrounded by the "far and wide entanglements of power's disguises and infinite forms" and experienced a need to respond to power's consequences and operations.[50]

Utilizing BAM, I remained reflective and reflexive in my role as a researcher, while I co-performatively witnessed these dialogic performances with my interviewees. Madison writes, "we don't stop at our mirror reflections, but recognize the resonances that ripple and expand to a thinking about thinking—a metasignification—that inherently takes our contemplations and meanings further out, beyond our own mirrored gaze."[51] As an approach that embraces the borderlands of identity struggle, embodies contextual soundscapes of power, and enacts an ethic of response(ability), my Summer of FSOHP is rooted in the "feeling/sensing home" of the body to undertake the dangerous work of entering "what is often hidden in plain sight—the convolutions and complications below the surface, the systems that generate and keep surfaces in place."[52] Additionally, as a project rooted in decolonial thought, a move to valuing and uplifting body epistemologies is a political move that directly confronts the scriptocentrism of the academy.[53]

Trusting Yourself Is Part of Love. Take the Jump into the Unknown. Even If It Scares You to Death. As a dialogic performance and an act of co-performative witnessing, the Summer of OHP remembers the memories and members the subjectivities of the teller and the told in the cuento being shared.[54] Shopes describes this phenomenon: "interviews record what an interviewer draws out, what the interviewee remembers, what he or she chooses to tell, and how he or she understands what happened, not the unmediated 'facts' of what happened in the past."[55] These memory performances are "stories performed, re-membered, to create knowledge" of the past.[56] As explained in Chapter 1, Chicano/Xicano communities draw on indigenous traditions of orality in their everyday lives, such as cuentos, chismé, that represent "years or centuries of knowledge woven into indigenous cultures passed down orally from one generation to the next."[57]

Therefore, the OHP interview, as a historical/cultural interpretation of an interpretation with a tendency toward contextualizing the teller's individual and personal life, understands communication as both a process and a product, which ultimately is an ontological and epistemological stance that acknowledges how performance and performatives verify the existence of resistance and agency.[58]

Fall: Poetic Transcription and the Found Poems

> Autumn is the cool down; it is exhilarating and intoxicating to reach a sense of completion that is dangerously misleading. —González, "Four Seasons"[59]

The image of Figure 6.3 perfectly epitomizes the affect and experience of the Fall season. The image depicts a bright and blooming frontier range with large purple and black/gray mountains rising high into the distance. The sky has large, pink, fluffy clouds into which an outline of a celebrating figure is lifting up their arms—a jubilant release. In the corner, a black bird serves as a warning that the Fall has its own challenges within its own cycle from which to learn and grow. As mentioned before, the metaphors for the Fall are harvesting, release, celebration, and adulthood.[60] The nature of the Fall is: "compiling all gathered forms of data, theoretical saturation is reached, memos have been developed and tried in the field, celebration of completion of field work, leave-taking behaviors which respect the relationships formed, leaving the field, organization of materials, decisions about focus begin to be made, personal journaling."[61] Listening to de la Garza describe the Fall, you almost have to laugh at that celebratory figure. There is still so much work to be done.

Figure 6.3: Fall celebration. Source: Author

I met Andres in a local Starbucks in Aurora, Colorado. In the background, I can hear the busy hustle and bustle of the coffee shop, but undaunted, my youngest participant is a storyteller expertly weaving theories in the flesh in the forms of cuentos, consejos, y testimonio. Listening to the recording, I am caught up in the process of classification: is this moment chismé or is it an example of a plática? However, each time I listen, I am back in that coffee shop co-performatively witnessing this narrative again and again and again. I am beginning to understand that the basic nature of the Fall is: " 'reaping what was sowed,' community celebration, 'gestalt' of experience begins to form, winding down, breaking away, self-knowledge, feasting and celebration of accomplishments."[62] Andres is a 20-year-old gay Chicano with deep roots within the undocumented community as the U.S. citizen son of two undocumented parents. How can I classify such a complex human being into a single narrative form? It is wrangling betwixt and between this external/internal tension where "decisions on the perspectives for analysis must be made."[63]

For example, Figure 6.4 depicts the labor of the Fall as an external and internal battle for control—a striving for balance/harmony. The image of a cracked white mask draws the eye to the center of the depiction. Lightning cuts across the top in a spectrum of pink to yellow to orange to the center. Yet, there is a centrifugal force erupting out shattered glass-like fragments in those same colors. The ripe fruit growing from the staff symbolizes how "the 'fall,' or harvesting portion of a ceremony is the time when the fruits of the ceremony are shared and celebrated communally."[64] The moon is again watching, but this time in the form of a crescent just to the left. In the background of this transformational chaos is a wise, kneeling figure in gray assuring that this labor is all part of the season.

Transforming Huitzilopochtli

What type of warrior will you be?
smoking your last toke
praying for affirmations
needing   to face fears
of failure, truth,
owning your own poverty
of spirit

reading, witnessing,
willing to fight with
not against

It won't be as hard   as
you're thinking   trust me

It is what the world wants
Ehecatl blowing, breaking,
busting my pipe
my bank account
my looks
my precious
ego

To sit between new worlds
cloudy, disorienting, yet
more real

It is scary moving to the
frontlines, La Frontera

Dressed in pink, screaming con La Llorona
nalgas por fuera
serving justice up   another head
on a stick

How do you plan to fight?

Figure 6.4: Striving for internal/external balance. Source: Author

Poetic Transcription and Found Poems

Poetic transcription is a performance method that aims to share the narratives of marginalized community members in a form that captures the visual, tactile, olfactory, and aural aspects of the original performance. For example, Madison used this method of "placing words on a page to resemble the rhythm of the human voice" in her work collecting Black women's oral history traditions as a way to come closer to "capturing the depth inherent in the indigenous performance."[65] Poetic transcription attempts to enter/contain the spirit of the narrative and its range of meanings, give ownership of the words to the narrator, and make visible the depth of the narrator's performance.[66] Following Sandra L. Faulkner's process of transcribing poetically, I began by "highlighting participants' exact words and language from interview transcripts with colors" that symbolized the six narrative forms I was looking for (i.e., cuentos, pláticas, chismé, consejos, mitos, and testimonios).[67] Later, I cut and pasted "the essential elements in an effort to reveal the essence of a participant's lived experience."[68] However, it wasn't until I began to transform the narratives into found poems that these performative utterances began to embody the meanings, rhythms, and aesthetic choice of words my interviewees were trying to convey.[69]

Found poems are poems created from research that "was not intended as poetry, but you will declare it such through your choice of 'found' parts in your research."[70] Utilizing cuentos, pláticas, chismé, mitos, testimonios, y consejos as found parts, I gravitated to narratives that were "most interested in storytelling"[71] and embraced these performative utterances by placing words "symbolically in relation to how they are uttered."[72] Were these choices wrong? I met Aya through a local community leader, and because it was Christmas, Aya would be in Denver instead of in San Francisco. We conducted the interview in the same cold, community room as Jay, the first interviewee for this oral history performance project. Aya is 28 years old, and she grew up in the Northside neighborhood of Denver. She identifies as transgender and Chicanx, and listening to her narratives, she is clearly a musician and artist. She moves through the world to her own rhythm, and it was only after performatively placing the words on the page with an eye toward the poetic that I could *feel* her. How can I practice a "tentative certainty" about my findings and choices during the Fall?

de la Garza discusses how in the Fall you might be tempted to believe that "one has certainty about the culture."[73] However, the year is not yet over, and a Fall researcher must practice a kind of tentative respect for boundaries while simultaneously not forgetting that "it's a work of art even as s/he interacts with it as if it were reality."[74] For example, I met Toni at Hamburger Mary's in Denver the day it was changing its name/franchise/sign to M Uptown. As the oldest interviewee, Toni is a 40-year-old gay/bisexual Xicano who has been involved in local Chicano activism his whole life. He brought his assistant with him to the interview, and as we drank and chatted, the assistant sat there on his phone the whole time. When trying to classify some of Toni's narratives, I originally had one as a *consejo* but later changed it to *chismé* as I remembered how Toni told his story of empowerment and self-esteem with a mischievous glee—an activist fire in his eyes. Additionally, when placed alongside the other narratives, Toni's narrative seemed to demand a different place in the meta-narrative enfolding in the act of writing. If Winter will be a time of writing, sharing, and publishing ones' work, then Fall is about harvesting and enjoying the fruits of ones' labor.

Staging a Winter Performance

"It is time
to consider what
the human instrument has experienced
subjectively.

It is a time
to anticipate one's
future
life, having been through
the ethnographic
experience.

It is a time
to journal honestly
while simultaneously
explicating one's
theories
and ideas
about the culture"[75]

Imagine a simple stage with five performers standing on a double-tiered choir stand—a spotlight on each of their faces. There is an emptiness between them, and to highlight this lack, scattered lights shine directly down onto the choir stand highlighting the nothingness. Each empty spot honors the lost history of Jotería ancestors forgotten. de la Garza argues that "the human instrument should write to *say something* [emphasis in original],"[76] so although the metaphors for the Winter are incubation, hibernation, retreat, waiting, solitude, and elder, don't be fooled—"Winter is the deadliest of seasons if one is not prepared."[77] In the Spring, we cultivated seeds that took root, and bravely, we inched out into the sky only to endure the heat of the Summer. By trusting ourselves and co-witnessing others, we bore fruit, and what a celebration we had in the Fall! But the year is not over. There are several narratives to share, and even now, my lower back hurts from the repetitive bending and lifting required of Fall's harvesting and sorting. Ahora, we are in a "time of rest and waiting" and a "time when the meaning of the ceremony is received and understood."[78] Pero, looking at the faces of all my friends and community members spotlighted on the stage, I need to make sure I am prepared to write and share.

Upstage to the left is Toni (Age: 40) behind Andres (Age: 20), because at the end of our interview when I asked them about where they wanted to be in 10 years, they both wanted to run for political office. They are connected somehow. Center left, Positivo (age 28) and Jay (age 35) stand on the lower tier, and there is a space between them and Andres, which is marked by a light. Aya (age 28) stands solitary on the lower tier downstage right. There are several lights marking the space between her and the cisgendered males. At 4 a.m. just before sunrise, I feel moonlight wake me up and urge me to the computer screen:

> If what you do will reflect back, or come back, to you, then actions must logically be careful. What one writes about the people will inevitably come back to the writer in his or her life. It is not a light enterprise. In fact, it is quite serious.[79]

Words are powerful, spiritual, and "the very act of recording in writing the essence of culture changes it to something it is not. It freezes it."[80] Utilizing poetic transcription, I have transformed the narratives collected through oral history interviewing into found poems, but it is in the Winter that decisions must be made about how one shares the gifts given to you by the community.

Shhhh! It is starting. Toni opens up the performance with his cuento, and then, he moves downstage center and kneels as if starting a fire. A warm red, orange, and yellow light crackles up from the stage as Toni tends the hearth. Positivo, then Aya, then Andres, then Jay share a cuento and join Toni around the hearth. It is a moment of chatter and laughter. Performative writing *embraces* the reader with care and passion; *enacts* evocative imaginings that lift the words from the page and places them in motion; *embodies* the sensations, experiences, and knowledge from the interview in the act of writing through a particular body with a particular political voice; and *effects* people and space, because as a performance, performative writing champions the political struggles, tensions, and advocacy with/to its subject(s).[81] Suddenly, the performers freeze and the stage goes dark. A spotlight highlights Positivo who shares a plática downstage left, then returns to the hearth and freezes. Afterward, Jay shares a plática downstage right, returns to the hearth, and the action returns.

The basic nature of the Winter is a slower pace, a conservation of energy, wisdom, an incubation period of creativity, success is determined by previous "year," confrontation of "mortality," cold.[82] It is lonely writing. My partner is getting agitated. Even now, his text messages bing across my screen: "Can you change the laundry to the dryer?" "My boss is being such a jerk right now!" "I love you." Performative writing turns "the personal into the political and the political into the personal"[83] and features lived experiences invested in a world that is communicatively co-constructed and interconnected.[84] de la Garza explicates that writing about a culture during the cold of the Winter transforms the researcher because they must make public private narratives and experiences.[85] The tasks during the Winter are: writing the ethnography, submissions, revisions, performances, decisions regarding the extent to which your knowledge will be shared, journaling about new tacit knowledge, theoretical sensitivity, personal development, speculation on future directions (personally and professionally), decisions regarding how relationships from the field will be maintained, and rest.[86]

The action continues near the community fire as Toni shares some chismé from his youth in San Francisco, and Andres shares some about his gay Mexican-American uncle. Bolstered by the eldest and youngest, Positivo shares un mito about down low or in-the-closest Chicano culture. I think it is because of this disclosure that Andres is willing to share his testimonio about being gay, invested in the undocumented community, and Chicano. After Andres' narrative, the five, starting with Toni and Jay, embrace on stage, and as all the cisgendered men move away from the fire into the darkness upstage, Aya remains behind tending the fire. The firelight is dimmer now as Aya tells her own testimonio of empowerment and struggle. It is telling that she is alone on stage as she remembers her history in Denver. After her testimonio, she, too, moves into the darkness of upstage, and the fire slowly goes out. However, after a dramatic pause, the spotlight on the performers faces and missing Jotería returns for Andres then Aya to give a brief consejo. The performers stand silently as the spotlight on their faces go out one by one; the missing Jotería lights remain for just a few seconds longer before also going out. Like Anzaldúa, as I am "putting images together into story (the story I tell about the images), I use imagistic thinking, employ an imaginal awareness. I'm guided by the spirit of the image."[87] For the remainder of this chapter, I utilize performative writing to present the found poems from the FSOHP process as a kind of staged production on the page. Like Johnson, I have chosen to share these narratives uninterrupted by description and analysis to allow the reader to have a role in the performance.[88] It is my greatest hope to one day share these theories in the flesh beyond the page to the stage as a gift back to the community that has embraced me.

Theories from the Fringes

Cuentos

Toni: "Our Struggle Has Been One of the Hardest for Centuries"

> You know that would probably make a lot of sense
> why there was such a rift between the older generation and the
>   newer people coming out 'cause we felt there were
> years between each generation.
>
> We couldn't relate to each other
> we were kinda thrown into this adult world
> there was no middle ground
> Now that you ask this question
> it makes a little more sense
> 'cause there weren't
> generations upon generations
> of people to learn from and
> the older guys were totally
> jaded
>
> You know
> They were jaded and mean
> and so, we
> experienced our own form of
> being jaded
> or mistreated
> by the adults, but
> now, thinking back
> they had probably had
> a lot   of   barriers
> a lot   of   hurt
>   hatred
>
> towards society
>
> They were just

reflecting on us
You know,
we had to grow up—really quickly
it's cool
to look
at this newer generation
and they're—actually—looking and expecting love

I don't think I actually expected love
until I was almost 30
when I was younger
I think I would have really liked to have it
but after being out
for a few years

I didn't think it was possible

Now, I see
21–22-year-olds
wanting marriage
and love
and families
and stuff
and that was something
we didn't even think of
Like, this new generation
doesn't have to experience that
because of the education they've been given
and all of the different inroads that
a lot of the older generations had to give them
and I would just wish that they would
respect that
a little more
'cause our struggle has been
one of the hardest
for centuries

Positivo: "That's the Only Spots I Was Able to Go"

I actually went to Tracks for the first time 'cause I had a friend who was a lesbian and she came out.

She's like, "Do you want to go?"

At the time I was pretending to be straight.
I didn't really say it. I was like, "Cool, I'll go.

Yeah, like I was just you know 'Girl, suuuure!' "

We went the first time it was just an eye-opening experience.
I was 16.
I think I remember trying my first cigarette.
I got this big   old   headache
in the club.
I'm just laying there.

>   She was all like, "Don't lay like that
>   at a gay club."

It was the second time that I went with her
No, one time I think I went by myself.
I met this guy there
He was wanting to dance
He was touching me

I was like, "Um, neeeever had this before?"

That was like the first
and he was the first guy that I was with.
I remember just getting his number
talking to him more
That's when we actually went and hung out at Cheesman Park.
Cheesman Park was the spot to go.

>   He was the one that told me,
>   "You've got to be careful about Cheesman Park, because
>   if you do come by yourself
>   and you park,
>   people are going to think
>   you're looking for sex
>   or looking to hook up."

He basically gave me the rules
of this is what the park is,
this is where people come hook up.
Obviously this is regulated.
Cops come at 11
because it had that image.

If you'd go on Sundays,
you could just go cruise by,

but you could also sit there and hang out
but also it was an opportunity for you
to kinda just see what's out there.

Nowadays people have the Facebook,
but I remember
when I was in college
Facebook was only
if you went to college.
Again, it's like thinking about
social media and all that.
At least for my days,
that was the only outlet:
going to Tracks
or going to Cheesman.

I know this is bad
but I had a fake ID
I've had two fake IDs.
They're pretty legit
because I wasn't taking someone's identity
It was my picture and my name
It just was a different address.
But, it wasn't for the alcohol
it was more just to go into the bars.
I want to get to know more.

I feel that from my experiences
being a 17 and 18-year-old
and being in that community

guys were like, "So what's up?
Oh, he's a youngin'"

They knew
when there was prey there
that they could prance on
I think for me
it was a shock
it was sort of
wanting to figure out who I was
in this community
trying to figure out
what is there to offer in this?

That's the only spots I was able to go to.

Aya: "Am I Ready to Bring This Up? Are They Ready to Change
their Language?"

Knowing that there are some places where   I
will have to kind of   hide that
mostly around my family   was
definitely at the foreground
of my mental preparation   for coming
to Colorado.

Getting ready today   I
kinda put my ambiguous
like, androgynous
boy drag
like boyish drag on
but then I have my makeup on hand
when I'm
walking into a space where   I
don't feel like I'll see any of my family members
because I'm not really ready
I think
to have that conversation
today

We did talk about   what

like what

pronouns she would use for me, or
if any
We pretty much determined that
not using pronouns
might be the easiest

I asked her if it would be hard for her to use he pronouns

and she was like, "Yes,
that would be very hard for me
and I don't want to do that."

I was like,
"I fully respect that."
We agreed on just
not gendering me
She is fully expecting
my parents

to refer to me as
Albert,
he, his,
son.
After everything,
my parents call me son.
I haven't really realized
how much
that happened
until   this   recent
this trip right now
which I know is
another kind of factor   in
Am I ready to bring this up?
Are they ready to change their language?
I want to say yes to all of those
but in actuality
I'm not sure.

Andres: "I'm Not Cool with That"

I don't think I have a type.
I mean, I hope I don't.
When I was younger
When I was 16, when I was barely coming out
I was really looking for that masculine man
who was probably 6 foot.
I was probably attracted to White men.
Now I'm like,
no   White men
They colonized.
That's the oppressor.

This is all going on the interview? Whatever.

Now I'm like sort of in this space where
racially I'm kind of anti-White right now
and I'm people of color power
That translates into my romantic life

I don't talk to White men.
I don't want to be attracted to White men.
If a White man is attractive,

I remind myself that:
He is not Brown
He probably will never understand
the full range of identities,
and expressions,
and oppressions
that our people have faced.

That's a very close-minded way of thinking about it,
but maybe in the future my mom says I'll end up with a White person
so maybe in the future I'll have a White husband or something.

In terms of this spectrum of masculinity
I used to be attracted to the hypermasculine
I wanted that.
I would tell myself
"I'm attracted to men.
Why would I want like—a woman?"

I was very unaware of about like
power structures and things like that.
This was pre-college.
Now, I find myself attracted to
a wide range of individuals.
They can be very feminine
and very flamboyant,
or they can be very masculine.

I find that
the men who are more masculine
are the ones that
I don't find a lot of connection to
because, they express their power
in different ways
than I do.

I don't like that.
I don't like that.
There's a difference between the way I
express power and the way that I
communicate and like the men that I
  might be attracted to, right?

  There was this guy
  that I was talking to.

He had been
in a really abusive relationship.
He shared way too much the first time,
but he showed me pictures
of his eye, it was black
broken ribs
and stuff like that.
I was like,
   "Whoa, that really sucks.
      I've never been in a relationship like that.
         I would never
            let it get that far, I think.
I would make sure I was communicating enough with my partner."
We've been talking for a while.
At one point
he started to yell.

He said, "If you don't shut the fuck up,
I'm going to throw this cup at your face."
That was the end.
He was very hypermasculine.
He cared a lot about how he sounded
He cared a lot about not sounding gay
I was so turned off by that.
I was like, that's not what I want, you know?

I'm attracted to a wide range of people,
but it really comes down to how you
present masculinity

If you're presenting it in
a way that's oppressive
for me or for other people
or for anyone around you

I'm not cool with that.

Jay: "Changed the Game"

The worst one was
we were   four years in deep
we were   obviously at the
comfortable level of our sex life

we were young
we were young
early 20s

He started talking about
introducing someone else to our bedroom
and I was very curious
because he was my first boyfriend
and my first sexual experience
in terms of penetration
    So I was
    I was like,
if this is who I'm going to be with for the rest of my life
I need to kinda be interested
in what's happening out there
I'd be open to it
It was really his idea but I'd be open to it
    He said,
     "But I don't want you to get jealous and
     I don't want you to blah blah blah."
"I'll be fine." You know,
back then, it was really funny
It's very much the same now.
       I don't care.
       We're together.
       You're coming home with me, so
       this is just sex, right?
So we engaged in that for a while
multiple   instances where we
invited someone
into our bedroom
had sex and
it was fine
until one of the suitors
showed interest more in me than him

Changed the game.

We were coming back from the bar.
We were having
ups and downs at that time
It was toward the end of our relationship   (we were really struggling)

We'd break up for a week
get back together
you know that whole thing   (we were young)
He was drunk
telling my older brother
in the car   (drinking and driving, according to him)
telling him that he
just loved me so much
that he just loves me
just wants to be working

My older brother is extremely outspoken like I am
if not worse
He said, "Well if that's the way you feel that's the way you should treat him
and blah blah blah blah blah"
Then they started going back and forth.

Back and forth
Back and forth
Back and forth

My brother had bought him a chain
for Christmas you know
a little silver chain and
Cruz was crazy
was in the backseat
was pissed
that this conversation was taking place

so he opened the door
so he could be let out
while the car was moving

Of course I'm driving
I slam on the brakes
I'm like, "What   are   you doing?"
He jumps out of the car and starts walking
I'm like
you know
following him trying to get him in the car
He rips the chain off
and throws it in my brother's face
'cause my brother's car window
he was the passenger

his window was down
trying to get him to get back in the car too.
That pissed my brother off
        so I stopped the car
        I get out
        I go to him
        and I'm like, "Cruz,
        you need to get in the car."
        I open the door for him
        I'm like,
            "Get in the car."
            and he just
            pop me
            right in the mouth

That was it.

My brother got out of the car
literally beat the liv-ing
crap out of him
Threw him in the back seat
Took him to my apartment
   where my little brother
   was living with us at the time
bring him upstairs   bloody
I throw him in the shower
clean him up
I had to take him to the hospital in the morning
   broke rip
   and just beat his face up real good and . . .

I stayed with him.

Kind of shunned my brother off a little bit
'cause I was a little angry with him for the experience
until   we broke up
we broke up
and I let him
live with me still 'cause
   financially he was just so unstable
   he never could hold a job
He started
sleeping with a gentleman in the apartment complex

that *we* lived in
even though we weren't together
I was just like   that's   so disrespectful
I eventually kicked him out
That was the end of it
    But yeah, his issues with jealousy and rage
    were just to this day
    still cause problems
    I still hear that he has issues with alcohol.
    I still hear that he abuses his current boyfriend.
        Pretty sad.
        Pretty sad.

Pláticas

Positivo: "A Whole New Can of Worms"

I remember
I went through a depressive state
It was very depressing
I always knew I was gay
since I was 5 years old
I've had an attraction
but I didn't know what it was
For me, it was hard
to channelize that
and to share that

I remember
in high school
there was a low point in my life
I remember
I went to my brother's house
He wasn't there at the time
but his wife was there
then my second oldest brother
was there

I remember
at one point
I had told them

I was thinking about committing suicide
They didn't know why
and I didn't really share it with them
but before I could even
share my feelings
I had a cousin
and my sister-in-law had said:

"Was it because of what your brother did to you when you were younger?"

That's where I was like, "Wait, what?"

What they had said
was that some family
had mentioned that
my older brother had molested me when I was younger
until this day
I don't know
if that was true or not
because I haven't confronted
  it was just that moment
  where I didn't talk about my sexuality
  It just completely took me out of my motive

"No   I was completely talking about a whole other thing,
but you opened a whole new can of worms."

Jay: "It Just Wasn't Talked About"

Mm-hmm.
Absolutely, we do not talk about it.
For example,
my   mother   has
three siblings:
one sister, two brothers

One of her brothers is gay.

As a matter of fact—well
The one brother who is gay,
my uncle,
had gotten married to a woman had two children and then divorced and
had lived downtown forever. As far as we were concerned that's what he did.

He had a roommate named John for-ev-er

like, 15 years
then John one day just moved to a different state   (broke up)
and I didn't actually know my uncle was gay
until I was 18 and he came out to me
after I came out to him
then all of it made sense

Now, I'm starting to get suspicious,
because he had some
rainbow beads hanging from his car's rearview mirror.
I noticed the rainbows,
so I started talking
more about myself
'cause I was like, "You have to be gay
or this wouldn't be hanging in your car
basically."

He picked me up every morning for work.
One day
one morning
he goes, "Well mijo,
I'm gay too.
I'm sure you already know that."
I was like, "I didn't know for sure, but."

He opened up a lot about that.
I was like,
"Why doesn't anyone in our family ever talk about this?
It would've been so much better for me."
The sad thing is,
his oldest son is gay
and his daughter's oldest daughter
is a lesbian.

He's a grandfather now.
He just said
It's just something we don't talk about.
and I said, "Why did you—
Did you know you were gay?"

He said "Yes."

"Then why did you get married?"

He said, "Truth?"

I said "Yeah."

He goes, "I thought she was a lesbian."

I said, "Well,
how did you get by
so long
without it being talked
in front of the children? and
how did you talk to my dad about this?!"

He said, "Me and your dad didn't talk about this.
We still haven't talked about this."
I said, "What the hell?
He has to know what these beads meant"

He said,
"No,
he never questioned it
so if he questioned it
he didn't question it with me"
he goes "one day we were driving in the car,
and he asked me why I had these beads hanging up
from my rearview mirror.
I said, "Oh,
I'm part of Jessie Jackson's Rainbow Coalition."

and my dad believed him

and so
it just
wasn't talked about

Chismé

Toni: "It Changed My Whole Way of Thinking"

I remember   meeting
a guy that had visited
the gay and lesbian community at CU[89], because
he was in a CU fraternity
and he was visiting Colorado
so he got to stay at the frat house for free

so him and I had a little rendezvous
and friendship

I remember seeing him out there
and he introduced me to one of his friends
It was almost 2 in the morning I had never been out that late in the city
and it was still kinda scary to me
So I started to cry

This guy is like   why are you crying
Well   I have never been alone in the city by myself
So   he let me stay with him
for the night
and was totally cool
I told him about my situation
and he had a couch bed ·
and he told me I could stay with him
for 200 a month   if   I were to   clean his house
in a thong
once a week

Well   I was a cheerleader
in a size 27 waist
with a kick-ass everything
So   I agreed

That is when I learned
that I could be empowered
by who I was and my sexuality
and it changed my whole way of thinking
and I learned to really utilize
different ass-pects
of myself   in order to   spring myself   into the community
and after that
I don't think I have been fearful
at all   about my sexuality

Andres: "We Don't Talk About My Uncle"

My uncle
who we don't talk to
not because he's gay
but because he's a horrible person

For Halloween
every year
he dresses up as a woman
and he performs in drag
and I'm pretty sure he's trans
or something
There are so many rumors that he has sex with men
My dad
He's okay with it
He loves his brother
even though he's a horrible person

He only dresses up as a woman in drag   out of a joke
but he performs really well
I think that's how he feels most comfortable
He's not really somebody I look up to but
He's somebody I know
in the family
that is also probably LGBT
but he'll never come out.

There was this whole thing where he bought a club
with one of my dad's friends
My uncle is undocumented
My dad's friend is documented
He needed the friend to sign for the club
The guy   invested   thousands of dollars into
buying the club

My uncle was supposed to pay him back
because my uncle can't get a loan from the bank
to pay for the club
My uncle started
going and being a part of the club
and being a part of the scene
He started money laundering
   He would say he made X amount
   but didn't really make X amount
   then he would put the money elsewhere
      and that was fine for him
      but the credit on the line
      and the people who were visible

about the club
were my dad's friend
   who he'd known for 20 years before I was born

The guy told my uncle, "Hey,
you need to pay me back this money
because I know you're making way more than you say you are
I know you're involved in illegal activities."
There was this huge fiasco
where my dad
was asked to choose between his brother
or his friend
My dad was like,
"You're my brother,
but what you're doing is really bad and
I can't stand by that, so
I'm going to stick with my friend."

It turned into this huge fiasco.
It was so chaotic.
My uncle ended up threatening our family on Facebook
and telling us he was going to kill us and
his wife ended up telling my mom, like
"If I ever see you on the street
I'm going to kick your ass."
My mom is not a confrontational person
My mom is typical, submissive
Mexican mom
where she's just going to go about her day.
This woman was threatening her.
We ended up calling the cops.
The cops were like, "Well,
they haven't done anything,
so we can't really take this
as an immediate threat."
   My dad's car was stolen.
   People broke into our garage.
   Somebody blew our tires.
      A bunch of things started happening.
      We know it's my uncle.
      Who else would it be?

There was this one point where somebody
almost killed the guy who owns the club
Like, they held him at gunpoint
so he is in a whole legal battle with
my uncle now
We are completely   detached
from that side of the family.
My dad still loves him, I'm pretty sure
   They hate my dad
   They are horrible   horrible
My dad cries a lot.
That's where his masculinity
is not shown in traditional ways
He is very vulnerable
with his immediate family. So yeah,
we don't talk to my uncle

Mitos

Positivo: "The Straight Whisperer"

I've had experiences
where I've had   Okay,
you're getting really into my life
I've been called
the straight whisperer
because what I've noticed is
that I get a lot of guys
that just feel comfortable
being around me

I've had experiences
where   I'll go out drinking with friends
and I've had friends
who will claim that they're straight
but then   when we go out
or do something
ended up having them touching me
or wanting to go
another level with me
I don't what it was or what not

but I still to this day
those are the experiences that I've had the most
which makes my gay experience interesting

I've had more
people that are in the closet
or don't know what they want
approach me
versus guys
who   know what they want
That was also   a habit I got into
of being with guys who are on the DL
because they are on the DL

That's what I guess attracted them
That's where I can see the privileges of
I'm masculine enough
that these guys were like, okay
Then when I would educate them
I felt like they were comfortable enough
to then share these stories

I've had people come to me and say
good friends
that are like, "I've messed around with guys,
but you're the only one I could tell
because I'm going to keep
a straight identity."

It's sad,
but those are the experiences that I got
that I was like
I don't want to live like that

I can't.

Testimonios

Andres: "I Can't Just Go Back to Colorado and Pretend Like It Never Happened"

I started doing sex education work
when I was 15 years old
     around the time

when I was still not sure
about coming out
    The biggest thing for any activism is
    storytelling. They were always like
    tell us your story.
My story was always about
the friend who was pregnant
and I wanted to help her
Poor Selena, she's so sad.
She's in eighth grade
She doesn't know what she was doing.
But, that was just a fake story
    The real story underneath was
    I'm gay
    and I don't know how to talk about it
For a whole year
I went with this organization
I went to D.C.
and I went to parts of the United States
telling this story that was not mine
telling a story that I didn't feel connected to
Finally, when I came out
it was then
that I could really
tell my story
and speak my truth
    I ended up coming out
    to the legislature
    in Colorado.
        I testified for a bill
        and told them I'm gay
        you're all Republican
        and you don't understand me
            That was very powerful for me
            to be able to do that
After I did that on the state level
other organizations have been reaching out to me
so I can share my story
and I can
speak up
I think that my

LGBT activism
and my activism around sexual health education
has been framed
by my story of being
closeted, a youth of color, by
being outed
by coming to terms with my sexuality
and what that was like
   On the other hand,
   my activism
   in immigration
   has been tough because
   I am documented
   I didn't know if I was going to be accepted
   in the immigrant community
   because I have a lot of privilege
   that they don't.
   But I took a trip to Tucson
      where I   walked
      part of the migrant trail in the desert
      I met with people in detention
         I spoke with an 18-year-old
         and I was 18 at the time

         who was gay and Brown
         and wanted to study theater
         and I was studying theater at the time

He was like a reflection of myself

I was like, "oh shoot!"
I need to do something
I can't just go back to Colorado and
pretend like it never happened

Aya: "One of the Most Powerful Political Moments"

                             Since moving
                            to California
                     my sense of politics
                 has expanded exponentially
          and also gotten stronger over time

Here, it was

it didn't seem like anything needed to change
I had the family
We all
took care of each other.
There were other people around
but they were all doing their thing
It didn't feel like
gentrification was a thing, really
when I was growing up
You know it wasn't a concept
that had hit
an area like Denver.
In that way
my politics were just a little shut off

I knew

I knew I was queer
and that shaped a lot of how   I
viewed the world
like sixth, seventh, eighth, ninth grade
in high school
Right now I guess the most
recent political action I was involved in
was in San Francisco a couple weeks ago
There's been a tug-of
a push-and-pull kinda fight
to not have a jail built in San Francisco
My partner has actually been spearheading a lot
of   the actions
around getting that jail
not to be built
I've been to No SF Jail
Coalition meetings and
board of supervisor meetings
where they vote on the actual project
and tried to shut that down
with our voices

That's something   that I never really   felt here
other than

when the Democratic National Convention was in town
That was Obama's first year, maybe
For me,
that was my first large political   moment
was during a critical mass bike ride
that went through downtown
zig-zagged up and down 16th Street Mall
We eventually got stopped by the cops
for getting too close to the Pepsi Center
I was in the front of this mass ride
There was a moment
when the police stopped us
and I looked back
and saw 500 people
with bikes in the air
behind me (I'm already getting like)
That was   one of my most powerful political moments
that I think I have had as a teenager
being able to feel
that tension between the people and the police
taking over
our town
pretty much
for that you know two weeks of time
It pretty much felt like a police state
which was something I'd never felt
prior to that
In a way   that
was an eye-opening experience
to see that cops could so easily take over our city
in a way that was   actually
hurt a lot of the people
who have lived here
their whole lives

Consejos

Andres: "Shifting the Way I Think About Myself"

We give advice to   other queer people
What I would say is

there is a lot of power
in your multiple identities
there is a lot of power
in every single part of who you are.
    You are not just queer.
    You are not just Chicano.
    You are not just American
    or undocumented.
You are a
whole lot of things at once
and you have a lot of
privilege also

I would really ask them to
think critically about their privilege

I would ask them to think critically about
power and why they have power
and how they are willing to execute that power
in ways that are not harmful to other people

I would also ask that self-pity
is not going to
do anything for them
that it won't do anything for me

There's a lot of power in their identity
and they should find that
and work really hard to find that
    It gets better with time
    not like the next day
    but that feeling of self-pity
    and feeling bad about yourself
    is not going to improve your situation at all
Maybe that's too American of me to think that way, but
for a long time I felt a lot of self-pity
and then afterward I was like
my mom can only love me so much
before I actually start believing it
you know, and actually start
shifting the way I think about myself

Aya: "A Space Where I Am Ready"

That Sylvia Rivera speech
has been something that
I always think about
She points out so many
accurate observations
of the way that cis-gay people
and the invisibility
the trans invisibility
that exists within the LBGTQ community.

With so many trans women of color
losing their lives
at the hands of street violence
police violence
male violence
I feel is another source of sadness
but also power
that brings a lot of people
within the   trans community
in the Bay Area   together.

Any time
I find out
about a situation
that's happened recently
or something in the past
that I didn't know about
or someone connected
to somebody else
a friend that lost another friend
and hearing these stories
just hearing them so much
is overwhelming at times

It is
a combination of my Latino roots
in Colorado
and my queer and trans
roots flowering
for lack of a better word

provides me with so much   empowerment
which is something
with recently coming out to my close circle of friends
I'm needing that   sisterhood
and that   empowerment
and finding that
I've been navigating it slowly
mostly internally
but now I feel like I'm in a space
where I'm ready

Notes

1. González, "Four Seasons," 641.
2. Lumbersexuality is a masculine aesthetic that responded to the earlier metrosexuality aesthetic movement on the 2000s. Ryan Seacrest, the host of American Idol and the aesthetic forms he practiced and later started a clothing line around, is a good example of metrosexuality. A focus on beards, flannel, and other stereotypes surrounding lumberjacks are utilized to cultivate an appearance of rugged, cisgendered masculinity; however, this aesthetic is often attributed to men or male-identified individuals who live in urban rather than rural areas. In the Denver area, informants would make references to this style in regards to affluent "hipsters" that were (in their view) responsible for the increasing gentrification of Chicano neighborhoods in the city.
3. Della Pollock, "Introduction: Remembering," in *Remembering: Oral History Performance*, ed. Della Pollock (New York: Palgrave Macmillan, 2005), 4.
4. Ibid., 1.
5. D. Soyini Madison, *Critical Ethnography: Method, Ethics, and Performance*, 2nd ed. (Thousand Oaks, CA: Sage, 2012), 34.
6. Ibid., 34–5.
7. D. Soyini Madison, " 'That Was My Occupation': Oral Narrative, Performance, and Black Feminist Thought," *Text and Performance Quarterly* 13, no. 3 (July 1993): 214.
8. González, "Four Seasons," 628.
9. Ibid., 632.
10. Ibid., 632.
11. Ibid., 636.
12. Ibid., 633.
13. Ibid., 633.
14. Ibid., 635.

15. Anzaldúa, *Light*, 38.
16. González, "Four Seasons," 634.
17. Ibid., 634.
18. Anzaldúa, *Light*, 4.
19. González, "Four Seasons," 637.
20. Dwight Conquergood, *Cultural Struggles: Performance, Ethnography, Praxis*, ed. E. Patrick Johnson (Ann Arbor: University of Michigan Press, 2013).
21. Conquergood, *Struggles*, 70.
22. González, "Four Seasons," 638.
23. Ibid., 638.
24. Ibid., 634.
25. Ibid., 645.
26. Anzaldúa, *Light*, 53.
27. Ibid., 63.
28. Sarah Amira de la Garza, *María Speaks: Journeys into the Mysteries of the Mother in My Life as a Chicana* (New York: Peter Lang, 2004), 14–8.
29. González, "Four Seasons," 639.
30. Anzaldúa, *Light*.
31. González, "Four Seasons," 639.
32. Ibid., 643.
33. D. Soyini Madison, "Co-Performative Witnessing," *Cultural Studies* 21, no. 6 (2007): 829.
34. Conquergood, *Struggles*, 77.
35. D. Soyini Madison, "The Dialogic Performative in Critical Ethnography," *Text and Performance Quarterly* 26, no. 4 (2006): 320–24.
36. E. Patrick Johnson, "Introduction: Opening and Interpreting Lives," In *Cultural Struggles: Performance, Ethnography, Praxis*, ed. E. Patrick Johnson (Ann Arbor: University of Michigan Press, 2013), 1–14; Madison, "Dialogic."
37. Madison, "Co-Performative Witnessing," 826.
38. Johnson, "Introduction," 7.
39. D. Soyini Madison, "Dangerous Ethnography," in *Qualitative Inquiry and Social Justice: Toward a Politics of Hope*, eds. Norman K. Denzin and Michael D. Giardina (Walnut Creek, CA: Left Coast Press, 2009), 189.
40. Madison, "Co-Performative."
41. E. Patrick Johnson, *Sweet Tea: Black Gay Men of the South* (Chapel Hill: University of North Carolina Press, 2008).
42. Madison, "Co-Performative."
43. Ibid., 828.
44. Ibid., 829.
45. Ibid., 828.
46. Ibid., 829.

47. Madison, "Dangerous," 192.
48. González, "Four Seasons," 643.
49. D. Soyini Madison, "The Dialogic Performative in Critical Ethnography," *Text and Performance Quarterly* 26, no. 4 (2006): 323.
50. Madison, "Dangerous," 193.
51. Madison, "Dialogic," 322.
52. Madison, "Dangerous," 190.
53. Conquergood, *Struggles*.
54. Pollock, "Introduction."
55. Linda Shopes, "Oral History," in *Collecting and Interpreting Qualitative Materials*, 4th ed, eds. Norman K. Denzin and Yvonna S. Lincoln (Thousand Oaks, CA: Sage, 2013), 120.
56. Kate Willink, "Domesticating Difference: Performing Memories of School Desegregation," *Text and Performance Quarterly* 27, no. 1 (2007): 22.
57. Charles E. Trimble, Barbara W. Sommer, and Mary Kay Quinlan, *The American Indian Oral History Manual: Making Many Voices Heard* (Walnut Creek, CA: Left Coast Press, 2008), 15.
58. Chon A. Noriega and Teresa Barnett, "Introduction," in *Oral History and Communities of Color*, eds. Teresa Barnett and Chon A. Noriega (Los Angeles: UCLA Chicano Studies Research Center Press, 2013), 1–18.; Della Pollock, "Moving Histories: Performance and Oral History," in *The Cambridge Companion to Performance Studies*, ed. Tracy C. Davis (Cambridge, MA: Cambridge University Press, 2008), 120–35; Shopes.
59. González, "Four Seasons," 644.
60. Ibid., 640.
61. Ibid., 637.
62. Ibid., 640.
63. Ibid., 645.
64. Ibid., 637.
65. Madison, "Occupation," 217.
66. Bernadette Marie Calafell, "Disrupting the Dichotomy: 'Yo Soy Chicana /o?' in the New Latina /o South," *The Communication Review* 7, no. 2 (2004): 175–204; Bernadette Marie Calafell, *Latina/o Communication Studies: Theorizing Performance* (New York: Peter Lang, 2007); Sandra Faulkner, *Poetry as Method: Reporting Research Through Verse* (Walnut Creek, CA: Left Coast Press, 2009).
67. Faulkner, *Poetry as Method*, 31.
68. Ibid., 31.
69. Calafell, "Disrupting"; Madison, *Critical*.
70. Faulkner, *Poetry as Method*, 133.
71. Ibid., 24.
72. Madison, *Critical*, 240.

73. González, "Four Seasons," 645.
74. Anzaldúa, *Light*, 41.
75. González, "Four Seasons," 646.
76. Ibid., 646.
77. Ibid., 644.
78. Ibid., 637.
79. Ibid., 646.
80. Ibid., 645.
81. Madison, *Critical*, 220–32.
82. González, "Four Seasons," 640.
83. Ron J. Pelias, *Writing Performance: Poeticizing the Researcher's Body* (Carbondale: Southern Illinois University Press, 1999), 420.
84. Pelias, *Writing*, 419.
85. González, "Four Seasons," 646.
86. Ibid., 640.
87. Anzaldúa, *Light*, 4.
88. Johnson, *Sweet Tea*.
89. "CU" stands for University of Colorado, and in this case, it is referring to the campus in Boulder, Colorado.

Part Three:

Jotería Performance Rhetoric

7

Queer of Color Performances of Generational Dis/Continuities, Culture(s) of Silence, and the Labor(s) of Intelligibility

I am in a space where I can see the past as a long journey up a mountain. I am about to reach the summit, and I am afraid. I know when I arrive at the highest point, and I inhale the view that I will see this was only a way station. A momentary stop on the path. I do not know what mountain or lake or broken bridge may come next for me. Looking back at that long, rocky, and bloody trail, it feels good to stop and remember. It is bittersweet. The wind blows from the west prompting me to turn around and watch the sun set. In the darkness, I (re)start my journey.

(Re)membering of Jotería, specifically the oral history performances captured in the prior chapter, challenges master narratives of history, culture, and politics through a multiplicity of theories in the flesh. As a theory of identity, multiplicity "understands social identities as *mutually constitutive* (rather than as discrete and separable) [emphasis in original]."[1] Not only do each of these identities mean something different to each interlocutor, but additionally, meaning is generated internally as ascribed identities clash intersectionally with avowed identities (i.e., ethnicity, citizenship status, sexual orientation, gender). Theories in the flesh are created within the clashes, fissures, critical junctures, and traumas experienced within this matrix of domination.[2] For instance, disidentification and the labor of intelligibility are two theories in the flesh co-witnessed by queer Latino scholars from within and outside of communication.[3] Theories in the flesh carve out spaces to survive and thrive from the fringes by purposefully working through a process of praxis turned theory turned praxis or a cyclical process of "decolonizing reality consist[ing] of unlearning consensual 'reality,' of seeing through reality's roles and descriptions."[4] As part of this shift in reality, multiplicity radically claims that what happens to me is a reflection of you—we are in this together.

For instance, throughout this book, Jotería are challenged by inter and intragenerational divides that make "coming out," regardless of age in this historical/political moment, a traumatic event where one's intersectional cultural identity is under attack from multiple vectors. Thus, the labor of intelligibility, or the labor of making sense of being Chicano or *Mexicano* and Jotería, is an everyday trauma that can only be understood in juxtaposition with other identities. I have aimed to remember the cuentos of GBTQ Chicanos de Colorado in Chapter 6 uninterrupted by description and analysis to honor the experiences of my ancestors and co-witnesses; however, to member these same cuentos (as discussed in Chapter 1), I revisit various borderlands narratives or rhetorical discourses shared throughout the book to highlight theories in the flesh and queer of color performance. In essence, I am asking: how can we "see" the communicative interconnections between us through multiplicity as a centralizing theory?

Like most borderlands narrative forms, cuentos blur and bleed together and make categorization difficult for researchers of communication. In fact, as a queer Chicano, it is important to note how because of my own identity each dialogic performance co-witnessed performatively together in this book was also an example of knowledge production within a plática. At times, these pláticas were part of the cuento told, or they were the entire cuento co-witnessed. At other times, cuentos, pláticas, mitos, testimonios, and/or consejos involved some sort of chismé. As part of the Jotería community, GBTQ Chicanos are only part of the story, and there is a need for more research on queer and trans Chicanas and Latinas. Rather than attempt to create six different analytical lenses for six different analyses, this chapter follows the wanderings of these narrative forms betwixt and between three thematics: the multiple inter-/intragenerational silences within (GBTQ) Chicano communities; the traumas and subsequent theories in the flesh created from coming out as a GBTQ Chicano; and the multiple vectors and levels of identity, culture, and power GBTQ Chicanos navigate to make sense of themselves and to make sense of themselves to others.

Generational Dis/Continuities

Articulated by Johnson in *Sweet Tea* in the co-witnessing of Gay Black men of the south, I, too, encountered generational dis/continuities during my dialogic performances of co-witnessing with GBTQ Chicanos.[5] Specifically, I was struck by the rift between the older generations and the newer generations of (GBTQ) Chicanos and how this rift affectively registers in both inter- and intragenerational communication within the family and within romantic relationships. As I highlighted spatially in the performative staging of these cuentos in Chapter 6, there is a culture of silence that (dis)allows theories of the flesh to be narrated intergenerationally between GBTQ Chicanos. Further, this culture of silence is also intragenerational in that GBTQ Chicanos (young and old) are not "out of the closet" to their families in the Euro-American construction of this term. Instead, as Jay, one of my co-witnesses, explains, "It just wasn't talked about." How does one make sense of themselves and make sense of themselves to others in this culture of silence? How does one resist and have agency in this cultural context?

Intergenerational Culture(s) of Silence

Toni, the eldest co-witness from the Colorado study, discusses this intergenerational culture of silence as an embodied historical and political inheritance from prior generations. He yearns for the newer generations to understand that "our struggle has been / one of the hardest / for centuries" and that we inherited this struggle (its victories and failures) from our queer elders in the form of cultural disciplining onto/into our bodies. In his cuento, Toni explains how the "older guys were totally / jaded / You know / They were jaded and mean" and how his generation "experienced our own form of / being jaded / or mistreated." Later, Positivo reiterated this generational dis/continuity when he discussed his first experiences at a gay club at 16 as a kind of predator/prey relationship: "guys were like, 'So what's up? / Oh, he's a youngin' / They knew / when there was prey there." As GBTQ Chicanos undertake the labor of finding community support and backup, they encounter a predator/prey gay male culture that objectifies their bodies, fetishizes their youth, and exoticizes their mestizaje. Rather than create communities of understanding and sharing, GBTQ Chicanos encounter a culture that continues patriarchal, White supremacist, and capitalist hierarchies within gay spaces and places.

Navigating the multiplicity of gender, Whiteness, and capitalist hierarchies is an intersectional labor of intelligibility for GBTQ Chicanos in LGBTQ spaces. John T. Warren, a White bisexual communication scholar, defines Whiteness as a privilege enjoyed simply because one appears white.[6] For Latinos, Whiteness stereotypes Brown male bodies as the "Latin Lover" or the heterosexual, affectively excessive, and hypersexualized "Latin Papi."[7] In LGBTQ spaces, these stereotypes mirror the dominant heterosexual culture and refract it into social scripts that drain queer Latinx bodies of their subjectivity. Fetishized and eroticized to fit a capitalist impulse, GBTQ Chicanos have little power within the hegemonic construction of Whiteness and masculinity in LGBTQ spaces In Chapter 5, I discussed the unique yet challenging homeplaces that Jotería create to bend but not break White cisheteronormativity and patriarchal constructions of the LGBTQ nightclub.

However, Toni, in a moment of telling chismé, discusses how he used this hierarchical, predator/prey culture to his advantage to survive away from Colorado in San Francisco as a younger man. Toni describes himself at this time in his life: "I was a cheerleader / in a size 27 waist / with a kick-ass everything." Toni's body fit easily into the fetishized image of the fit, portable, and young "Latin Lover" who could and would fulfill all your desires. Utilizing his "kick-ass" body, he finds shelter during a scary night wandering alone in the city, and further, he secures a stable and affordable place to stay. "And he told me I could stay with him / for 200 a month if I were to clean his house / in a thong / once a week." For Toni, the ultimate lesson from this chismé is that he could use his raced sexuality and the predator/prey culture to feel and be empowered as a GBTQ Chicano. By working with and through a harmful ideology rather than against, Toni disidentifies to create space to resist an impoverished living situation and a possibly violent circumstance (i.e., wandering around alone at night). It must be acknowledged how this script relies a system of fatphobia, yet how gossip and rumor challenge master narratives through the theory of disidentification is an example of this cultural norming/disciplining process. These everyday power differentials divide and disempower Jotería in the micro, meso, and macro structures of intersectional control.

By using rumor/gossip to open up pláticas about sexuality and gender, GBTQ Chicanos transform spaces and challenge binary understandings of gender and sexuality because the intent is to break silence. Within the cultural logic of machismo, queerness is connected to the feminine, so one is seen as weak, disempowered, and monstrous if one does not perform masculinity correctly.[8] For example, Ricky Martin, a Puerto Rican pop singer and performer, publicly navigated the difficult terrain of gossip and rumor about his gender and sexuality in the early 2000s. Drawing on Muñoz's theory of disidentification, Calafell charts Martin's public performances of politics that utilized ambiguity to disrupt gender/sexual binaries to maintain a masculine identity through chismé rather than against.[9] She writes that because of Martin's light-skinned status he "carried the privilege of visibility, enabling him to pass from the terrain of Latina/o Otherness into the public space of whiteness and imbuing it with difference."[10] Some of this difference was cultural navigating and competing with understandings of masculinity and sexuality that Martin bridged with his public performances of dance, resistance, mestizaje, and passing.[11]

In media portrayals and commentaries, Martin's body is simultaneously eroticized and Othered by playing a sexually ambiguous game of "is he or isn't he."[12] In a (in)famous interview with Barbara Walters in 2000, Martin was pressed to answer rumors of his sexuality, yet rather than adhere to binary understandings of sexuality, Martin "remains staunchly, discursively ambiguous."[13] Working through both the politics of naming (refusing to answer the question) and the Latin Lover stereotype (Martin's body as spectacle/object) to disidentify and resist hegemonic structuring. Of importance for this study, Martin essentially does not dispute or directly challenge chismé, but he works through and with it to transform the rumor into an international space to discuss the politics of coming out for the larger Latina/o culture. In 2010, Martin officially came out of the closet, but in order to maintain his career and public acceptance of his gender and sexuality performances, he utilized chismé and disidentification to protect himself and survive the onslaught of two competing cultural expectations on his body and identity.

GBTQ Chicano generational communication is full of fissures, cracks, and empty spaces because each generation has had to grapple with the violent realities of being GBTQ and Chicano in different historical/political moments. Speaking about the older gay generations, Toni notes how "They were just / reflecting on us" because "they had probably had / a lot of barriers / a lot of hurt / hatred." For example, Toni explains how his generation never expected to find love but "this newer generation ... they're—actually—looking and expecting love." Growing up as a GBTQ Chicano in the 1980s and 1990s, Toni witnessed many friends and mentors lose their lives to the HIV and AIDS epidemic. In the midst of Reaganomic policies of silence on the epidemic, Toni faced a different historical/political environment than Andres who is beginning his adult life in the current post-gay marriage moment. In this case, love and the possibility for love mark a significant political and historical rift between the generations. Whether old or young, GBTQ Chicanos face a culture of silence within the LGBTQ community that upholds oppressive structures of power based on race, gender, and class, and within their own Chicano community, GBTQ Chicanos face a culture of silence that pits them against their own brothers and sisters, fathers, mothers, and extended family members.

Intragenerational Culture(s) of Silence(s)

Passing on and/or forgetting to pass on historical and political traumas to the next generation is rooted in a culture of silence that is intragenerational. Meaning that fissures, cracks, and junctures left unaddressed within a generation (familial, communal, global) are passed on for the next generation to grapple and struggle with. In the narratives co-witnessed, intragenerational struggles within the family and within romantic relationships effected and affected future GBTQ Chicano experiences of identity, culture, and history. In the plática between Jay and his older gay uncle discussed in Chapter 6, Jay's uncle explains how he is still not out to his own brother: "he never questioned it / so if he questioned it / he didn't question it with me." Likewise, Andres notes that his "horrible" gay uncle is not officially out to the family, but instead, his sexual orientation is the topic of many rumors. These unaddressed silences and rumors at the intragenerational level of communication have ramifications for future generations.

For example, Positivo, in a mito of "down-low" or DL culture, explains how his ability to pass and perform a cisgendered masculine identity has resulted in the majority of his sexual and romantic exploits being with Latino men who identify as "straight." At the intragenerational level, Positivo is a GBTQ Chicano grappling with a dualistic culture of competing ideologies of sexuality and gender alongside and with other GBTQ Chicanxs. This socio-cultural ideological matrix was inherited from prior Chicano generations, yet at the intragenerational level, the struggle to hold an empowering view of one's sexuality and gender is a similar story of silence and violence that echoes throughout the centuries. GBTQ Chicano men internalize the modern/colonial gender system, and in an insidious fashion, they begin to view their intersectional performances of gender and sexuality as monstrous, sinful/blasphemous, criminal, or unnatural. For instance, the majority of my interviewees had experienced deep depression because of their identities that led to either suicidal thoughts or attempts at suicide. Although each of my interviewees from Chapter 6 are out of the closet to their families, GBTQ Chicanxs are still forced to live double lives where their desires and performances of gender/sexuality must be hidden or carefully performed to maintain community support and safety. For those not out of the closet, living two, three, or sometimes four lives depending on the context takes a mental, emotional, spiritual, and physical toll on GBTQ Chicanxs, which manifests in addiction, aggression, and violence.

In these collected cuentos and pláticas, violence materialized in the form of abusive relationships. Jay and his first boyfriend clashed not only because of a lack of positive gay relationships to model but also because the maintenance of the activo-passivo binary and machismo led to physical violence. Even in Andres' cuento of being threatened by a DL man, the potential boyfriend "was very hypermasculine / He cared a lot about how he sounded / He cared a lot about not sounding gay." Further, the threats of violence came after the potential boyfriend shared that he was recently in an abusive relationship: "he showed me pictures / of his eye, it was black / broken ribs." Intragenerational silences maintain the conditions in which each new generation must grapple with the baggage of the prior generation. Unaddressed pláticas and chismé within the family, community, or world sit like a grain of sand in an oyster irritating and agitating the mouth. Each generation adds its own layer to the irritant until consciously or unconsciously someone or something cuts it out and removes it. Now, the traumas of generations past and present are a pearl of knowledge (conocimiento) to be shared with others as cultural currency—a kind of equipment for living.[14]

Utilizing Pláticas and Chismé to Address Culture(s) of Silence

Within GBTQ culture, there are generational dis/continuities that reinforce dominant narratives, and GBTQ Chicanxs work with and through these master narratives to resist and survive their material realities. Generational dis/continuities are a consistent theme throughout GBTQ Chicanx cuentos and pláticas because silence is all that GBTQ Chicanxs can expect when trying to make sense of themselves and make sense of themselves for others. For instance, Andres lacks an elder role model to help him undertake his labor of intelligibility. Even though Andres has a gay uncle who "dresses up as a woman / and he performs in drag," this potential ally within the family is "not really somebody [Andres] look[s] up to" because of his uncle's violent and criminal behaviors toward his friends and family. In the case of Jay, he shares a plática of when he came out to his older gay uncle, and in response, his uncle finally came out to him. Jay asks his uncle, "Why doesn't anyone in our family ever talk about this? / It would've been so much better for me." Like Jay and Andres, GBTQ Chicanos face a culture of silence within their Chicano communities and families because nonheteronormative performances of sexuality and gender are tolerated as long as they can be ignored or excluded from the space. These performances are tolerated as long as they are neutered and remain marginal within the cultural logic of the everyday communicative life being socially constructed within the space.

Indeed, highlighting generational dis/continuities is an attempt to heal the historical/political divide through the personal because culture(s) of silence are ingrained inter-and intragenerationally in the everyday. In the narratives cowitnessed, pláticas and chismé were utilized by the participants to address the condition of being silenced and the culture of silence in LGBTQ and Chicano communities. In the plática shared by Positivo, he was only able to access a memory of sexual abuse by his brother by engaging in chats/conversations with his family. Further, it is worth noting that, facing depression and suicidal thoughts, Positivo utilized pláticas to reach out for support from his family. However, pláticas can open up "a whole new can of worms" because addressing familial silence is a dangerous labor that GBTQ Chicanos engage in to understand themselves.

Holling researches the dynamics of the Chicana/o familia and Chicano masculinity within a case study of *Resurrection Blvd.*, which aired three seasons between 2000 and 2002 on the cable network Showtime.[15] The Chicano familia is viewed as extending beyond a blood lineage-based view of family, and la familia is male-dominated, patriarchal, and maintains a gender-based family structure.[16] Chicana/o familias have varying degrees of egalitarian relations among marital couples and a strong emphasis on family solidarity, extended relations, affectionate and close bonds, and celebrations of life-cycle rituals.[17] These characteristics of familia fluctuate depending on the degree of urbanization, industrialization, acculturation, and socioeconomic status, not to mention the influences of one's spirit, qualities, and respect for elders and genders.[18] In discussing how hypermasculinity or machismo comes into being within the familia, Holling cites the colonization of Mexico by the Spanish: "one view presupposes a pathology among Mexican and Mexican American men who suffer from feelings of inferiority, weakness, and powerlessness for which outward demonstrations of masculinity compensate."[19] However, she offers a second view that claims the association between hypermasculinity and Mexican males is an assimilation to the Spanish cultural value system and worldview, which emphasized masculinity, patriarchy, and strict gender role adherence.[20] Holling writes, "Within that context, Chicano masculinity is born from experiences of colonization, oppression, and resistance, as well as influenced by cultural attitudes of what constitutes a 'man.' "[21] Meaning that:

> the "tough macho" reflects behavioral characteristics of machismo, whereas the "tender macho" reveals the expression of emotions and behaviors most associated with femininity, that is, adoration and sensitivity toward children, expressing vulnerability, and close, perhaps even intimate, physical contact between men.[22]

GBTQ Chicanos navigate the difficult terrain of gender and sexuality by utilizing pláticas and chismé to address familial cultures of silence that upholds binary, hierarchical thinking, such as the "tough macho" over the "tender macho."

In the case of Jay, his plática with his gay uncle opened up a space where they both could reach across the generational divide to come out of the closet to each other. Moreover, Jay becomes a resource and confidant for his uncle to share the secrets of his former marriage and the trauma of the intragenerational divide. By addressing silence, pláticas are opportunities to utilize listening and dialogue toward the goal of alliance building, which are all powerful forms of advocacy. These alliances can provide critical support for GBTQ Chicanos within the family to maintain a positive self-image in the face of negative images at the local, national, and global level. Each participant utilized pláticas to build knowledge by addressing culture(s) of silence, and GBTQ Chicanos utilize these familial or personal pláticas to resist and have agency within a complex and dynamic social system.

Oftentimes, gossip and rumor can be part of the violence of heteronormativity that queer folks must grapple with in order to carve out spaces for themselves.[23] In my own experience, chismé has been an oppressive narrative form, yet it is also one of the few tools at my disposal to defend/protect myself. There is an element of breaking silence or "narrative trespass" within this narrative form that makes the theories in the flesh communicated within *chismé* particularly potent for resistance and agency.[24] For Toni, gossiping about the first time he felt empowered by his sexuality was a moment that I couldn't help but share. Without positive images and histories to draw from, it felt important to share a narrative where same-sex desire and sexuality protected and defended Toni against master narratives where GBTQ Chicanos should be ashamed of their bodies. In Andres' chismé about his gay uncle, he humanizes the experiences of an older generation of GBTQ Chicano—we are not without flaws. Further, Andres' *chismé* addresses how undocumented communities navigate a system that does not want them to be business owners and how not all fathers within the Chicano community are afraid to be vulnerable with their feelings. In sharing the chismé about sexual empowerment, undocumented experiences, and male vulnerability, remembering GBTQ Chicano cuentos and pláticas challenges the colonial/modern gender system and other master narratives of control, such as citizenship, class, and coming out.

Politics of Coming Out

As the previous section discusses, bodily and boundary violations, border shifts, and identity confusions shock GBTQ Chicanos into a new way of reading the world, and in confronting culture(s) of silence, GBTQ Chicanos create theories in the flesh in a process of praxis turned theory turned praxis.[25] These fissures and cracks are inherited from prior generations, yet they operate within the current historical/political moment in the form of intragenerational dis/continuities. In co-witnessing these narratives, I was surprised by the amount of "coming out" narratives that emerged from our dialogic performances and how each interviewee utilized different performativities of disidentification to open up space for their identities. Specifically, "the phrase 'coming out of the closet' refers to the experience of coming out into a queer identity ... It also refers to coming out into a community of other similarly identified people, which entails personal and political dimensions."[26] To further explicate the effects and affects of generational dis/continuities, I highlight how GBTQ Chicanos create theories in the flesh out of their "coming out" narratives, and how they then turn and utilize these traumatic experiences as a praxis of resistance in their everyday lives.

For instance, Aya, as a transgender Chicana from my Colorado research, articulates an understanding of identity as fluid and contextual, and through her *cuento*, we glimpse at the complex cultural history navigated by transgender Chicanas. Transgender communication grapples with the historical baggage of the medical/psychiatric models that view "transsexualism as a mental illness that, uniquely, could be treated with a combination of psychological, hormonal, and surgical interventions."[27] Indeed, the term "transgender" is a more recent label that emerged from the community to combat the static and pathologizing medicalization model.[28] As an umbrella term, transgender "describes a subject-in-motion" for "any gender expression, identity, or presentation that varies from what we might understand as normative."[29] Prior to Christmas, Aya was worried about how or if she should come out as transgender to her family because transgender narratives of coming out challenge dominant narratives circulating that maintain the gender and sex binary and the assumed Whiteness of transgender experiences. She was preparing to have a plática that would break silence within the family.

For instance, further complicating the visit, Aya's transgender girlfriend was going to be arriving in the next few days to meet the family for the first time. As two transgender women in a romantic relationship, Aya challenges the woman/man, feminine/masculine, and gay/straight binary narrative that the Chicano familia and the U.S. and Mexico promulgate. Her cuento articulates how she performed her identity differently depending on the context. At home, she was prepared with her "boy drag," but she was ready with her "makeup on hand" for those spaces more inclusive of her evolving identity. Aya, as a Chicana, understands how the family surveils and constrains gender categories, so in this context, non-normative identities are marked as different and cissexism and transphobia manifest in often violent and domineering forms of privilege.[30] Transgender experiences "challenge the dominant cultural assumption that gender is invariant and that a misalignment between body and identity is deceptive or less 'real' than someone whose body and selfhood are congruent."[31] Addressing cissexism and transphobia, Aya and her girlfriend undertook a plática before the visit to discuss tactical ways to resist the gender-norming practices of Aya's family. As a form of disidentification, Aya and her girlfriend decided to work on and through the Chicano family ideology instead of against by purposefully not gendering Aya in their interactions.

As Aya undertakes the labor of articulating her identity to others and herself, she challenges the assumed Whiteness of transgender experience. From within and outside the discipline of communication studies, transgender studies has been critiqued for centering the experiences of White folks and marginalizing trans of color narratives.[32] In a speech in the wake of trangendered teenager Leelah Alcorn's suicide in 2015, Lourdes Ashley Hunter, National Director of the Trans Women of Color Collective, describes the current moment for transgender women of color:

We are dying and what are you doing? What are you doing to stop the murders of trans women of color . . . . Right here in the United States, 12 trans women of color were brutally murdered. Trans women of color are 50 times more likely to be impacted by HIV, the average income of a trans person is less than 10,000 dollars, over 40% of trans people attempt suicide . . . . If you want to fix something, we need to fix this shit now.[33]

As an intersectional experience, Aya's narrative highlights the importance of race and class in constructions of gender and sexuality. Focusing on the materiality of transgender subjects, the politics of coming out are a complex and fluid terrain that GBTQ Chicanxs navigate within and outside of their familias.

Looking deeper into the coming-out narrative of Andres, he narrates the process of praxis turned theory turned praxis necessary to create a theory of the flesh. At 16, Andres was "barely coming out," and at that time, he "was really looking for that masculine man" who was "6 foot" and White. Later, he notes how internalized racism, classism, homophobia, and heteronormativity materialized in the form of the passivo-activo binary. He "was very unaware of about like / power structures and things like that." However, after exposure to critical texts in college, Andres creates the following theory: "Now I'm like sort of in this space where / racially I'm kind of anti-White right now / and I'm people of color power / That translates into my romantic life." Andres puts this theory created out of praxis to work in his love life by rejecting White men and White beauty as the ideal ("I don't talk to White men / I don't want to be attracted to White men"). Further, after threats of violence from love interests within the community, Andres "find[s] that / the men who are more masculine / are the ones that / I don't find a lot of connection to," and he puts this theory to use by rejecting hypermasculinity, masculine gender norms, and patriarchal forms of aggression and violence. Theories in the flesh transform everyday traumas into equipment for living that Jotería utilize to resist dominant narratives and to have agency over their circumstances.

As a different performance of culture with different historical affective registers, "coming out of the closet" is a performative act that must be (re)performed over and over again for GBTQ Chicanos. As Jay explains in his plática, his gay uncle "had a roommate named John for-ev-er / like, 15 years / then John one day just moved to a different state (broke up)." Although his uncle had found love, it did not translate to him coming out to the rest of the family. In fact, earlier in his life, Jay's uncle "had gotten married to a woman, had two children and then divorced" and claimed that he thought his wife was a lesbian when he met her. Even after both of these events in his life, Jay's uncle is still not out of the closet to his family, and although his nephew, oldest son, and granddaughter are LGBTQ, he has chosen to be "out of the closet" to varying degrees with each. Jay's uncle is struggling within multiple cultures of silence to come to terms with his identity as an elder GBTQ Chicano. In this coming-out narrative, we glimpse the struggle of the older generations as they find themselves in a historical/political moment where coming out of the closet at the inter- and intragenerational level is a new and frightening expectation.

Coming out is not a one-time, one-size-fits-all performance of empowerment,[34] and "the coming out process can be long and complicated."[35] In Jay's narrative, we are co-witnesses to Jay's uncle coming out to his nephew; remaining in the closet with his brother-in-law, son, and goddaughter; yet out to his ex-wife and out enough in certain spaces to have had a 15-year-long gay relationship. This narrative challenges the "simplistic definition of queerness: closet—coming out—happiness!"[36] Indeed, "the metaphor of coming out of the closet and the politics of the closet have been central to contemporary western queer experiences,"[37] and although the politics of coming out can be inclusionary, the politics have a radical dimension within this Western construction, such as "to declare their presences, demand systemic changes, and resist and disrupt assumptions of normative culture."[38] However, as the previous examples showcase, non-White and non-Western constructions of identity, family, and culture do not have the same privileges or norms, so coming out for GBTQ Chicanos is often a traumatic experience. They are not safe to perform "coming out" as a performative act because to mark desire and publicize gay sex is taboo within Chicana/o culture, and as a community-oriented culture, we need our families to survive our material realities on the fringes of society.[39] GBTQ Chicanos regardless of age undertake different labor(s) of intelligibility that must be repeated over and over because of this cultural, historical, and political context.

Intersectional Labor(s) of Intelligibility

The labor of intelligibility is a reoccurring theme throughout each cuento y plática (and throughout this book) regardless of categorization because this labor is an intimate part of the process of transforming traumatic experiences into theory into praxis. As a reminder, the labor of intelligibility is a process of making sense of oneself to others and making sense of oneself to oneself.[40] This is the everyday labor of being seen as a legitimate bearer of knowledge, of interpreting one's life accurately, of finding community backup and solidarity, and of resisting oppression.[41] By resisting oppression, I am referring to the labor of how one grapples with confusion and fear, with ridicule and violence, and displacement through social isolation.[42] Throughout the previous sections, I have discussed this labor in reference to generational dis/continuities and coming-out narratives, but in this final section, I want to highlight how every narrative grappled with oppression in some form.

For Jay, his lack of access to the older generations, to understandings of his identity in popular culture and history, and to social services geared toward LGBTQ issues landed him in an abusive relationship with few options to leave. Although Jay's brother is also a GBTQ Chicano, internalized homophobia and heteronormativity affected all three cisgendered men, such as strict gender and sexual role adherence, aggression, alcoholism, and domestic violence. After a failed attempt to move from an exclusively monogamous relationship to one of polyamory, Jay's relationship turned emotionally and physically abusive. Jay's repeated mentions that "we were young" throughout the narrative means that he has since utilized this traumatic experience to understand what love is and is not. In the process of understanding what it means to be a GBTQ Chicano, Jay creates a theory in the flesh, or an awareness and sensitivity to machismo, that he deploys to avoid issues of jealousy and rage within other possible relationships. Additionally, this cuento has a pedagogical function in that Jay's narrative describes the tell-tale signs of abuse and how, through family support and personal growth/empowerment, Jay was able to survive that relationship and repair his relationship with his brother. His abusive partner did not undertake the same difficult labor of intelligibility to create theory out this moment of jealousy and rage ("I still hear that he has issues with alcohol / I still hear that he abuses his current boyfriend"). To create a theory of the flesh, one must be willing to work on and through a traumatic experience—it doesn't just happen.

Throughout each narrative and each theme, GBTQ Chicanos undertake particular labors of intelligibility because of the multiplicitous and intersectional nature of the culture(s) of silence. "Being Brown" or the affects of race and ethnicity on masculinity and sexuality can be traced along the vectors of class. Class arose as a persistent theme within the narratives gathered in the Colorado study, and what is interesting about this theme is that the interviewees seem to conflate being Brown with masculinity. For example, Jonathan Xavier Inda makes the argument that race operates in performatively similarly ways as gender (a la Judith Butler), and Inda outlines how "the place that Mexicans have historically occupied within the United States' racial hierarchy has depended strongly on the pigmentation of their skin."[43] He discusses how if one is light-skinned they often receive privileges associated with Whiteness, and if one is dark-skinned, then one is often racially marginalized. He writes that "their skin was not only read as a sign of their inferior social status, it also served as a justification for keeping them in that position."[44] This marginalization of people based on skin pigmentation occurs in Mexico as well as in the United States (and all over the world). This stratification of society inhibits upward mobility for dark-skinned Xicanos, and class is often conflated with sexuality as well as gender.

Irwin, in *Mexican Masculinities*, discusses how working-class men are often considered more macho than upper-class men because of class biases and clothing fashions.[45] Irwin analyzes Mexican literature during the early nineteenth century and points to this time when "lower-class masculinity was being marked as sexually dangerous and roughly masculine."[46] On the opposing side, "civilized upper-class men were not committing violent crimes, but it seemed their soft, cultured style was leading them into dreaded effeminacy."[47] It is not that upper-class men are not considered masculine, but it is that effeminacy during this time became connected to homosexuality.[48] Thus, "lower-class versions of masculinity, then, reflected degeneration into barbarous historical patterns while upper-class versions reflected the decadence of modern civilization."[49] Class intersects with sexuality for Chicanos because of this historical conflation of how one dresses and its connection to effeminacy; if one is upper class, then one could afford and wear the clothing of the privileged soft laborer.

Scholars of Latinx rhetoric and Latina/o communication studies offer excellent examples of how class perceptions and its intersections with race and sexuality operate on Chicanos. Delgado questions the continuing beliefs that Chicanos are not worthy to be in the privileged space of the academy because of race/ethnicity: "Do they see me as the dean? Do they only see me as Brown? Does my Latino identity subvert my credibility and authority?"[50] Essentially, Delgado, because of his skin color, is viewed as part of the lower-class, and even as a well-accomplished scholar, his legitimacy is constantly questioned. In addition, Márez notes how working-class style is often judged as inappropriate for Anglo spaces, and exhibitions of this Brown style are avoided or shoved to the margins.[51] He writes, "To those who do not appreciate it, working-class brown style can be too ornate, too gaudy, too florid, too loud, too busy, too much—an embarrassment of riches."[52] However, working-class aesthetics are the preferred choice for Chicanos/Xicanos who want to maintain a masculine gender performance according to the culturally dualistic logics of Latino culture. This is seen in the scandal of El Baile de los 41 Maricones and in Chapter 5 within the aesthetic forms archived in auto/ethnographic form from the LGBTQ Latinx nightclub. They are caught in a kind of catch-22 where their gender and sexuality performances are always already oppressed because of race or class hierarchies, yet because of patriarchy and heteronormativity, they experience privileges and benefits that they will defend (sometimes violently) from women and LGBTQ people. In their everyday lives, GBTQ

Chicanos/Xicanos deal with the politics of class and race, and their perceived performances of excess are in fact biases related to maintaining meso-level structures of oppression mutually constituted alongside gender and sexuality.

The labor(s) of intelligibility are intersectional acts that inform how GBTQ Chicanos utilize their available choices to learn about themselves and about how to explain themselves to others. For example, in Positivo's cuento, he articulates that, for GBTQ Chicanos of Denver, the only spaces available to build community were Tracks and Cheesman Park. As a community on the periphery, politics of shame have an effect on urban zoning, whereas LGBTQ businesses and spaces are often (un)consciously targeted and shut down.[53] Meaning that LGBTQ folks have fewer and fewer spaces to undertake the labor(s) of intelligibility, and given the hierarchical, predator-prey culture, these places are not necessarily the safest spaces to learn about oneself. Positivo explains that because of this isolation and lack of knowledge, he suffered from deep depression and suicidal thoughts, yet in the face of sexual abuse and mental/emotional issues, Positivo used these traumas to create theories of the flesh by working through his past and present oppressions to arrive at place where he has graduated with a doctoral degree. By examining intersectional labor(s) of intelligibility, GBTQ Chicano narratives offer a pedagogical function that seeks to guide others through the difficult moments of their own lives.

(Re)Starting the Journey

In his final consejo, Andres demonstrates the pedagogical function of sharing one's labor of intelligibility with others as a form of narrating theories in the flesh. Andres makes the argument that GBTQ Chicanos should embrace their intersectional identities as a form of empowerment. He states: "You are a / whole lot of things at once" and "there is a lot of power / in every single part of who you are / You are not just queer / You are not just Chicano / You are not just American / or undocumented." Andres faces ridicule and violence from his queer and Chicano identities because of larger structures of power, including homophobia, heteronormativity, xenophobia, and racial injustice. Additionally, he experiences, like many GBTQ Chicanos, a split between his identities that can be confusing and can incite fear (i.e., Chicano, American, undocumented), but still, Andres advocates for wholeness and embraces the power of self-love as a radical act of resistance. He proclaims that "self-pity / is not going to / do anything for them / that it won't do anything for me," and instead he asks us all to "think critically about /

power and why they have power / and how they are willing to execute that power / in ways that are not harmful to other people." In this consejo, Andres narrates a theory in the flesh that pushes back on master narratives, such as self-hate, self-pity, and "it gets better" by arguing for an embrace of borderlands identities and cultures. All of them.

In this chapter, I have wandered between cuentos, pláticas, chismé, testimonios, mitos, and consejos of GBTQ Chicanos de Colorado and highlighted some of the themes that a borderlands lens to narrative theory (re)member. Looking back on the path that we have taken together, I can't help but wonder what other forms disidentification and the labor of intelligibility can take. I wonder what other theories in the flesh are being utilized by GBTQ Chicanos across the U.S. Southwest? And I wonder what theories in the flesh are created and deployed by Chicana lesbians? As a way station, this project is a snapshot of Colorado from a very particular location at a very particular time, but the generational dis/continuities, politics of coming out, and labor of intelligibility archived here are not particular. For instance, these themes were also located by Johnson in the oral history narratives of Black gay men of the South, and Roque Ramirez in the oral history narratives of LGBTQ Latinas/os of the San Francisco Bay Area.[54] Additionally, many of the theories of the flesh utilized by GBTQ Chicanos have been articulated by Chicana feminists and queer of color scholars.[55] GBTQ Chicano experiences of culture, politics, and history are particular, but given the cultural dualism of this community immersed in the modern/colonial gender system and in histories of settler colonialism, these narratives implicate a multiplicity of persons of all races, classes, sexualities, and genders. As a tactic to (re)member cuentos of GBTQ Chicanos, this chapter is not a complete rendering of experience, but through the theory of multiplicity, I invite the reader to fill in the gaps with their own experiences, identity, culture, and history. I invite you to look back at our journey and ask: where do I fit? Rather than leave these oppressions as particular, I hope you will shift with them and integrate them fully into your reality. This is your story too.

Notes

1. Michael Hames-García, *Identity Complex: Making the Case for Multiplicity* (Minneapolis: University of Minnesota Press, 2011), xi.
2. Gloria Anzaldúa, *Light in the Dark/Luz en lo Oscuro: Rewriting Identity, Spirituality, Reality* (Durham, NC: Duke University Press, 2015); Patricia Hill Collins, *Black*

Feminist Thought: Knowledge, Consciousness, and the Politics of Empowerment (New York: Routledge, 1991).

3. Bernadette Marie Calafell, *Latina/o Communication Studies: Theorizing Performance* (New York: Peter Lang, 2007); Robert Gutierrez-Perez, "Disruptive Ambiguities: The Potentiality of Jotería Critique in Communication Studies," *Kaleidoscope: A Graduate Journal of Qualitative Communication Research* 14 (2015); Ernesto Javier Martínez, *On Making Sense: Queer Race Narratives of Intelligibility* (Stanford, CA: Stanford University Press, 2013); Jose E. Muñoz, *Disidentifications: Queers of Color and the Performance of Politics* (Minneapolis: University of Minnesota, 1999).

4. Anzaldúa, *Light*, 44.

5. E. Patrick Johnson, *Sweet Tea: Black Gay Men of the South* (Chapel Hill: University of North Carolina Press, 2008).

6. John T. Warren, *Performing Purity: Whiteness, Pedagogy, and the Reconstitution of Power* (New York: Peter Lang, 2003), 185–86.

7. Shane T. Moreman, "Rethinking Dwight Conquergood: Toward an Unstated Cultural Politics," *Liminalities: A Journal of Performance Studies* 5, no. 5 (2009); Shane T. Moreman and Bernadette Marie Calafell, "Buscando Para Nuestros Hijos: Utilizing La Llorona for Cultural Critique," *Journal of International and Intercultural Communication* 1, no. 4 (2008): 309–26.

8. Bernadette Marie Calafell, *Monstrosity, Performance, and Race in Contemporary Culture* (New York: Peter Lang, 2015); Robert Mckee Irwin, *Mexican Masculinities* (Minneapolis: University of Minnesota Press, 2003); Octavio Paz. *The Labyrinth of Solitude: Life and Thought in Mexico*. New York: Grove Press, 1961.

9. Calafell, *Latina/o*.

10. Ibid., 90.

11. Ibid., 87–8.

12. Ibid., 100–4.

13. Ibid., 108.

14. Kenneth Burke, *The Philosophy of Literary Form: Studies in Symbolic Action* (Baton Rouge: Louisiana State University Press, 1941).

15. Michelle A. Holling, "El Simpático Boxer: Underpinning Chicano Masculinity with a Rhetoric of Familia in Resurrection Blvd," *Western Journal of Communication* 70 (2006): 91–114.

16. Ibid., 93.

17. Ibid., 94.

18. Ibid., 94.

19. Ibid., 96.

20. Ibid., 96.

21. Ibid., 96.

22. Ibid., 97.

23. Gust A. Yep, "The Violence of Heteronormativity in Communication Studies: Notes on Injury, Healing, and Queer World-Making," *Journal of Homosexuality* 45, no. 2/3/4 (2003): 11–59.

24. Abdi, Shadee, "Staying I(ra)n: Narrating Queer Identity from Within the Persian Closet," *Liminalities: A Journal of Performance Studies* 10, no. 1 (2014): 1–19.

25. Anzaldúa, *Light*, 86.

26. Karma R. Chávez, "Pushing Boundaries: Queer Intercultural Communication," *Journal of International and Intercultural Communication* 6, no. 2 (2013): 83–95.

27. Vernon A. Rosario, " 'Qué Joto Bonita!': Transgender Negotiations of Sex and Ethnicity," *Journal of Gay & Lesbian Psychotherapy* 8, nos. 1–2 (2004): 91.

28. Spencer, Leland G. IV, "Introduction: Centering Transgender Studies and Gender Identity in Communication Scholarship," *Transgender Communication Studies: Histories, Trends, and Trajectories*, eds. Jamie C. Capuzza and Leland G. Spence IV (Lanham: Lexington Books, 2015). ix–xxii.

29. Ibid., xi.

30. Julia R. Johnson, "Cisgender Privilege, Intersectionality, and the Criminalization of CeCe McDonald: Why Intercultural Communication Needs Transgender Studies," *Journal of International and Intercultural Communication* 6, no. 2 (2013): 135–44.

31. Ibid., 137.

32. Chávez, "Pushing"; Francisco J. Galarte, "On Trans* Chican@s," *Aztlán: A Journal of Chicano Studies* 39, no. 1 (2014): 229–36; Johnson, "Cisgender;" Benny LeMaster and Amber L. Johnson, "Unlearning Gender—Towards a Critical Communication Trans Pedagogy," *Communication Teacher* 33, no. 3 (2019): 189–198. Rosario, "Qué Joto Bonita!"

33. Mitch Kellaway, "WATCH: Trans Leader's Speech Perfectly Explains Why We Must 'Fix Society,' Not Trans People," *Advocate,* January 13, 2015, https://www.advocate.com/politics/transgender/2015/01/13/watch-trans-leaders-speech-perfectly-explains-why-we-must-fix-society; Lourdes Ashley Hunter, " 'We Need to Fix This Shit Now' Says Director for Trans Women of Color Collective," *News2Share*, January 10, 2015, https://www.youtube.com/watch?v=Qu1niZYDzsk

34. Abdi, "Staying I(ra)n."

35. Rita E. Urquijo-Ruiz, "Coming Home," *Aztlán: A Journal of Chicano Studies* 39, no. 1 (2014): 251.

36. Giorgia Aiello, Sandeep Bakshi, Sirma Bilge, Lisa Kahaleole Hall, Lynda Johnston, Kimberlee Pérez, and Karma Chávez, "Here, and Not Yet Here: A Dialogue at the Intersection of Queer, Trans, and Culture," *Journal of International and Intercultural Communication* 6, no. 2 (2013): 111.

37. Karma R. Chávez, *Queer Migration Politics: Activist Rhetoric and Coalitional Possibilities* (Urbana, Chicago, and Springfield: University of Illinois Press, 2013), 84.

38. Chávez, *Queer Migration*, 84.
39. Robert Gutierrez-Perez, "Brown Fingers Ran Down," in *Queer Praxis: Questions for LGBTQ Worldmaking*, eds. Dustin Bradly Goltz and Jason Zingsheim (New York, NY: Peter Lang, 2015), 41–54.
40. Ernesto Javier Martínez, *On Making Sense: Queer Race Narratives of Intelligibility* (Stanford, CA: Stanford University Press, 2013).
41. Ibid.
42. Ibid.
43. Jonathan Xavier Inda, "Performativity, Materiality, and the Racial Body," *Latino Studies Journal* 11, no. 3 (1996): 77.
44. Ibid., 79.
45. Robert McKee Irwin, *Mexican Masculinities* (Minneapolis: University of Minnesota Press, 2003).
46. Ibid., 60.
47. Ibid., 60.
48. Robert McKee Irwin, "The Famous 41: The Scandalous Birth of Modern Mexican Homosexuality," *GLQ: A Journal of Lesbian and Gay Studies* 6, no. 3 (2000): 353–76.
49. Irwin, *Mexican Masculinities*, 64.
50. Fernando Delgado, "Reflections on Being/Performing Latino Identity in the Academy," *Text and Performance Quarterly* 29, no. 2 (2009): 162.
51. Curtis Márez, "Brown: The Politics of Working-Class Chicano Style," *Social Text* 48 (1996): 109–32.
52. Ibid., 122.
53. Michael Warner, *The Trouble with Normal: Sex, Politics, and the Ethics of Queer Life* (Cambridge, MA: Harvard University Press, 1999).
54. Johnson, *Sweet Tea*; Horacio N. Roque Ramírez, "Gay Latino Histories/Dying to Be Remembered: AIDS Obituaries, Public Memory, and the Queer Latino Archive," *Beyond El Barrio: Everyday Life in Latina/o America*, eds. Gina M. Pérez, Frank A. Guridy, and Adrian Burgos Jr. (New York: NYU Press, 2010), 103–28.
55. Anzaldua, *Light*; Martínez, *Making Sense*; Muñoz, *Disidentifications*.

I Put a Spell on You

Because you're mine
I toiled and troubled
over cauldron

I let it bubble in cathexis
I let the fire burn
no matter the consequences
I eyed your newts and glutes
Batted my winks your way
and invoked the Goddess

I had to have you, so
I put a spell on you
Prayed to Xochiquetzal
Practiced ceremony with Xochipilli
I sat, twisted and turned,
Yearning for your entrance
into my life, my loins

It feels good to be filled

but you just wouldn't be predicted
no matter how long I looked into the obsidian mirror,

you could not be controlled
It made me want you more.
The challenge. The hunt. The late-night fantasies. A chance to catch
your eye.

You put a spell on me
Because I'm yours

Back to Love / A Jotería Myth

For Juan

I'm trying to find
   my way   back
   to you
Laying beside your heat
I find you at night
staring, peaceful   a stalker in a tree
searching the map of your face
memories shared, forgotten   in the past
Do you miss me when you dream?

Scissors cutting up rocks
papering the path
barefoot   bleeding   beating up
my souls   sending them out
shocked   soaring
heart off   hiccupping   having
a fucked-up year

I gotta find my way back
my way back

to you
rhyming riddles
with guilt, shame, injected over time
your insecurities on top of mine
mirroring, reflecting, each other's shadows
endlessly

Is this why
I hunt you, crave you
always coming back for more
please   let me   please you
no one gets me in line like you
pigged onto the abuse
leashed   I want it
craving the echo   slapping my ass
baring my secret
I love it   deeper

Can you make ceremony through latex?
Can the ritual still invoke?
desiring   dictating   distancing us away
too much asked, too little given
feelings escalate
pressuring a release

Silence
Aye papi,
I have to find my way back
my way back to love
loving you like a tattoo
honoring you like an altar
dripping honey and rose petals
over your hip bone   your chest   those lips
praying for a vision
licking every drop of the bath water
toweling up your perspiration

Aye papi,
I have to find my way back

La Hambre

Did you catch it?
A glimmer of milk-chocolate skin
melting inked delicious
dark complex lines
taco de ojo

It would take a lifetime to trace him
drool over his complexity
lick that look right off his beard
fated for one night
I am pissed
howling moon to ceiling
I throw away my halo
Let go of inhibitions
anxiety un-wounding
around your head
self-doubt melding away
to your tempo, clip-ping petals
hungry with tongue
hummingbird wings beat-ting
sweat puddles on your back

our favorite tool:
your pillow

Feeling like a cannibal, you scream   desire
decolonial porn star
searching for my next snack
flights of the imagination
taking a nibble, then a bite
marking your fingers
something to sniff and remember me by
for your journey
        wink

once in the woods   back to mamá
you're confused   smelling me then touching your lips

Didn't you say harder?
can't text *me* anymore
need time to think
wanting to be torn
versatile

I knew you would message me first

Smirking, I let you think
The basket was for me
convinced, you take off your red hood
move closer, so I can feel your breath

"Oh how big you are papa!"

A Thriller ensues   growing fangs, spiky hair
Engorged with lunacy, chill
no Netflix but Mars in Aries
foraging grown men for sustenance
Oh death, stalking me as a reminder
Let me have this last juicy taste
Gaze at that cake one more moment
Admire this xochitl like a jewel
Perfect fit to the hilt
Not ready
        Don't blink
    Feed

Jotería Resistance

I don't like going to the doctor
Because I am afraid
You will find out

That one prick of my blood
From the tippity top of my finger
Will drop a bomb on my existence

You will find out

That I am an alien to this world
A visitor from another dimension
Like this but different
Like me but different
Like something or someone that has never existed before:

A bridge.

A short giggle to the side of my mouth
A kinda sarcastic exhale
I laugh at the thought of a monster so dangerous
Incendiary
Radical
Resistive

A bridge.

Asking questions
Not commands, Not
a colonial stack of paperwork
a forced volunteerism with a gun
nor an exhausted and nihilistic opinion
or a moralistic, imperial
sermon

Will you burn it?
Will you ignore it?
Or, will you cross it? Defend it? Repair it?
Demand that this bridge stay

Invitational
Celebrational
Worth remembering

To be a bridge
To risk the resources
To face the vast chasms between us/them
Who says this, also,
Is not healing?
Is not worth claiming/loving/feeling
anger/passion/desire for
self-care and self-esteem
and ultimately
self-love

Anzaldúa says
dive into your navel
Take out the toads

Shake it
And dive in again

Think about it
Like an orbit
The seasons changing
The circular rhythm of the drum
Not marching forward
But moving, vibrating, returning,
singing, surviving, tuning
our hearts
toward each other
like magic

The Lifeguard Station

Look at "It"
Standing there proud
The only one on the sand
Tone down your colors beach
Against a million grains
You're too bright
Too happy
Too much

Extra

It   draws them to   It
Like a lighthouse or shrine
I bet for them It is like Delphi
A visit to the oracle of truth,
light, knowledge, Apollo blessings
across the navel
tongue on the thigh
bronze curls up the spine

Mad love
forbidden love

smeared red raspberry, orange blossom
Yellow predictability in a poem
Greening your desire, turning you
blue   purple
Rage rabidly spewing forth
curses   slurs   fear

No one told me I could be happy in my skin
No one told me that I could dance in the sun

Your presence reminds me
I am afraid.   I need stability.
hurtling on a speck of dust
nothingness   scares me

Why aren't you afraid?

Protecting the beach
Watching the waves
Witnessing the moon
Calling las otras
locas, Jotería, personas de otros mundos
to play on your floorboards
to hang from your railings
to take pictures
kissing   hugging
Loving publicly

How dare you?

The Secret

For Michael

I press send and hold my breath
No response
Twirling fingers
Write then delete
Write then delete
Waiting   Write
then delete

Each version of my imagination
leads to some tragedy
Heart ripped out
Ego shredded on the floor
Murdered   I contemplate rebirth
Pulling my story back together
I try on new clothes
(paid for on credit)
This one too tight
That one too loose
Will I ever fit?

Life feels like a test
Check a box
Pick a number
Multiple-choice questions
all feels wrong

But I studied all night
crammed in websites and books
drank coffee and smoked a pack
dissected fake news and masturbated
I survived

Relax hermano

emojis of love
words of wisdom and support
I exhale   eyes dilate
A temporary utópico
Palm trees and sunsets
Harmony in difference

Breathe

Prepare   to bare
your soul
again
Write and delete
Write then
delete

Write.

Welcoming the Shadow

Charisma
Uniqueness
Nerve
Talent
Commander of the Pack
Destined to be on the front lines

It is lonely work

Who will coddle you when you put down masks,
political manipulations, comparing egos,
you're a fucking loser
unreliable, selfish, stubborn
I wish you were never born
Holding me back. I blame your independence,
broken promises, dark depression, my shadow
my inheritance

I carry you everywhere

Suddenly, your eyes squint and I get a glint
That you want this ass, these lips
Damé papi, give it a try   taste the tip

I'm good at getting in your head chulo
Finding your pain, massaging your prostate
making sure to knead you lower back
place my girth on that burden you carry
Let's share our pain
let it crack out our knuckles   toes
curl up your feet   feeling it up   staring

I often feel disconnected   on my own path
I often feel bored   too smart for my own good
I often feel alone   not with you

You did this feeling
drilling deeper dominating desiring destiny
gripping your back I hold you
A miracle spoon transforming into a fork
bending you backward
opening all our chakras at once
letting the celestial in
through and between
lighting up all our secrets
I woof protections in your ear
Is this what you felt?

I am
naturally connected
spirit of my ancestors
beautifully crafted to achieve my mission
to touch me is to feel divine
an alert for your soul
an awakening, a balancing
a coming to reality
an enfleshment of revolution

you're welcome

MUERTE DEL MACHO /
Death of the Macho

I came here to hide
from my diagnosis
Two pills every morning
keeping me alive but
am I living?
You say, "Let me love you"
Silently, I wonder   do I deserve it?
Leashed to fetishized
Castilian slurs, hipster margaritas,
a white socialite with her bloody hands
around my throat
a public display of a   "free city"
a selfie within a selfie
posted to Instagram

#welcometoLA

I say, "How do you define love?"
a lap dance in the back of a rental car
a gaze, a carefully laid stiletto on my neck,
a necklace from Reno gifted by a man
without a home

without a fuck to give
without an artist
painting his story
with her pinche chocha
I am not ready to tattoo your names on my leg
A vision of my own death made real
stalking me, just over my left shoulder
shocks me
I pick up the pace   Anxious
run to transform space   Anxious
A wall of bodies keeping me from my goal
Fifteen pairs of hands
Holding me down
Pulling at the headband you gave me
Stretched, immobile, locked down
at your mercy
Did I just die again?

I feel naked
ass showing every time my hand lowers—strapped
the jock of a transnational bunny

Papi, we love your body still
Chulo, show us your body facedown sideways
Mi corazón, "I will miss you."
Will you? I'm not dead yet.

Conclusion: Interview with Robert Gutierrez-Perez by Luis M. Andrade

Preface to the Interview

Robert, we have collaborated numerous times, talked over the phone and Internet frequently, and even danced once at the NCA queer party. Remember? We have written a number of essays together and learned to appreciate our styles, voices, and lives. We've chatted endlessly about our experiences as queer of color scholars in academia. And, yet, I don't know you very well. Perhaps, we never truly know each other, because even in the closest relationships we have built with others, we never truly fully know the difference of others. In the eternal dance of our souls and bodies, our differences remain, as you beautifully set forth in the introduction of this book.

Siéntate conmigo, Robert, mi colega, para platicar. Siéntate means "sit down," though I want to invoke the term in the sense that my abuelita used it: to relájarte, take a moment, be present, listen to yourself, your heart and soul, and your surroundings as we speak. Siéntate to calm the rushing veins, blood, and thoughts, and express yourself freely. In this context, I am also speaking metaphorically because this interview will truly break the (non)traditional format and mode of interview as we exchange emails, talk over the phone, Skype, and text to capture your responses to my questions. As you and I have written elsewhere, sometimes our interpersonal communication for coping and survival is influenced positively by digital mediums. Hence, we text and talk on the phone often as our only means of communication, which is also effective since we live in vastly different areas of the U.S.—you in the "Biggest Little City" of semi-arid Reno, Nevada, and I in the busy and rapid-paced Hollywood, California, area. This interview melts digital and physical worlds. Siéntate because time and space run fast, but we can slow it down in this moment to hear your teorias in the fringes.

I see our interview as a plática in the same way as my tías, abuelita, and amigxs did over lunch, dinner, or un cafecito. A plática is no small chat or conversation. It is intimate, honest, and liberatory. Our pláticas are spiritual. Healing. And we don't just sit with any person for a plática, because it is based on trust. For me to sit with you and you with me means that we care for what we want to say and share. Your thoughts and responses will, in fact, not die in your mind and memory. A plática transcends time and space. A moment, or two, or three away from the institutions, politics, egos around us. Just us. Plátiquemos.

I sent you these questions digitally first to allow you to answer them and formulate responses to them. My original questions began with a cue (Luis) that separates them from your responses (Robert). After reading the questions, you sent me your typed responses. Then, I reached out to you with probing questions to get richer description and understanding. The final form of our transcribed plática comes from a series of textual and verbal dialogues that capture what you feel best describes your thoughts and bodily responses. As such, the reader should prepare themselves to time travel betwixt and between political moments within the United States over a period of a year in which we both lived through intense division and hate in Aztlán during the Trump administration. The following questions and responses are separated into themes related to you and your identity, academia, writing, health and wellness, Pulse and violence against Jotería, queer marriage, and spirituality.

You, Your Identity

Luis: Robert, ¿cómo estás? It's a pleasure to have this plática with you as one of the few queer/gay Mexican cis men in our field with similar experiences. It's quite a coincidence that we crossed paths at the National Communication Association a few years ago and that we continued our communication. I've learned so much about you, and yet, I don't know you very well. Tell me, what is your aspiration in telling us your story in this book?

Robert: Luis, you know that you can call me Rob, and I am also grateful that you have agreed to this plática for the conclusion of this book. In fact, I love that we instinctively understood that this conclusion was a dialogue, not an argument, and only loosely an interview. I wanted this chapter to showcase the method of interviewing but not as a gathering data device like in many other areas of this book. In *Interviews/Entrevistas*, Anzaldúa constructs theory and method by assembling each chapter as a different interview conducted at different times in her life—not as a memoir but a circular, creation-centered approach to understanding identity, culture, history, and society that was layered, reflexive, activist-oriented, and dynamic in its aesthetic and rhetorical movements. It isn't easy to find someone who you can write and speak with because, to get to the heart of the matter, you have to be willing to be intimate with the other. I say this loosely to indicate all kinds of relationalities to other people, places, animals, nature, or objects. You are so special to me because I trust you, and for me, it isn't easy to trust anymore. I see this as a fault. You ask me what is my aspiration for sharing the collected data within this book? I desire connection. I desire respect and influence. I desire to help myself and others let go of our collective and individual traumas and egos. Hahaha! I guess I am in nepantla. I don't know what is to become of me. In fact, if I am to be honest with you, I wrote this book because this may be my only accomplishment before I die. I had to write it. I don't believe in safe spaces anymore.

Luis: Rob, thanks for your honesty. We've written about the many reasons why our surrounding spaces are violent and unsafe, and you mention this throughout your responses in this chapter. For the readers of this book, what would you say makes spaces unsafe, particularly for those in our communities?

Robert: There are so many ways in which spaces become unsafe for Jotería because we hold so many identity categories that are oftentimes hegemonically made lower in the material spaces that we occupy. There are many layers, including lack of safety within our own communities, in White academia, and in broader society. I am not safe going to the gay bar, Walmart, my classroom, and so on. It's almost like walking through a field of landmines. It looks beautiful and you want to run across it, but there's always the risk of danger. You cannot run free because there's always the possibility of a mine clicking, capturing your weight, and exploding. Boom!

It's just like . . . I don't know. I keep thinking of what Anzaldúa and bell hooks say about how your skinfolk are not always your kinfolk. Just because someone is gay, Latino, or working class does not mean they got your back. All those things you look for on the surface doesn't mean they will step up when it matters. Especially in academia.

These places are unsafe because of betrayal, backstabbing, and gossip. Gossip is one of the worst ones. I often use gossip to push back on gossip, but then, it becomes a matter of ego. And I have to let go because I am disenchanted with the potentiality for academia to emancipate Jotería. Then, there is Whitetalk—usually done unconsciously—where White-appearing folks speak about you with other White-appearing folks and use these exclusive spaces to tell *your* story. Over and over and over again. Microaggressions, which are still macroaggressions, telling you that you are not worthy and that you are not supposed to be there. That your work is not enough. But then when you go into other social worlds, there are mass shootings. I think it's a mistake to tell Jotería that they are safe because they are not. Believe me, I wish I could let my guard down. I dream it. I wish for genuine connection, but everything in academia makes me want to give it up. Academia flares my paranoia. And I don't think my colleagues understand that this really is the frontlines of combating White supremacy, patriarchy, heteronormativity, and so on.

Our spaces are unsafe because they are inauthentic. Charades and scripts that we have acted out over and over, and in order for us to reach a new level of consciousness, we need new/old stories. And Luis, we are not going to find these stories on some Rosetta Stone buried underneath the U.S.-Mexico borderlands. If you dig there, all you will find is bones and an open wound. When institutions and interlocutors utilize the language of feminism and anti-racist or queer advocacy but then agitate the system only for those who look and think like them, then they are part of the problem. This futurity sentences many queer people of color to live lives constantly questioning the motives and motivations of the networks around them. Chismé is a powerfully disciplining force in our lives, and you know what, words fucking hurt because they often turn to bullying, gaslighting, and mental or physical violence. These spoken utterances cast hexes on us creating the worlds we must navigate, so we are always unsure of when someone will throw their own shadows, misrepresentations, and misrecognitions onto our positions. This social construction creates an endless series of miscommunication with other interlocutors, and the labor of making oneself intelligible to others and oneself is exhausting and violent.[1]

We are unsafe because these negative messages become internalized, and some of these values and beliefs about what it means to be Jotería have been literally beaten into our bodies. When I was attending the Association of Jotería Arts, Activism, and Scholarship (AJAAS) conference in Portland, Oregon, in October 2019, I went to the business meeting, and during the check-in, many members (including myself) vulnerably shared their tears as they expressed deep emotions about how good it felt to not have to translate yourself for once or how this wonderful world we created together allowed us to heal. At this conference dedicated to "Reclaiming Jotería Kinship and Futurity," it was clear that our community is under attack from multiple vectors and at all levels, which isn't new, but there is a palpable fear at the level of extreme duress being navigated by the artists, activists, and scholars within our community. I knew that I had been feeling lost and depressed, but it wasn't until a moment at that business meeting when we engaged in a playful plática when I finally understood. It was here where one of my favorite people in the room joked, "if you are over 35, then you are an elder here." The room laughed, including myself as a 37-year-old cisgendered male at the time, because it was meant to poke fun at herself (the jokester) and the four to five other 30- to 40-year-olds in the room. However, on my plane ride home looking above the clouds in Temochoan, I was sad because she was right. I am a Jotería elder. It is sad that we have to grow up so fast, and we die young. With the HIV/AIDS crisis of the 1980s and 1990s, we lost so many elders, and we have yet to heal from this generational trauma. The loss of so many, and now, I have to be a leader? Who would want to follow me?

Luis: In all your intersections, your sex and sexuality are one layer that you focus deeply on in this book. Sex and sexuality have been both traumatic and empowering for you. What is it about sex and sexuality that, despite the trauma from it, has helped you become who you are today?

Robert: I think of myself as a scholar and practitioner of sex and sexuality, and I often joke that it would be my dream to be a scholar by day and a GoGo boy by night. I have heard it said by other Jotería like this: "I am a mijo in the streets but a cochino in the sheets." Hahaha! But, Luis, I am not sure if I want to label this book as focused on these same dimensions of identity and desire. For example, you mentioned that I am one of the only Mexican cisgendered men doing this kind of work in communication studies and academia at large, but I am mixed-raced. Yes, I am Mexican-American, but that is a transnational ethnic identity. In general, we all hold complex and complicated histories on and in our bodies. So I have always struggled as an intersectional scholar because I am not focused on single-axis issues, problems, levels, or contexts. There is a radical interconnectedness to identity, culture, and society because of the inherent social co-construction of communication. It is like a drum or a gong. Just because you hit one side and not the other doesn't mean that the whole instrument doesn't resonate, vibrate the air, and share the waves of sound. It is the same thing when speaking about sex and sexuality. I am not simply discussing one thing. I am beating a drum across the matrix of domination, so you can hear the resonating, normalized songs of oppression and privilege.

I guess this is a long way of saying that just because I am looking at Chicanos and Latinos doesn't mean I am only talking about Chicanos and Latinos. Just because queerness is uplifted and centered doesn't mean I am discussing only LGBTQAI concerns, theory, or life. I am theorizing power and how to resist and have agency in multi-layered, multi-dimensional, contextual, and dynamic social systems of power and control. That is what is empowering about working with this community and with these theories and methods.

Luis: On the largely commercialized *RuPaul's Drag Race* show, RuPaul often asks the competitors what they would tell their 6-year-old selves. This came to mind as I was reading about your upbringing in the Introduction. As you reflect on your experiences of childhood, what would *you* tell the 6-year-old mini Robert?

Robert: Oof! I knew when we agreed to do this that I was going to have to go to some tough spaces, and I hate revisiting my childhood. As a defense mechanism, I largely have blocked a lot of my childhood experiences out. I recently wrote a piece with my brother on fathers and fathering, and I am always so shocked by how much he remembers versus how much I remember of our childhood. In that "testimonio talkback," I discuss how much more important my brother is to me now that I know that he is carrying my burden/memories for me. If I look at my childhood, I remember being a mostly happy child who was bullied almost constantly in school or from family. However, I was lucky that I never experienced physical bullying like described in Keith Berry's recent book titled *Bullied: Tales of Torment, Identity, and Youth.*[2] Also, I experienced sexual abuse as a child from a female cousin; however, I mainly experienced sexual abuse/assault when I came out as gay as an adult. I, honestly, thought that was how men were supposed to court and mate with each other. It wasn't until a friend was pushing me to dive deeper into a piece I was working on that I realized that my boundaries had been crossed in violent ways multiple times and that it wasn't normal to experience these things as normal. I find that I am very easy to abuse. Maybe that is why people always find me. I've been working on no longer being a victim, but my ego keeps convincing me to perform my old habits, roles, and stories over and over again. I know that I learned these from childhood experiences to cope with fears of physical/verbal abuse, neglect, abandonment, and betrayal.

If I could speak to my 6-year-old self, I wish I would have fought back more against my bullies, and I wish I didn't have to be a parent for my parents or my siblings. These are wishes, and you asked me what I would *tell* myself. (Sigh). I would tell him: "You are going to feel alone and confused for a long time, and the ways that you learn how to cope with all these feelings of separation and too much responsibility will determine what makes you both strong and powerful. It is also what makes up your shadow side because so much of what you do and say comes from remembering the pain, fear, and hurt . . ." I'm sorry. I feel like I have more to say, but I can feel myself getting upset. And without you here physically (Luis), I feel myself shirking back. It is like touching fire, or better yet, it is like rubbing out a knot in a muscle. You know that if you are diligent and move toward the pain, you will be able to heal from this kink in your shoulder, but fuck! It hurts doesn't it?! I am not saying that I am not willing to address this topic, but can we perhaps come back to it? It's like I'm getting a massage, and I need like a 5-minute break. Hahahahaha.

Luis: Take a break. It's okay. Memory, like childhood memories, is often fragmented and painful. Yet, as you have suggested, massaging our mind and body through these inflictions is healing. I see your affective responses here as what Anzaldúa meant by a path to conocimiento or a process of piecing together our pained and fragmented memories and bodies toward spiritual healing and self-transformation. We'll revisit this point later.

Luis: In the Introduction, you mention, "I am searching for others like me," which I view as more than a personal purpose in this book. Why is this search for others like us important for you, our community, and field?

Robert: Because I am desperate for connection. I have started a gratitude practice recently and that has been very helpful. Every night before I go to bed, I make sure to list off a few things (and some days more than just a few) that I am grateful for. Small or big. I try to remember my day and pick out the moments, people, places, animals, things, or whatever that I am grateful for. Over time, I have been able to feel more connected and alive, but until this practice, I found it very hard to feel connected. When you are the darkest person in the room, the most queer, the poorest, the most feminine, then you are often unintelligible to the people, culture, or social organization with which you are trying to connect to or be a part. This book is for anyone like me who feels like a monster or an alien in most spaces. Not because I am, but because it is rare for me to connect with other people. Also, I don't think that this is just a "me" thing.

For the last several years, I have had the honor of instructing some amazing undergraduate communication studies students in research methods, and as a final project, we work over the semester to create oral history performances of "What it means to be an 'Other' in Reno, Nevada?" Luis, you would just flip over the images, movements, and careful attention to details that these students create. It is essentially a class on research ethics, so these students head into the local community to interview one person who self-identifies as an other or who has experienced otherness. Because the interviews are all located within the same geographic space, woven together they create an ethnographic sketch of Reno, and these students feel an immense amount of responsibility to get their interviewees' story right. Many times, these same interviewees are in the audience when the students perform their final, 60-minute-long, staged performance. I tell you all of this because "otherness" is a very human experience and a social construction. The truth of the matter is that we are never alone, and the more I have studied otherness and difference the more I see how much we are united through these differences, these shared and unshared aspects, these samenesses in our experiences. This is why I felt I had to share the oral history narratives and borderlands narratives collected in this book. By going out into the world and talking with other Jotería, I have never felt so connected and whole—I am part of something bigger than myself. I want other Jotería to know that too. You are fighting on the frontlines of change every day. Every day, you are pushing back, agitating, surviving, making space, moving toward a utopian horizon, shifting language, and disidentifying with what is deemed normal and ordinary. And, you are not alone. It is my greatest hope that people can see themselves in this book even if all the pieces don't completely fit.

I am not sure if I am representing my community well right now. I do not mean to be nihilistic or cynical. In all honesty, I am quite a happy person with so much to love and so many to love. I am blessed with so much wealth in terms of friendships, familial relations, and lovers. When I am discussing connection, I am discussing love in the definition of bell hooks, which is thinking of love as a verb and not a noun.[3] Love cannot exist in spaces of neglect or abuse, and love is the will to lift one's own or another's spirit.[4] It is about care, affection, respect, commitment, mutual recognition, and open and honest communication.[5] And Luis, I love our Jotería. We are so beautiful, creative, fierce, and courageous. The bravery our community displays makes me so proud to be a joto. I often feel unworthy to be part of this history.

Finally, the search for others is always a search for the self, and in academia, I have found that I would rather work with and for people deemed other than invest in the normalized and everyday ways knowledge is being generated in our society. I can never forget that I am part of the machine, so finding connection, valuing connection, and searching for connection has been a tactic that I have been able to use to resist the ideological state apparatus of school. Instead of trying to hide from or push my otherness to the shadows, I have embraced my monstrosity, and by being unwilling to leave my poor and working-class value system behind, I use that feeling of otherness in spaces and places as a kind of barometer. What I mean is that, if I ever do not feel like a monster or alien, then I know I have left my community behind. You know, I drank the Kool-Aid. Does it make you sad to know that I am still working on feeling connected? Sometimes, I feel it, especially during sex. That radical interconnectedness to all things. Other times, it is gone—cloudy, too wordy, too many thoughts. I guess it is my perpetual crux to bear, or perhaps that is my ego playing out the role of the victim again.

Luis: You've now mentioned this circle of victimhood several times. Academics and many social and political conservatives often accuse our work of overly relying on self-victimization. They accuse us of being too attached to our suffering and see this as a downfall in our work. What are your thoughts on this?

Robert: It's interesting you ask this question. I mentioned earlier by phone that I spent a good three to four hours checking in with a Latinx friend who is trans and prefers they/them pronouns. I met this kind human being through a Jotería mentor who has taken me under his wing. They arrived in the area after me with their partner, but we have really connected over our shared Californian heritage and our need for spaces of connection without our partners. Many Jotería believe that one person should be able to be everything for you, but after being married for over 16 years to a first-generation Mexican-American cismale, I can tell you that this is unrealistic and unfair to your partner to burden them with this expectation. No, you need lots of people and animals and beings to support you, so we value our friendship as a lifelong partnership because it is authentic, caring, and without the need to translate.

I hadn't seen my friend in two to three months. In order to relay what's been going on in my life, I found it really challenging to let go of my ego, not make my colleagues into monsters, and be strategic and tactical with the ways I am trying to tackle my work life. Still, I fell into the narrative of me as a victim. That's the challenge! We *are* suffering, and violence is happening to us. Yet, we have to find a way to survive things that we don't necessarily have control over. So, we are victims, but we go through this process of confronting betrayal, sabotage, etc. that brings us power, perspective, and agency. It is cyclical. How do you resist being a victim when you are constantly made a victim through violence?

We have to go back to the concept of language and how we use language. What are the old patterns of communication holding us back? We are restricted by language, so breathe, take a step back, and recognize your voice in your head is not you. You are the witness watching the voice. For example, I am not a writer. I am the watcher who writes. It might be a generational thing because I grew up during a time when you didn't come out of the closet at a young age. There was nearly no positive representation of LGBTQ lives in the media or politics. I think I still have a lot of internalized homophobia I need to deal with, so I have to remind myself that I am who I am and that is enough.

Luis: I've sensed some sadness in you lately. I feel it. I've seen your Facebook posts about feeling burned out and overwhelmed. And this is one primary reason why I've wanted to have this plática with you—to listen to the sources and forces that are causing this burnout. Many studies document that scholars of color, particularly Black and Latinx scholars, face burnout because of the tremendous pressure placed on them by institutions. In your particular case, what is causing this burnout? What consejos can we take from this book and your life that may help us survive this burnout?

Robert: I don't know if I want to summarize the book into simple terms. With this book, I think I have made some modest and humble gains in terms of "progress" by pushing knowledge generation into new cartographies. Yet, I think there is a depth to this book that is radical and beyond the paradigms driving what stories we tell and are told and who gets to tell them and for whom. Eve Sedgwick calls this "restorative" or "weak" theory as opposed to the dominant paradigm in research, which is often considered "strong theory" (and the race to discover strong theory is part of this comparison), but in reality, she calls this drive "paranoid" theory.[6] In communication studies, I have seen this idea articulated by Deanna Fassett, John T. Warren, and Keith Nainby as a cultural myth called "Progress is Progress" that is a strategy utilized through communication to avoid dialoguing and communicating about power and social justice issues.[7] For instance, you ask about my well-being as a scholar of color in a system of schooling that historically has marginalized my body, my ideas, and my way of moving through the world. And what did I do? I started quoting theory and authors and making claims about what this book progresses. Why am I avoiding the issue? In a recent introduction to *Border-Lines: Journal of the Latino Research Center*, I discussed the differences between surviving and thriving and how as Jotería academia is not a safe space for us.[8] It often feels like I am on the frontlines of a war (perhaps like Cherríe Moraga writes), and I am tired, hermano.[9] Maybe, I am not a warrior after all, or maybe, I am. I'm not sure anymore. Anyway, I am trying to get to my point, which is that I really struggle with identity. Do you remember when we had that check-in, and I ended up sitting in my car in the garage talking to you on the phone forever? I remember my husband came into the garage with such a funny expression on his face because he wanted to know what I was still doing in the car. Hahaha! In fact, I wrote it down because it felt so profound, and like normal, you cut through my bullshit (corazón desnudo). You are one of the few people who know how to talk to me. Here are some of the things you said:

> "I remember praying for the life I'm living today."
> "Your uniqueness will never be paralleled."
> "You are your only competition."

I know you are worried about me. I'm worried about me too. I remember you warned me that this quest for fame wasn't the right path for me. You said that you had been listening to Lady Gaga's album *The Fame Monster*, and you kept getting visions of me, which is why you decided to check in. I laughed. You told me that I had changed. Before I received my appointment as a tenure-track professor at an R1 / Tier 1 university, I was always able to stay disconnected from the flow of the machine by not allowing my ego to root itself in that identity, but now, I was different. I sat with that for a long time. I'm reading a couple of books right now that have really been helpful to processing your words to me. Both are by Eckhart Tolle, and they are respectively called *A New Earth: Awakening to Your Life's Purpose* and *The Power of Now: A Guide to Spiritual Enlightenment*. They have really helped me to understand how the ego and the mind work (individually and collectively) to hold us into patterns of suffering. Old stories on replay. We are all suffering from these socially constructed framings of understanding reality. How can we shift this paranoia that grips the entire human race? We need to choose weak or restorative theory because we know where the other story of fear and paranoia will take us. This undertaking isn't about fame. This book is about speaking truth back to power.

Academia

Luis: Why did you choose academia as a profession given that Anzaldúa and many others proclaimed it as unsafe?

Robert: My friend, I really didn't want to write today, but my sister-in-law is taking a summer class, which is the last she needs to completely transfer into the University of Nevada, Reno. We are listening to Christina Aguilera sing "Express" from the movie with Cher called *Burlesque*. We are doing pomodoros. Those are when you work on your project (homework, this conclusion, writing, etc.) for 25 minutes, then you take a 5-minute break to do whatever you want. I think I am going to go stretch on this foam roller I have nearby. We are on the dining room table. Completing a round of work and rest constitutes one pomodoro. After three pomodoros, you take a longer 15-minute break. It is a great productivity technique that I picked up from Chicana feminists while in graduate school. It continues to help get the work done of researching, teaching, and service with/for my communities.

Haha! Now, it is Katy Perry singing "Never Really Over." :)

I can feel my shoulders shake to the rhythm as the timer counts down, and I complete the task that we agreed to do together. This is on the third day of me tackling your questions. The dialogue is unfolding over time and space, yet in this moment, the rhythm of this interview is being created by a strange synchronicity. In the previous question, I did not take the bait to dehumanize my aggressors in academia by name or by anecdote. In the past, I have often utilized my writing to record the abuse of my oppressors whether in code or theme or narrative format, but right now, you aren't letting me escape having to confront academia directly again. Without trying to challenge me in this temporal moment, you still are somehow. It feels synchronistic. How did you know I would try to dodge these questions?

Dodge is the wrong word. ("Without You" Halsey). Tired. I'm tired of translating my existence for others, but the answer to this question is actually very easy—my students. As a young man, I remember accompanying one of my first girlfriends to get Plan B treatment at our local Planned Parenthood. I had always wanted children early, and I had wanted three kids. But after that experience, I was relieved. We didn't last too much longer after that, but ("Wolves" Selena Gomez) I knew that if I was ever to make something of myself, I couldn't have children young. I gave up the dream of creating the family that my parents couldn't create for me. I'm not saying I will never have kids. In fact, a close friend has asked me to be a surrogate, and I have agreed. I'm saying that my students are my children sometimes. I want them to succeed. I want them to make their dreams come true. Academia is unsafe, and my students need me to be their first line of defense. I have to get into those rooms where decisions are being made about them and for them. If I am not here, then our needs and wants are being narrated by people who don't understand our imposter syndrome due to colonial regimes and imperial capitalism. If you have never had a family member in jail or living on the streets or suffering from drug addiction, how will you understand the incredible worth of the students who make it into this place that was never made for us to make it?

I arrived in academia partly by accident, partly by fate, and partly by an intense will to not become my parents. I wasn't going to have kids early. I wasn't going to drop out of college. I wasn't going to use drugs to regulate the highs and lows of my life. I worked as a server and bartender to get myself through all the 16 years it took me to get my Ph.D. in Culture and Communication from the University of Denver. I had started working to help my family by not being too much of a financial burden at age of 14. At that time, my dad still was selling cocaine and marijuana to his blue-collared friends and former high school friends (and their friends). He did it to pay the bills and give us a life in which we did not want for much. However, he also did it because he liked to be that guy who bought everyone at the bar a drink. A real O.G. Everyone knows my father in San José, California. My mom tells me stories of when my father would get his paycheck and spend it immediately at the bar buying drinks for everyone there. Rent, food, and utilities all out went out the window just for one night of being "that guy." My mom was the financial rock for our family in those days, and I wanted to help her and him. By the way, he still has this problem, and only recently have I accepted that my father plans to ride into the sunset living his entire life like a 21-year-old. It is scary sometimes, and I worry. Yet, that will to "live my life my way" runs through my blood as well. I am queerly in this plática on this page because of that willpower. I write about some of this complexity within queer cultural heritages in Chapters 2 and 3 of this book.

I guess I am trying to say that everywhere is unsafe. I chose to be here because my students need me, but my family needs me as well. Who was going to teach my sister-in-law about pomodoros? Like me, she is a first-generation college student from a Latinx family where poverty (and in her case sexism) hold her back from stories that might help her on her path or where she is held back from writing her own story. I do suffer, but the more and more I learn from the suffering, the more I see through it—the mental abstraction of it, the false separation of mind/body/spirit/soul, and the socially constructed nature of values, norms, and beliefs. This is supposed to be part of my story. I have accepted it, and now, I am. I create. It is what it is.

Luis: Here, again, I see a full circle of sifting through your suffering toward a path of conocimiento, in Anzaldúan terms. But, this time, I vividly see how conocimiento is not self-centered; it is always already other-oriented. Thank you, Rob.

Luis: You live and breathe communication studies. Where are we going as a sub-branch of Latinx and Jotería communication studies in the field? Do you foresee any dangers to the discipline?

Robert: I've never been really good at popularity contests or predicting the next popular anything. People tend to have very visceral reactions to my presence, and I don't always understand why or what I do exactly. Sometimes, I think just loving myself and being confident in my abilities is enough to make the entire system come crashing down on me. However, I think others have pointed around the river bend for us already (see Gonzalez, Calafell, and Avant-Mier).[10] In terms of Jotería communication studies, I think that is an easier question to answer. There needs to be and will be more work for and with Jotería that will challenge, agitate, and expand our knowledge of communication. One of my biggest fears is that this book will be viewed as the end-all-be-all when it comes to this subdiscipline, and it simply is not. This is just the tip of the iceberg, and I truly hope that this work is viewed as an invitation to engage. The danger I see is that communication studies as an area of scholarship is racist, classist, sexist, and homophobic. It casts a long historical shadow of covert and overt oppression that makes those working on the margins vulnerable. Like the rest of academia and in the U.S., this shadow is a sickness, and we need to collectively and individually look at ourselves and choose to face our fear of otherness, our investments in Whiteness, and our complicity with our privilege.

Writing

Luis: Anzaldúa often spoke about writing as cathartic and a release of emotion to deal with trauma? Why do you write?

Robert: I write because I often feel misunderstood or mistranslated. Right now, I am resting in bed typing into my Apple iPhone 6 Plus, and I am thinking about my privileges and secrets, the ego and trauma, and the fact that our president just gave a White supremacist dream speech to the world after back-to-back mass murders. I was still hurting from the mass murder in Gilroy, California, and now, I can't help envisioning a target on my back everywhere I go. A red dot tracing my most vital organs while I shop, watch movies, dance, go to campus, go to concerts, public events, I mean the list goes on and on, and it isn't hyperbole. A great mentor for me has been Alberto González, who helped me navigate the tremors and tribulations of graduate school even though I was attending a Ph.D. program in Denver, Colorado, and he was at Bowling Green University. Today, as I scrolled through Facebook, he posted an ACTUAL ad for back-to-school shopping featuring bulletproof backpacks. Can you believe that?! My heart ripped out of my chest. I plan on following up with my own research to verify this, but if it is true, I will have to take action. I will have to take to the streets to protest. In my life, I have protested many times against this government and the policies and laws that exclude or dehumanize people.

When I first saw this question, I doubted myself. I thought, "What do I have to say that is important enough to be placed in conversation with Anzaldúa or communication theory in general?" I am just that kid from downtown San José, California. My accent sounds like a mix between a valley girl and a surfer bro. Now, after Gilroy, I know I have something to say about writing and power. You ask why I write? It is because I have something to say that is important, and the writing reminds me of my power. Writers have transformed the world. It is our function to dive into that inner void and bring consciousness into this world through our creative acts. It is a kind of magic or will that catalyzes minds, bodies, spirit, and soul to act as one. It can shift the collective consciousness of the planet. Artists are powerful, which is why they are often suppressed. The explosive orange and yellow of creativity (poeisis) and passion (eros) are how I imagine it. Like Jean Grey in the popular comic and movie series *The X-Men*, when flames erupt out of her and take the shape of the mythical bird called the Phoenix, she becomes ablaze and contains the power to create and destroy, both embodied into one beautiful yet monstrous form.

Luis: Many authors, including womanist and Chicanx/Latinx scholars, have seen writing and poetry as weapons to dismantle oppression. What is unique about your writing that may help us combat violence?

Robert: I think that I don't give a fuck. (Luis: Yes!) When people tell me not to do something, it makes me want to do it more. I can be very stubborn. For example, I have been working on bringing poetry and the rhetoric of writing aesthetics into my academic work for a long time now, and it still surprises me how disruptive it is for folks. When I first started as an assistant professor at the university, I joined a research club with colleagues from across the school, and I was happy to share my work. When I arrived the day of the meeting, I encountered several comments about how my colleagues thought that their printers were broken because of the poetry at the beginning. They lost their minds, and now, if my work doesn't shock myself or others shitless,[11] then I know my work is failing to connect to those spaces in/between. For me, I view my work as radical performance art, à la Guillermo Gómez-Peña, and I have studied with him and the performance troupe La Pocha Nostra as part of a five-day performance workshop.[12] Some of the poetry in this book came from working with La Pocha Nostra. I think that is what makes me unique, but I feel like I need to ask. Is this unique? We are all writing. It truly is all art (flower and song). I am just acknowledging this fact and pointing at it continuously in my work. I say this because I don't want the reader to create a false separation between my work and the work of other scholars. There are enough borders in the world. I want to create rainbows that bridge and provide. This connectivist impulse is discussed at length by AnaLouise Keating, and this impulse to sacrifice my own body and soul by staying in the room or by walking up the sacrificial pyramid utilizing my own volition—this is power.[13] This is agency. This is choosing to demand space for us to breathe and be. I am, and there will be no apologies for existing.

Luis: Researchers and critics have argued that writing and poetry is apolitical and insufficient to address structural violence. Although writers promise praxial transformation, critics view it as textual catharsis that does not result in material transformation. What is your response to that?

Robert: They are wrong. I suggest they read a book. (Luis: Very well! Hahahaha!)

Health and Wellness

Luis: José Esteban Muñoz's death weighed heavily on my mind. Hasta el alma. We've both read his powerful texts and used them as guidance in our own writing.[14] I've also been noticing the health of educators of color in academia slowly diminishing. We are dying perhaps because we are internalizing pain and trauma, especially in White spaces. I know you've experienced health complications in the last few years, especially when you started your tenure-track job. How have you navigated health complications with your responsibilities as an academic?

Robert: Up until this point, I haven't let the reader leave my mind during this interview and book. I've ducked and dodged an issue that is fueling my pain and trauma. I don't know if I can let the reader know this yet, but to you, I will be honest. Maybe, in the writing, I will find the strength to not delete this answer before publication. I have two different thoughts on this question of health and wellness.

Academia is killing us. Pushed to the margins of the margins, we are held to impossible standards of conduct. I've heard it called neutering by other critical/ cultural communication scholars who study queer theory. This is where intersectionality is an essential tool to understand what is happening to queer people of color when they enter higher education spaces and places. Yes, I am talking about Whiteness, White Privilege, and White Supremacy. I purposely capitalized White because I want to call attention to race and because we capitalize Black and Latino, yet I always have push back during the editorial process: "Please lowercase white throughout the document. I don't think the writer wants to insult people." This is a paraphrase because I respect the editorial process and the work this reviewer did to bolster my arguments and prose, but here we are, back to the everyday mundane world of grammar and the choices we make when communicating with each other and across difference. Before I proceed, I also need you to see the socially constructed nature of "race." It isn't real. It is real because we have, collectively as a human consciousness, continued to believe in and (re)tell this story over and over, but it isn't naturally occurring. There is only one race—the human race—and we are radically interconnected to each other and all life on this planet.

So, here we are, walking down the hallway and embodying centuries of some socially constructed role that we can never fully predict—when and where and how it will rise up out of a colleague, student, or administrator. We work in an incredibly White discipline and career. It is like teleporting to a completely different planet every day. Have you ever read *War of the Worlds* by H. G. Wells? It is a fantastic story of the Earth being completely overtaken by an alien invader, and (spoiler alert) it wasn't humanity that wards off the invaders. It was the microorganisms that our immune systems have attuned to defend against over the existence of life on this planet through various species and generations who rescued us. The invading monsters were destroyed because their bodies could not handle those things we see in a microscope during high school or college biology classes. That is what it is like to be queer and Latino and working class and this and that and and and ... do you see where I am getting at? It isn't necessarily the aliens I work with who are killing me. It is all the microorganisms that have been created over hundreds of years of socially constructed categories of difference. It's the taken-for-granted, normalized, everyday things that are "supposed to be" or "have always been this way." They eat at you. Constrict your throat, so you can't speak up about your suffering. Gnaw at your heart, so your circulation becomes irregular—you doubt your worth, your dream. And without a functioning heart, how can you be confident in your breathing? Passion fizzles and depression hits because your immune system was sabotaged and undermined by your White colleagues, students, and administrators.

You may say, "Rob, just teleport back to your own planet! If you don't like it here, then go back to where you came from."

The problem is that I come from Earth, so my own home planet is against me too because I am queer and brown and from the working class. I think my favorite part of the trip is the space in/between. That space between being a thing and a no-thing that occurs during the teleportation process. Sorry if this metaphor doesn't make a lot of sense. I loved *Star Trek* as a child, and I continue to think about television and film as I think about trying to work with and between multiple worlds. I loved watching those characters move from space ship to planet and back with whirling, magic sounds of digitalized light.

My other thought that is connected to this is: I was dying Luis. I was dying, and I couldn't tell anyone about it at work. In that first year of my diagnosis, I remember enduring sabotage and bullying from my colleagues, so I made the decision to suffer in silence because I felt like I could not trust anyone with my secret. I kept my HIV status to myself. I learned a lot about the people around me during that first year. This book is the first time that I have written about my status, and it frightens me to death to think about what others will think. I fear that by opening up about health and wellness I am telling many of my colleagues, family, friends, or lovers my secret for the first time. The poem in this book "The Secret" describes this feeling that overwhelms when challenged to break silence around HIV status, which is another form of "coming out of the closet." It has taken me over a year of therapy (a privilege) to finally be brave in this moment. I was deeply ashamed, and I didn't know what to do or whom to trust. When I started getting suicidal ideation in January 2020, I knew I needed to seek out help. It took me over two years to tell my parents. I wasn't trying to hurt anyone, and I am sorry for anyone I have hurt with my silence. I can only hope that they will forgive me because I need to move forward with my life. I refuse to see myself as a victim any longer.

Luis, I was so close to being diagnosed with AIDS when I finally found out that I was HIV+. My physician, who I am grateful for and who I trust completely, placed me on two pills instead of one pill. The first attacks the virus at the beginning of the process by preventing the virus from entering my white blood cells while the second pill attacked the white blood cells that were already taken over by the virus on the back end of the process. Frozen and malfunctioning, the white cell dies and is cleaned out by the body. These pills are not a cure, but they suppress the virus to a level that is so low that it cannot be detected. Being undetectable = untransmittable.

I first wrote the above answer to this question over a year ago, and subsequently, I have added and deleted this answer several times with the last time being on October 25, 2019. Now, it is January 24, 2021 (the three-year anniversary of my diagnosis), and I think I am ready to finish this answer and let go of my fears surrounding my status change. What does it mean to be undetectable? This means that you and I could have unprotected sex, and you would not seroconvert. Luis, I need the reader to get this fact through their skull, so I hope you will forgive my shocking statement, but if you and I fucked raw, then you would still be HIV – because I am undetectable. We could try all we wanted, but

I would not be able to seroconvert you. My sexual partners are safe from HIV with me because I cannot transmit the virus. Moreover, I cannot contract other versions of HIV. Currently, I have been switched to a single pill (BIKTARVY) that is basically a hybrid version of the prior medication I had been taking. Like my prior regimen, I have to make sure to take it about the same time everyday. It is challenging, but HIV is known to mutate and adapt quickly, so lapses between medication might mean my drug regimen would need to change. It takes about three-to-six months of malpractice with my regimen to become a person who could be transmittable again. The drugs suppress the virus, and I am grateful to be alive. I am grateful that HIV/AIDS treatment is at the point where it is more manageable than diabetes.

Honestly, I don't mind the blood work twice a year because it means that as a person who is HIV+ I am statically more likely to live longer than someone who is HIV−. What do I fear? I am afraid of the stigma. My ego, or that part of me who loves to be a perfectionist, is shattered. Look at that handsome, smart, funny, and successful man over there! He is walking death. (Sigh). I am undetectable, so I am not a threat to anyone, but everyone is potentially a threat to me. It is strange to be healthy and untransmittable but feared, hated, and desired.

During the return to this specific answer, I am living through a pandemic and a Republican political party that is hell-bent on taking away healthcare away from millions of people, including removing protections from pre-existing conditions. HIV/AIDS status and treatment could return to being something that would get you kicked off your health insurance and left in the gutter. My life potentially is on the ballot this presidential year. Breaking precedent set by themselves, the Republican Party, now simply a shell for White nationalism and fascist idealism, is forcing a nomination to the Supreme Court while voters have already started voting. In a recent argument with one of my Republican aunts to whom I recently disclosed my HIV status, she did not connect her vote to my survival but was going to vote Republican because her taxes were lower. I was hurt that capital meant more than me, and I had to end the conversation. By making a blatant power grab to replace Justice Ruth Bader Ginsburg with Judge Amy Coney Barrett, it is clear that communities on the periphery are under attack. It took me two years after my diagnosis to tell my parents, which led to a watershed of disclosures that each revealed new insights into my relationships. With the unconditional love of my family and friends, I think I am now ready to include this answer in this book because the divisions between us are deep, and I do not choose fear over my values and responsibilities.

Early HIV/AIDS medications were extremely toxic on the body, and the side effects were painful. Andy, my gay White uncle, died of AIDS in the late 1990s in San Francisco, California. He lived with the virus for nearly 10 years. He was cremated, and we scattered his ashes in the bay for his funeral. I still remember that funeral boat ride, and the strange eulogies that testified that he had renounced his sins before he died. As a young queer boy, I listened to the chismé being revealed, and I learned that death demanded heterosexuality. Every time I cross the bay bridge to Oakland, California, or the Golden Gate Bridge, I can feel the presence of my uncle. His life story told through me returns, and I feel the pressure of proving that funeral wrong. To live with HIV has been a blessing in disguise for me because it allows me to see and sort through the bullshit that our societies and cultures lob at us to keep us in line and under control. But, why is it that he had to die and I get to live?

I was congratulated by my doctor after one month of treatment because I had reached undetectable so quickly. Like the good student I am, I had aced the HIV positive final and was a model patient. My doctor often brings in other doctors that he is training during my visits now, yet my white blood cell count isn't returning to normal quickly, and we are watching it every six months. He is happy it is climbing, yet I know what is happening. I'm stressed. My job is on the frontlines of social and cultural transformation, and because I am a threat to the White Supremacist, capitalist, cisheteropatriarchy, I am a target. I don't know how long I will survive. Internally and externally, I am not safe, so it is important for me to mention that I was able to include this answer only because I sought out therapy. It has been really helpful.

Luis: I remember the day you told me about your diagnosis. I was on my way to Mexico to buy medicine for my family members. The irony! My husband was driving while I spoke to you, and as my throat clenched and my eyes got watery, I kept asking myself how I could be strong and provide advice if you needed it? I kept the tears in, but they exploded out of me later that night when I was at a gay club, embracing my husband, and saying silent prayers for diosito and La Virgencita to give you strength. Rob, what consejos does this book and you offer for us to positively navigate health complications?

Robert:

Yoga

Mindfulness

Gratitude and Self-Compassion Practices

Therapy

It may sound glib, but these actions are about balance, healing, opening up, and being in the body. Part of my conditioning as a cisgendered male is I am expected to not show emotions or vulnerability because these are performances expected for women, and the number one rule (supposedly) for being a man is to not be a woman. For example, I just mentioned how therapy has been key to overcoming my fears and anxieties around my HIV status. Therapy is manly. You have to face your fears in the face, and the best part is that you have a trained professional there to help you fight. I encourage any men out there reading to get a therapist, and do not be afraid to talk about mental health and wellness. Trans or cis, there is power in going to therapy, practicing yoga, mindfulness, and gratitude/compassion practices. There is a racial/ethnic dynamic to this fear of discussing mental health as well, but I have come to realize that personally these practices are what will bring me peace and happiness. Also, I will say that this book is full of consejos. I encourage the reader to check out the endnotes for further gifts. I often like to utilize footnotes and endnotes to provide treasures hidden within the text.

Pulse and Violence against Jotería

Luis: You've written so much about the shooting at Pulse nightclub. Why is this such a significant and historically meaningful event in the lives of queers of color? Why should our future generations look back on this moment as truly important?

Robert: My partner and I are polyamorous and in an open relationship with our own separate boyfriends. We have been together as a couple for about 17 years now, and it was a necessary shift in our partnership to maintain intimacy and trust. One of the men whom I encountered while playing solo showed me a beautiful tattoo on his arm. It was simple: a heartbeat pulse in black with rainbow-colored ink as part of the accentuation. He was Latinx, young, and handsome. As I am now a 39-year-old man, I find myself often placed within the role of "Papi." Given my interest in Jotería narratives surrounding tattoos, I asked him about it. He told me that the massacre at Pulse nightclub in Orlando, Florida, deeply affected him. He got the tattoo in commemoration of those lost at that moment of violence and hate. He got it to remind him to live because life can be cut short at any moment. He was going to live life for those lost.

This is how significant this historical moment was for queer people of color. I had to write about Pulse because it shook our people to their core. And can you believe it? One of my evaluators/"mentors" had the audacity to tell me that although all three of my essays on Pulse were published in three different high-level journals, they are all short, so they won't count much for tenure. Do you see how sick academia can be for queer people of color? I never looked at her the same way again. Maya Angelou has a quote that my administrative assistant has posted on her door: "When someone shows you who they are, believe them the first time."

Pulse reverberated and continues to reverberate through our communities. We are not healed. There was no retribution. U.S. mainstream culture and society is based on a system of heteronormativity and homophobia, and there is little to no mention of this atrocity except when it can be exploited for ratings and capital along with the rest of the Pride festivities during June (Pride Month). I am currently writing a (re)turn to those pieces for a special forum on rhetoric, race, and violence, and I have started to work on a short speculative fiction of this same piece to help me think through the violence, erasure, and trauma of this massacre. I am nervous. I have been avoiding it, but my unconsciousness has been brewing and bubbling for some time. I finally have a sketch of the alternate history I am trying to voice, but am I ready to embody this again? I can't tell you how many times I cried and had to stop writing for all three of those essays. Remember, I called you very upset because I knew this was the work I was being called to do, but emotionally, I could not complete the final of the three essays alone. Thank you for agreeing to write that piece with me. I still feel like the performative writing in that piece is very radical and unique. I wish more folks would read and utilize work by Jotería scholars in their own research, art, and practices. I wish more Jotería would utilize more work by Jotería scholars. I also remember that, in that award-winning special issue, the editors created a poem at the end that took the last line from every published work. I remember reading the poem, and my ego was eager to see our last line in that piece alongside the myriad scholars that I value and acknowledge as exceptional folks. To my dismay, the last line of our essay wasn't included in that intertextual final poem. We decided not to reach out to the editors because we didn't want to be disrespectful to scholars that we TRULY love and value, but it just shows you that in an issue with too few Latinx authors writing about the deaths of Latinx queer bodies—are we valued? Do you remember what our final line was?

"We matter."

Luis: The Age of Trump is upon us, and it is incredibly violent, particularly for many in the LGBTQ community. What are your thoughts on this historical moment? What dangers has Trump brought to life that we may continue to face for years to come?

Robert: It is frightening, huh? When you think we/you have hit a breaking point, we/you wake up the next morning to some new horror awaiting us. Our collective nightmares are policy proposals so normalized, repeated, and unchallenged that it has become a reality.[15] Right now, it is just a few days after the president's lackluster reading of a speech written to address the recent back-to-back massacres in El Paso and Dayton by domestic terrorists. There was a picture taken from behind him that showed the teleprompter as he messed up and added Toledo (a Canadian city) to the list of cities to which he wished his condolences. I was shocked.

No empathy.

We, as a collective, have no empathy, and in these late stages of capitalism, are we surprised? The culture of greed that we swim and breathe in is dehumanizing, and as part of the problem, we keep (re)performing this narrative of mine and yours.[16] It would be easy to blame one person, but it just isn't so. That gives too much power to an ephemeral tick on the clock. This is the final expression of our collective desconocimientos, and whether we are asked to or not, each of us has to choose our side. Do you choose the path of conocimiento or not? It is a choice that will determine the form and content that life will take on this planet for the next millennia. Can't you feel the shift? Do you see why and how all old structures are being broken down and falling apart? They don't work anymore. As a world, we need to shift to a radical environmentalist consciousness where economic, social, political, and spiritual systems are driven by finding harmony and balance with our global ecosystem. This will transform everything, and we have to do it. Our very survival as the human race demands we become the caregivers for this planet that we were meant to be.

I feel like my answer to this question isn't working. Let me try again. Right now, I am writing because I am nervous for my dog Penny. She is at the vet for some emergency surgery. I'm currently waiting to get the call about the x-ray and blood work results. She may have pus filling her uterus, and poor thing, she has been having diarrhea for about a day now. She is dehydrated, and if I wouldn't have taken her in this morning, she could have been dead right now. There is also reporting (images, texts, editorials, etc.) of approximately 680 people being abducted by ICE in a raid in Mississippi.[17] Of course, the owner of this business is walking around freely, but these folks were targeted during the first day of school, so their children never got picked up. Volunteers fed them, and many were sheltered in the school for the night. Can you imagine the trauma? The specter of death and hate is everywhere around me as I write this on August 8, 2019.

You ask me about the future and the effects of these kinds of state-sponsored (and instigated) terrorist acts?

Tragedy.[18]

Luis: Why might theories from the fringes offer some hope in light of the violence in these war years?

Robert: I want to be careful here because I am not trying to appropriate the work of (queer) women of color and make it my own cisgendered male property. The theories that I am bringing to the table are "theories in the flesh" as articulated by Moraga and Anzaldúa and explicated in my opening chapters.[19] These theories in the flesh are often located in the embodied locations of interlocutors on the fringes of society and culture due to the everyday, intersectional oppressions they are forced to navigate in their everyday lives. It is important to maintain this connection to theories in the flesh because I am utilizing restorative theory as a telos. So I am not interested in stealing to satisfy my ego or a tenure and promotion committee. What you have here is a collection of borderlands narratives placed into multiple forms of content to create a larger theory of power circuitries operating in the U.S. Southwest/Mexico borderlands; to intervene in and critique the Western assumptions inherent within methodological conversations and explorations occurring in research practices across the world; and to share these cuentos, platicas, chisme, mitos, testimonios, y consejos for and with Jotería artists, scholars, and practitioners. These borderlands narratives are theories in the flesh. Some may help more than others, or some may be helpful at a different time in your Jotería life. But these are not my narratives. They are ours. These narratives offer hope and concrete actions that can help you survive in these war years. I always wished I had a handbook growing up that would help me navigate this Jotería life. I hope this book serves a similar role for the reader.

Queer Marriage

Luis: In one of our collaborative pieces, we wrote about the worldmaking possibilities of queer marriage. Our biggest struggle was justifying queer marriage, despite the inherent violence and coloniality of the institution. What additional thoughts do you have, particularly in light of theories from the fringes, which may provide useful insight about queer marriage? What can queers of color learn about the radical potentials of queer marriage that is potentially socially transformative?

Robert: I am sick and tired of talking about marriage. You always make fun because you really had to push me to continue with that piece until the very end. I'm glad we did it because it is one of my favorite pieces; however, as an LGBTQAI community, we have placed too much merit, gold, and time into marriage law and policy. One of the things we do in that piece is create a map of the power circuitries that marriage wields intersectionally in both text and the embodied repertoire of acts. Marriage is dangerous and violent, but it is also resistive. And as LGBTQAI folks, we need to utilize our marriages to agitate the system more. Given the work of activists for over 25 years, <marriage> is inextricably linked to the LGBTQAI community, so with this powerful social and cultural organizer, we must be queer as fuck.

One of the ways that I challenge this construction of hetero and homo normativity is not new for heterosexual folks but is often marginalized and placed on the fringes. Currently, I am polyamorous and in an open relationship, which is often an unacceptable sexual behavior that marriage attempts to regulate ideologically and legally. By utilizing the social stabilizing and privileges of <marriage>, I advocate and demonstrate a healthy relationship that doesn't rely on monogamy or heterosexual acts of desire. Like we argue in our piece (and others like Goltz and Zingsheim have noted this fact as well), these moments of resistance are ephemeral, and the intersectional system of control wielded through <marriage> quickly re-establishes normalized values and beliefs through the communication of other interlocutors within your familial and social circles.[20] For me, <marriage> for LGBTQ folks is important because we have to have access to those narratives legally, so we can then disidentify and tell/embody new narratives that challenge the existing oppressive status quo story. What do I mean?

When I lived in Colorado for my graduate program, my husband had an uncle who lived nearby. One of the ways in which we felt like we could survive when we moved from California to Colorado was that we had at least some biological family nearby. We quickly learned that this family operated under the "to be seen, not heard" motto that I explicated in Chapter 7 through the analysis of borderlands narratives. In fact, later we would befriend and support/mentor one of their closeted children, and we would be shocked by the years of homophobic language and toxic heteronormativity that this cousin had to endure under the guise of Christianity. Specifically, I remember my husband calling to ask if we could come over for Thanksgiving, and his Tia said excitedly, "Yes! Please come!

We would love to have you. We are having friends over on Thanksgiving, but you are more than welcome to come the next day."

Hahaha! The next day? Can you believe that? What kind of love is that supposed to be? Anyway. I tell this all to say that when one of the children of this Tio and Tia got married, we were invited to the wedding. It is hard to explain how you can be very well liked and valued within your Latinx family and enjoy being with them, yet the violence of heteronormativity, intergenerational violence, gender role policing, and religious intolerance are blatant and normal. To question them is taboo. Either way, my point is that at this conservative Christian Latinx wedding ceremony and ritual, there is often a game played. The DJ invites all the married couples to the dance floor, and over the course of a single song, the DJ counts upwards every 20 to 30 seconds. The numbers symbolize how many years of marriage that a couple has been committed to each other, so once the number passes the length of your marriage, then you leave the dance floor. This proceeds until there is only one couple left.

My partner and I enter the dance floor when the DJ announces for all married couples to get ready to play. We hold hands and wrap the other hand around each other like when we got married, and just like then, he holds me so close that I am locked into an awkward position. It forces me to slow dance in a kind of penguin-like motion where I am shifting weight back and forth from left to right in a circle. He feels their eyes on us too. 1... 2... 3... 4... Couples are leaving the dance floor slowly. 5... 6... There is a sudden exodus. 7... I don't think the crowd can believe how long we are lasting in this game. 8... We leave the dance floor. At the time, we had only been married for seven years. I smile and hold his hand as I recognize the incredible and brave thing we just did and how much this moment must have meant for all his family in the closet who are attending this wedding.

Spirituality

Luis: I want to end this interview with a discussion about spirituality. We've spoken before about your spirituality and how it is important for your activism. It's been a fundamental force in our survival. In fact, we often refer to Anzaldúa as a spiritual guide for our writing and academic paths. Explain your spirituality. What is it? Why is this spirituality helpful to cope, heal, and survive in our war years?

Robert: I was raised as a nondenominational Christian, so I went to a Christian preschool, kindergarten, and first grade before entering the public school system. My grandparents are both deaf and hard of hearing, as I explain in Chapter 2, and both were very religious. However, it was always a very social thing for them as well. They basically went to whatever church that their deaf pastor went to, and we followed him from church to church depending on how he secured a space for his congregation. I was hearing, so I went to whatever youth ministry was present. In this way, I experienced multiple pastors from different Christian sects over the first decade or more of my life. Between and betwixt, there is a lot that I loved about Christianity. Like Jesus, he is one of my favorite deities, and I still have crosses all over the house, wear crosses, and celebrate his birth and his teachings. He was so wise and loving, and he cared about people and children. I feel like he would be upset by how many human beings have been murdered and persecuted in his name. I no longer consider myself a Christian, but I continue to draw on what I learned from all those pastors, ministries, schools, and congregations to practice reverence for spirituality.

I might be classified as an agnostic, or one who believes in a higher power or order but who does not believe in organized religion; however, I use this term to help the reader understand where I am located. Personally, I wouldn't label myself an agnostic, but like agnostics, I tend to pull and pick and mix and match to create and practice spirituality in a cacophony of forms and content. In fact, we need to be careful about the word "spirituality" and the Western assumption behind the term because many indigenous peoples have critiqued this term and its impulses. For me, I practice what Anzaldúa has discussed as a spiritual activism, which I explain in some depth in Chapter 4.[21] It has been useful for me in these war years because our communities are under assault from multiple vectors and levels of control, and in these conditions, agency is being suppressed with physical, mental, psychic, and spiritual violence and oppression. Yet, by committing myself to an activism rooted in utilizing yoga, mindfulness, gratitude, and self-compassion practices, I challenge hegemonic systems of control and hierarchies of power from what Anzaldúa called "inner work, outer acts."[22] She discussed how "if I change myself, I change the world."[23] These are not slogans or verses, but she is explaining a process of working toward social justice in which balance and harmony are centered. I am still thinking through this idea, and I have lots more to work on. The idea from Anzaldúa is that outer acts matter, but it isn't "what" we do but "how" and "why" we do it. Luis, maybe we can talk later about writing about that one together.

Luis: I'd love to, Rob. For now, it is fitting to say that our work is far from over. One more piece of writing may or may not dent the oppressive structures we inhabit, but our healing will continue with and through our penned words—perhaps until we die.

As I (re)read my questions, your answers, and think about the new horizons in front of us, I cannot help but think of the immense privilege we hold for speaking, writing, and surviving in these war years. Thanks again for trusting me.

Notes

1. Ernesto Javier Martínez, *On Making Sense: Queer Race Narratives of Intelligibility* (Stanford, CA: Stanford University Press, 2013).
2. Keith Berry, *Bullied: Tales of Torment, Identity, and Youth* (New York and London: Routledge, 2016).
3. hooks, bell, *All about Love: New Visions* (New York: HarperCollins, 2001).
4. Ibid.
5. Ibid.
6. Eve K. Sedgwick, *Touching Feeling: Affect, Pedagogy, Performativity* (Durham, NC: Duke University, 2002).
7. Deanna Fassett, John T. Warren, and Keith Nainby, *Communication: A Critical/ Cultural Introduction* (San Diego, CA: Cognella, 2018).
8. Robert Gutierrez-Perez, "Editor's Introduction: Deconstruction as a Simultaneous Act of Reconstruction," *Border-Lines: Journal of the Latino Research Center* 11, (2019): 9–15.
9. Cherríe Moraga, *Loving in the War Years: Lo Que Nunca Paso por Sus Labios* (Cambridge: South End Press, 2000).
10. Bernadette M. Calafell, Karma R. Chávez, Fernando Delgado, Lisa A. Flores, Michelle A Holling, Darrel Wanzer-Serrano, Stacey K. Sowards, and Angharad N. Valdivia, "Conclusion: The Futures of Latina/o/x Communication Studies: A Plática with Senior Scholars," in *Latina/o/x Communication Studies: Theories, Methods, and Practice*, eds. Leandra Hinojosa Hernández, Diana I. Bowen, Sarah De Los Santos Upton, and Amanda Martinez (Lanham, MD: Lexington Books, 2019), 371–92; Bernadette M. Calafell and Thomas K. Nakayama, "Dialoguing about the Nexus of Queer Studies and Intercultural Communication," in *Queer Intercultural Communication: The Intersectional Politics of Belonging in and across Difference*, eds. Shinsuke Eguchi and Bernadette M. Calafell (Lanham, MD: Rowman & Littlefield, 2020), 259–66; Shinsuke Eguchi, Sophie Jones, Hannah R. Long, and Anthony Rosendo Zariñana, "Closing Thoughts: The Future of Queer Intercultural Communication," in *Queer Intercultural Communication: The*

Intersectional Politics of Belonging in and across Difference, eds. Shinsuke Eguchi and Bernadette M. Calafell (Lanham, MD: Rowman & Littlefield, 2020), 267–79; Alberto González, Bernadette M. Calafell, and Roberto Avant-Mier, "An LCSD & La Raza Microhistory: The Latina/o Communication Studies Division & La Raza Caucus of the National Communication Association," *Review of Communication* 14, no. 2 (2014), 12–37; Thomas K. Nakayama and Rona Tamiko Halualani, "Conclusion: Envisioning the Pathway(s) of Critical Intercultural Communication Studies," in *The Handbook of Critical Intercultural Communication*, eds. Thomas K. Nakayama and Rona T. Halualani (Malden, MA: Wiley-Blackwell, 2013), 595–600.

11. Gloria Anzaldúa, *The Gloria Anzaldúa Reader*, ed. AnaLouise Keating (Durham, NC: Duke University Press, 2009).

12. Guillermo Gómez-Peña and Roberto Sifuentes, *Exercises for Rebel Artists: Radical Performance Pedagogy* (New York: Routledge, 2011).

13. AnaLouise Keating, *Transformation Now!: Toward a Post-Oppositional Politics of Change* (Chicago: University of Illinois Press, 2013); AnaLouis Keating, "Risking the Vision, Transforming the Divides: Nepantlera perspectives on Academic Boundaries, Identities, and Lives," *Bridging: How Gloria Anzaldúa's Life and Work Transformed Our Own*, eds. AnaLouis Keating and Gloria González-López (Austin, TX: University of Texas Press, 2011), 142–152.

14. José Esteban Muñoz, *Cruising Utopia: The Then and There of Queer Futurity* (New York: New York University Press, 2009); José Esteban Muñoz, *Disidentifications: Queers of Color and the Performance of Politics*, (Minneapolis, MN: University of Minneapolis Press, 1999).

15. Center for the Study of Hate and Extremism, "Report to the Nation: 2019 Factbook on Hate and Extremism in the U.S. and Internationally," California State University, San Bernardino, 2019; Mikelle Street, "Hate Crimes Against LGBTQ+ People Are the Highest in a Decade," *Out Magazine*, August 1, 2019, https://www.out.com/news/2019/8/01/hate-crimes-against-lgbtq-people-are-highest-decade? fbclid=I-wAR2ovXbQH-f1y-26kR3uC9PDBe6Rp8qL-NADPWa2fx1YjTLH7JnjzJT-4Ww.

16. hooks, *All about Love*.

17. Rogelio V. Solis and Jeff Amy, "Largest US Immigration Raids in a Decade Net 680 Arrests," *APNews*, August 7, 2019, https://apnews.com/bbcef8ddae4e4303983c91880559cf23.

18. Andrew Buncombe, "Trump Administration Leaves Menstruating Migrant Girls 'Bleeding Through' Underwear at Detention Centres, Lawsuit Claims," *The Independent*, August 27, 2019, https://www.independent.co.uk/news/world/americas/trump-immigration-migrant-children-border-lawsuit-period-tampon-latest-a9081341.html?fbclid=IwAR0AONPO7FGIih1YkktvWqDDr5Gz-JGkuzXnSkfIY75Pbw1n0mscRNXSxdI8; Leila Fadel, "More Hispanic Kids Are

Depressed Than Their Peers as Anti-Migrant Rhetoric Rises," *NPR*, August 6, 2019, https://www.npr.org/2019/08/06/748565528/more-hispanic-kids-are-depressed-than-their-peers-as-anti-migrant-rhetoric-rises?fbclid=IwAR0xi3mCvPswvElV4y-h5wCyyiWkt_fDZO1MqYoqF0q0Q9bYQvHOz3WQzEqY; Richard Gonzales, "Sexual Assault of Detained Migrant Children Reported in the Thousands Since 2015," *NPR*, February 26, 2019, https://www.npr.org/2019/02/26/698397631/sexual-assault-of-detained-migrant-children-reported-in-the-thousands-since-2015?fbclid=IwAR3PK10XmUo-5K7rM3sS3D2x1iQ6NDiKInhrFsvLutYTgYK_9dB-mJ6h_As; Chris Johnson, "Trump Administration: HIV Status Used to Justify Family Separation at the Border," *Washington Blade*, July 25, 2019, https://www.washingtonblade.com/2019/07/25/trump-administration-hiv-status-used-to-justify-family-separation-at-border/; Naureen Shah, "At Detention Facilities, Legal Rights 'In Name Only,' " *USA Today*, October 25, 2019, https://www.usatoday.com/story/opinion/policing/2019/10/25/detention-facilities-legal-rights-for-immigrants-in-name-only/4089634002/?fbclid=IwAR3zJnjMmrXjxa34jqS1x8PXHtlrVEeCN-qZk1jVwgP6SGE94Pt57GGTelak

19. Cherríe Moraga and Gloria Anzaldúa, eds., *This Bridge Called My Back: Writings by Radical Women of Color*, 4th ed. (New York: Kitchen Table, 2015).

20. Dustin B. Goltz and J. Zingsheim (Eds.), *Queer Praxis: Questions for LGBTQ Worldmaking* (New York: Peter Lang, 2015).

21. Gloria Anzaldúa, *The Gloria Anzaldúa Reader*, ed. AnaLouis Keating (Durham, NC: Duke University Press, 2009).

22. Ibid.

23. Ibid.

Affirmations for the Jotería Community

A Full Moon Affirmation for Self-Healing and Liberation

I release fear
I release doubt
I release shame
I release my inauthentic self

Affirmation to Combat Body Dysmorphia

I love myself
I care and have affection for myself
I respect myself
I am committed to myself
I am open and honest when communicating with myself and others
I acknowledge my humanity and the flaws therein that make me beautiful
I am beautiful

Affirmation to Survive

> I am happy to be alive
> I am going with the flow of the cosmos
> I am grateful to be here with you on this planet
> I release any fear, shame, and guilt I have been carrying
> I am loved
> I love myself

Affirmation to Make It Through the Day

> I forgive myself
> I am amazing
> I am happy
> I am connected
> I am

Affirmation from White Buffalo Calf Woman

> I respect myself
> I respect the relationships, people,
> and beings   I encounter
> in the world
> On all levels and directions,
> I have surrendered to peace
> I am ready to live life fully
> and freely

Affirmation to Put Yourself Back Together Again

> I am impeccable with my word
> I do not take things personally
> I have the courage to ask questions and to not make assumptions
> I will always do my best because I am free
>> I surrender to the present moment
>> I have permission to be happy

Another Sun Rises

I am ready to finish this book
I am scared of everyone
    knowing my secrets

        judging me
        on high
        a Senate trial
        mocking my life story

I am ready to finish this book
I am afraid of change
        heartbroken
        aching, when
        you poke me
        desperate

I am ready to finish this book
I am hopeful for the future
        no more social isolation
        together fighting for change
        therapy, and
        you

I am ready to finish this book
　　I am empowered by my inner voice
　　　　a reminder that I love myself
　　　　I am enough
　　　　I can trust me

I am ready to finish this book
　　I release my obligations
　　　　assumptions of the future
　　　　failures of the past
　　　　who is going to live my life
　　　　but me?

I am ready to finish this book
　　I have permission to be happy
　　　　to fail, to lose
　　　　to win, to cry
　　　　to never accept anything less than
　　　　the minimum

I am ready to finish this book
　　I am free. I am.
　　　　singing in hallways
　　　　dancing in supermarkets
　　　　dreaming of Spanish-style
　　　　homes made
　　　　alone

I am ready to finish this book
　　I accept this loss
　　I accept this fear
　　　　the torture is over
　　　　I cut my own ropes
　　　　in the crowd, you saw
　　　　my magic, my heart,
　　　　it is time for my souls
　　to　　shift　　let　　go
　　　　another sun rises

The Promise

For Luis A.

I found you
Looking at me hazel-eyed
Late to the door
But of course, I waited.
How do I explain that I was lost?
That I was dying, crying
Empty inside, eye twitching
Overwhelmed.
In need, but no longer capable
Then, you opened up
And there was more
but I don't deserve more

Waking up
Hugging me close
It is that simple, dangerous,
Amor, I found you.
How dare you tell me:
"I think I will always be alone."
Hurt, I stare blankly
Begging silently

Believe in me
Instead of telling you, I cleaned your room
Folded clothes, arranged your things
Made the bed and cried when hugging you goodbye

Be   mine   papi
Not in ownership
Not in that put-your-hand-in-my-pocket bs
but that romantic cholo love
A smile that is only for you
A laugh that is your instrument to play
My heart breaks when you leave
I think your heart breaks when I stay
Like a desert flower in full bloom once
We are back to missed calls
We are back to moving through the motions
We are back to being in the crowd
Masks tightly to nuestras caras
Neon green gorilla teeth
baring, flashing, warning
I don't know how to leave you alone,
to be in two places at once, up in my feelings
Playing sad songs about tender kisses
Gone tomorrow, gone today
My own worst enemy.
I let me get me.
You can't fight this battle for me pa
This darkness is mine to face
I hope I live to see you again.

But, for everyone else, they kick rocks
They get fists and blank stares
A quick wit, a quicker temper
A Stereotypical OG with a low-rider
One hand on the wheel
The dream? You're in the passenger seat
Making everyone jealous
Wearing those pants and chonies that I like
Playing Chicano Soul
We become addicted to green lights,
Southwest sunsets, blunts and Latinx love,
cruising through life
our roads converge

I'm waiting for you

Bibliography

Abdi, Shadee, "Staying I(ra)n: Narrating Queer Identity from Within the Persian Closet." *Liminalities: A Journal of Performance Studies* 10, no. 1 (2014): 1–19.

Aiello, Giorgia, Sandeep Bakshi, Sirma Bilge, Lisa Kahaleole Hall, Lynda Johnston, Kimberlee Pérez, and Karma Chávez, "Here, and Not Yet Here: A Dialogue at the Intersection of Queer, Trans, and Culture." *Journal of International and Intercultural Communication* 6, no. 2 (2013): 96–117.

Alarcón, Norma. "Anzaldúan Textualities: A Hermeneutic of the Self and the Coyolxauhqui Imperative." In *El Mundo Zurdo 3: Selected Works from the 2012 Meeting of the Society for the Study of Gloria Anzaldúa*, edited by Larissa M. Mercado-López, Sonia Saldívar-Hull, and Antonia Castañeda, 189–208. San Francisco: Aunt Lute Books, 2013.

Alcoff, Linda. "The Problem of Speaking for Others." *Cultural Critique* 20 (1991): 5–32.

Aldama, Frederick Luis. *Brown on Brown: Chicano/a Representations of Gender, Sexuality, and Ethnicity*. Austin: University of Texas Press, 2005.

Alexander, Bryant Keith. "Standing in the Wake: A Critical Auto/Ethnographic Exercise on Reflexivity in Three Movements." *Cultural Studies <=> Critical Methodologies* 11, no. 2 (2011): 98–107.

Allen, Brenda J. "Theorizing Communication and Race." *Communication Monographs* 74, no. 2 (2007): 259–64.

Althusser, Louis. *On the Reproduction of Capitalism: Ideology and Ideological State Apparatuses*. New York: Verso, 2014.

Andrade, Luis M. "CAUTION: On the Many, Unpredictable Iterations of a Yellow Border Sign Ideograph and Migrant/Queer World-Making." *Text and Performance Quarterly* 39, no. 3 (2019), 203–28.

Andrade, Luis M., and Robert M. Gutierrez-Perez, "On the Specters of Coloniality: A Letter to Latina/o/x students Journeying through the Educational Pipeline." In *Latina/o/x Communication Studies: Theories, Methods, and Practice*, edited by Leandra Hinojosa Hernández, Diana I. Bowen, Sarah De Los Santos Upton, and Amanda R. Martinez, 313–31. Lanham, MD: Lexington Books, 2019.

Anzaldúa, Gloria. *Borderlands/La Frontera: The New Mestiza*. San Francisco: Aunt Lute Press, 1987.

Anzaldúa, Gloria. *Interviews/Entrevistas*, edited by AnaLouise Keating. New York: Routledge, 2000.

Anzaldúa, Gloria. *The Gloria Anzaldúa Reader*, edited by AnaLouise Keating. Durham, NC: Duke University Press, 2009.

Anzaldúa, Gloria. *Light in the Dark/Luz en lo Oscuro: Rewriting Identity, Spirituality, Reality*. Durham, NC: Duke University Press, 2015.

Arrendondo, Gabriela F., Aida Hurtado, Norma Klahn, Olga Nájera-Ramírez, and Patricia Zavella, eds. "Introduction." In *Chicana Feminisms: A Critical Reader*, 1–18. Durham, NC: Duke University Press, 2003.

Arrizón, Alicia. *Queering Mestizaje: Transculturation and Performance*. Ann Arbor: University of Michigan Press, 2006.

Avant-Mier, Roberto, and Marouf A. Hasian. "Communicating 'Truth': Testimonio, Vernacular Voices, and the Rigoberta Menchú Controversy." *The Communication Review* 11, no. 4 (2008): 323–45.

Avila, Elena. *Woman Who Glows in the Dark: A Curandera Reveals Traditional Aztec Secrets of Physical and Spiritual Health*. New York: Jeremy P. Tarcher/Putnam, 1999.

Ayala, Jennifer, Patricia Herrera, Laura Jiménez, and Irene Lara. "Fiera, Guambra, y Karichina! Transgressing the Borders of Community and Academy." In *Chicana/ Latina Education in Everyday Life: Feminista Perspectives on Pedagogy and Epistemology*, edited by Sofia A. Villenas, Francisca E. Godinez, Dolores Delgado Bernal, and C. Alejandra Elenes, 261–80. Albany: State University of New York Press, 2006.

Baldwin, James. "My Dungeon Shook: Letter to My Nephew on the One Hundreth Anniversary of the Emancipation." In *The Fire Next Time*. New York: Vintage Books, 1993.

Bañales, Xamuel. "Jotería." *Aztlán: A Journal of Chicano Studies* 39, no. 1 (2014): 155–66.

Bardhan, Nilanjana, and Mark P. Orbe. "Introduction: Identity Research in Intercultural Communication." In *Identity Research and Communication: Intercultural Reflections and Future Directions*, edited by Nilanjana Bardhan and Mark P. Orbe, xiii–xxv. Lanham, MA: Lexington Books, 2012.

Baugh-Harris, Sara, and Bernadette Marie Calafell. "A Tolerance for Ambiguity or the American Dream: Utilizing Anzaldúa to Disrupt and Reclaim Latina Lives from Multicultural Feminism." In *This Bridge We Call Communication: Anzaldúan Approaches to Theory, Method and Praxis*, edited by Leandra Hinojosa Hernández and Robert Gutierrez-Perez, 213–25. Lanham, MA: Lexington Books, 2019.

Berry, Keith. *Bullied: Tales of Torment, Identity, and Youth.* New York and London: Routledge, 2016.

Berry, Keith, and John T. Warren, "Cultural Studies and the Politics of Representation: Experience ↔ Subjectivity ↔ Research." *Cultural Studies ↔ Critical Methodologies* 9, no. 5 (2009): 597–607.

Blindjaw. "How to Clean Your Ass Before Anal Sex." Accessed October 31, 2019. https://howtocleanyourass.wordpress.com.

Bochner, Arthur P. "Narrative's Virtues." *Qualitative Inquiry* 7, no. 2 (2001): 131–57.

Bost, Suzanne. "Hurting, Believing, and Changing the World: My Faith in Gloria Anzaldúa." In *Bridging: How Gloria Anzaldúa's Life and Work Transformed Our Own*, edited by AnaLouise Keating and Gloria González-López, 191–96. Austin: University of Texas Press, 2011.

Buncombe, Andrew. "Trump Administration Leaves Menstruating Migrant Girls 'Bleeding Through' Underwear at Detention Centres, Lawsuit Claims." *The Independent*, August 27, 2019. https://www.independent.co.uk/news/world/americas/trump-immigration-migrant-children-border-lawsuit-period-tampon-latest-a9081341.html.

Burke, Kenneth. *The Philosophy of Literary Form: Studies in Symbolic Action.* Baton Rouge: Louisiana State University Press, 1941.

Butler, Judith. "Performative Acts and Gender Constitution: An Essay in Phenomenology and Feminist Theory." *Theatre Journal* 40, no. 4 (1988): 519–31.

Calafell, Bernadette Marie. "Disrupting the Dichotomy: 'Yo Soy Chicana /o?' in the New Latina/o South." *The Communication Review* 7, no. 2 (2004): 175–204.

Calafell, Bernadette Marie. "Pro(re-)claiming Loss: A Performance Pilgrimage in Search of Malintzin Tenépal." *Text and Performance Quarterly* 25, no. 1 (2005): 43–56.

Calafell, Bernadette Marie. *Latina/o Communication Studies: Theorizing Performance.* New York: Peter Lang, 2007.

Calafell, Bernadette Marie. "Mentoring and Love: An Open Letter." *Cultural Studies <=> Critical Methodologies* 7, no. 4 (2007): 425–41.

Calafell, Bernadette Marie. "Rhetorics of Possibility: Challenging the Textual Bias of Rhetoric through the Theory of the Flesh." In *Rhetorica in Motion: Feminist Rhetorical Methods and Methodologies*, edited by Eileen Schell and K. J. Rawson, 104–17. Pittsburgh, PA: University of Pittsburgh Press, 2010.

Calafell, Bernadette Marie. "Love, Loss, and Immigration: Performative Reverberations between a Great-Grandmother and Great-Granddaughter." In *Border*

Rhetorics: Citizenship and Identity on the US-Mexico Frontier, edited by D. Robert DeChaine, 151–62. Tuscaloosa: University of Alabama Press, 2012.

Calafell, Bernadette Marie. "(I)dentities: Considering Accountability, Reflexivity, and Intersectionality in the I and the We." *Liminalities: A Journal of Performance Studies* 9, no. 2 (April 2013): 6–13.

Calafell, Bernadette Marie. "The Future of Feminist Scholarship: Beyond the Politics of Inclusion." *Women's Studies in Communication* 37, no. 3 (September 2, 2014): 266–70.

Calafell, Bernadette Marie. *Monstrosity, Performance, and Race in Contemporary Culture.* New York: Peter Lang, 2015.

Calafell, Bernadette M., and Shane T. Moreman. "Envisioning an Academic Readership: Latina/o Performativities Per the Form of Publication." *Text and Performance Quarterly* 29, no. 2 (2009): 123–30.

Calafell, Bernadette M., and Shane Moreman. "Iterative Hesitancies and Latinidad: The Reverberances of Raciality." In *Handbook of Critical Intercultural Communication*, edited by Rona Halualani and Thomas Nakayama, 400–16. Malden, MA: Wiley-Blackwell, 2010.

Calafell, Bernadette M., and Thomas K. Nakayama. "Dialoguing about the Nexus of Queer Studies and Intercultural Communication." In *Queer Intercultural Communication: The Intersectional Politics of Belonging in and across Difference*, edited by Shinsuke Eguchi and Bernadette M. Calafell, 259–66. Lanham, MD: Rowman & Littlefield, 2020.

Calafell, Bernadette M., Karma R. Chávez, Fernando Delgado, Lisa A. Flores, Michelle A. Holling, Darrel Wanzer-Serrano, Stacey K. Sowards, and Angharad N. Valdivia. "Conclusion: The Futures of Latina/o/x Communication Studies: A Plática with Senior Scholars." *Latina/o/x Communication Studies: Theories, Methods, and Practice*, eds. Leandra H. Hernández, Sarah De Los Santos Upton, Diana Bowen, and Amanda R. Martinez, 371–92. Lanham, MA: Lexington Books, 2019.

Calvo, Luz, and Catriona Rueda Esquibel. *Decolonize Your Diet.* Vancouver, BC: Arsenal Pulp Press, 2015.

Carbado, Devon W., Kimberlé Williams Crenshaw, Vickie M. Mays, and Barbara Tomlinson. "Intersectionality: Mapping the Movements of a Theory." *Du Bois Review: Social Science Research on Race* 10, no. 2 (2013): 303–12.

Carballo-Diéguez, Alex, Curtis Dolezal, Luis Nieves, Francisco Díaz, Carlos Decena, and Ivan Balan. "Looking for a Tall, Dark, Macho Man ... Sexual-role Behaviour Variations in Latino Gay and Bisexual Men." *Culture, Health & Sexuality* 6, no. 2 (2004): 159–71.

Carrasco, Davíd. *The Aztecs: A Very Short Introduction.* Oxford and New York: Oxford University Press, 2012.

Carrillo, Héctor. *The Night Is Young: Sexuality in Mexico in the Time of AIDS*. Chicago and London: University of Chicago Press, 2002.

Cartwright, Mark. "Xochipilli." Ancient History Encyclopedia. September 6, 2013. https://www.ancient.eu/Xochipilli/.

Castaneda, Nivea. "Using Testimonios to Untame Our Silent Tongues: Exploring Our Experiences of Child Sexual Abuse Through an Anzaldúan Perspective." In *This Bridge We Call Communication: Anzaldúan Approaches to Theory, Method, and Praxis*, edited by Leandra Hinojosa Hernández and Robert Gutierrez-Perez, 3–16. Lanham, MD: Lexington Books, 2019.

Center for the Study of Hate and Extremism. *Report to the Nation: 2019 Factbook on Hate and Extremism in the U.S. and Internationally.* California State University, San Bernardino, 2019. https://www.csusb.edu/sites/default/files/CSHE%202019%20Report%20to%20the%20Nation%20FINAL%207.29.19%2011%20PM_0.pdf.

Cervantes, Vincent D. "Traces of Transgressive Traditions Shifting Liberation Theologies through Jotería Studies." *Aztlán: A Journal of Chicano Studies* 39, no. 1 (2014): 195–206.

Céspedes, Karina L. "A Call to Action: Spiritual Activism … An Inevitable Unfolding." In *Bridging: How Gloria Anzaldúa's Life and Work Transformed Our Own*, edited by AnaLouis Keating and Gloria González-López, 74–9. Austin: University of Texas Press, 2011.

Chasteen, John Charles. *Born in Blood and Fire: A Concise History of Latin America.* New York: W. W. Norton & Company, 2001.

Chávez, Karma R. "Pushing Boundaries: Queer Intercultural Communication." *Journal of International and Intercultural Communication* 6, no. 2 (2013): 83–95.

Chávez, Karma R. *Queer Migration Politics: Activist Rhetoric and Coalitional Possibilities.* Urbana, Chicago, and Springfield: University of Illinois Press, 2013.

Clair, Robin P., Stephanie Carlo, Chervin Lam, John Nussman, Canek Phillips, Virginia Sánchez, Elaine Schnabel, and Liliya Yakova. "Narrative Theory and Criticism: An Overview Toward Clusters and Empathy." *Review of Communication* 14, no. 1 (2014), 1–18.

Conquergood, Dwight. *Cultural Struggles: Performance, Ethnography, Praxis*, edited by E. Patrick Johnson. Ann Arbor, MI: University of Michigan Press, 2013.

Coronado, Raúl. "Bringing It Back Home: Desire, Jotos, and Men." In *The Chicana/o Cultural Studies Reader*, edited by Angie Chabram-Dernersesian, 233–40. New York: Routledge, 2006.

Crenshaw, Kimberle. "Mapping the Margins: Intersectionality, Identity Politics, and Violence Against Women of Color." Stanford Law Review 43 (1991): 1241–99.

Davalos, Karen M. "Sin Vergüenza: Chicana Feminist Theorizing." *Feminist Studies* 34, nos. 1/2 (2008): 151–71.

de la Garza, Sarah Amira. *María Speaks: Journeys into the Mysteries of the Mother in My Life as a Chicana.* New York: Peter Lang, 2004.

DeGuzmán, María. "Darkness, My Night": The Philosophical Challenge of Gloria Anzaldúa's Aesthetic of the Shadow." In *Bridging: How Gloria Anzaldúa's Life and*

Work Transformed Our Own, edited by AnaLouis Keating and Gloria González-López, 210–17. Austin: University of Texas Press, 2011.

Delgadillo, Theresa. *Spiritual Mestizaje: Religion, Gender, Race, and Nation in Contemporary Chicana Narrative*. Durham, NC: Duke University Press, 2011.

Delgado Bernal, Dolores, Rebeca Burciaga, and Judith Flores Carmona. "Chicana/Latina Testimonios: Mapping the Methodological, Pedagogical, and Political." *Equity & Excellence in Education* 45, no. 3 (2012): 363–72.

Delgado, Fernando. "The Complexity of Mexican American Identity: A Reply to Hecht, Sedano, and Ribeau and Mirande and Tanno." *International Journal of Intercultural Relations* 18, no. 1 (1995): 77–84.

Delgado, Fernando. "Rigoberta Menchú and Testimonial Discourse: Collectivist Rhetoric and Rhetorical Criticism." *World Communication* 28, no. 1 (1999): 17–29.

Delgado, Fernando P. "All Along the Border: Kid Frost and the Performance of Brown Masculinity." *Text and Performance Quarterly* 20 (2000): 388–401.

Delgado, Fernando P. "Golden, But Not Brown: Oscar De La Hoya and the Complications of Culture, Manhood, and Boxing." *International Journal of the History of Sport* 22 (2005): 196–211.

Delgado, Fernando. "Reflections on Being/Performing Latino Identity in the Academy." *Text and Performance Quarterly* 29, no. 2 (2009): 149–64.

Delgado, Richard, and Jean Stefancic. *Critical Race Theory: An Introduction*. New York: New York University Press, 2001.

Dicochea, Perlita R. "Chicana Critical Rhetoric." *Frontiers* 25, no. 1 (2004): 77–92.

Doring, Ernest. "Growing Up Gay and Latino." In *Queer in Aztlán: Chicano Male Recollections of Consciousness and Coming Out*, edited by Adelaida R. Del Castillo and Gibrán Güido, 17–24. San Diego, CA: Cognella, 2014.

Dunbar-Ortiz, Roxanne. *An Indigenous Peoples History of the United* States. Boston, MA: Beacon Press, 2014.

Duran, Antonio, Roberto C. Orozco, and Sergio A. Gonzalez. "Imagining the Future of Jotería Studies as a Framework in the Field of Higher Education." *Association of Mexican American Educators Journal* 14, no. 2 (2020): 67–86.

Eguchi, Shinsuke, and Bernadette Marie Calafell. "Introduction: Reorienting Queer Intercultural Communication." In *Queer Intercultural Communication: The Intersectional Politics of Belonging in and across Difference*, edited by Shinsuke Eguchi and Bernadette Marie Calafell, 1–16. Lanham, MA: Rowman & Littlefield, 2020.

Eguchi, Shinsuke, Sophie Jones, Hannah R. Long, and Anthony Rosendo Zariñana. "Closing Thoughts: The Future of Queer Intercultural Communication." In *Queer Intercultural Communication: The Intersectional Politics of Belonging in and across Difference*, edited by Shinsuke Eguchi and Bernadette M. Calafell, 267–79. Lanham, MD: Rowman & Littlefield, 2020.

Facio, Elisa, and Irene Lara, eds. *Fleshing the Spirit: Spirituality and Activism in Chicana, Latina, and Indigenous Women's Lives*. Tucson: University of Arizona Press, 2014.

Fadel, Leila. "More Hispanic Kids Are Depressed Than Their Peers as Anti-Migrant Rhetoric Rises." *NPR*, August 6, 2019. https://www.npr.org/2019/08/06/748565528/more-hispanic-kids-are-depressed-than-their-peers-as-anti-migrant-rhetoric-rises.

Fassett, Deanna, John T. Warren, and Keith Nainby. *Communication: A Critical/Cultural Introduction*. San Diego, CA: Cognella, 2018.

Faulkner, Sandra. *Poetry as Method: Reporting Research Through Verse*. Walnut Creek, CA: Left Coast Press, 2009.

Ferris, Kerry O. "Ain't Nothing Like the Real Thing, Baby: Framing Celebrity Impersonator Performances." *Text and Performance Quarterly* 30, no. 1 (2010): 60–80.

Flores Carmona, Judith. "Cutting out Their Tongues: Mujeres' Testimonios and the Malintzin Researcher." *The Journal of Latino-Latin American Studies* 6, no. 2 (2014): 113–24.

Flores, Lisa A. "Challenging the Myth of Assimilation: A Chicana Feminist Response." *International and Intercultural Communication, Annual Vol XXIII: Constituting Cultural Difference through Discourse*, edited by Mary Jane Collier, 26–46. Thousand Oaks, CA: Sage, 2001.

Galarte, Francisco J. "On Trans* Chican@ S." *Aztlán: A Journal of Chicano Studies* 39, no. 1 (2014): 229–36.

Garza, Teresita. "The Rhetorical Legacy of Coyolxauhqui: (Re)collecting and (Re)membering Voice." In *Latina/o Discourse in Vernacular Spaces: Somos de Una Voz?*, edited by Michelle A. Holling and Bernadette Marie Calafell, 31–56. Blue Ridge Summit: Lexington Books, 2011.

Ghabra, Haneen. "Disrupting Privileged and Oppressed Spaces: Reflecting Ethically on my Arabness through Feminist Autoethnography." *Kaleidoscope: A Graduate Journal of Qualitative Communication Research* 14 (2015): 1–16.

Godinez, Francisca. "Haciendo Que Hacer: Braiding Cultural Knowledge into Educational Practices and Policies." *Chicana/Latina Education in Everyday Life: Feminista Perspectives on Pedagogy and Epistemology*, edited by Sofia A. Villenas Francisca E. Godinez, Dolores Delgado Bernal, and C. Alejandra Elenes, 25–38. Albany, NY: State University of New York Press, 2006.

Goltz, Dustin Bradley. "It Gets Better: Queer Futures, Critical Frustrations, and Radical Potentials." *Critical Studies in Media Communication* 30, no. 2 (2013): 135–51.

Gómez-Cano, Grisel. *The Return of Coatlicue: Goddesses and Warladies in Mexican Folklore*. Bloomington, IN: Xlibria, 2010.

Gonzales, Richard. "Sexual Assault of Detained Migrant Children Reported in the Thousands Since 2015." *NPR*, February 26, 2019. https://www.npr.org/2019/02/26/698397631/sexual-assault-of-detained-migrant-children-reported-in-the-thousands-since-2015.

González, Alberto, Bernadette M. Calafell, and Roberto Avant-Mier. "An LCSD & La Raza Microhistory: The Latina/o Communication Studies Division & La Raza

Caucus of the National Communication Association." *Review of Communication* 14, no. 2 (2014), 12–37.

González, Juan Carlos, and Edwardo L. Portillos. ""Teaching from a Critical Perspective / Enseñando de Una Perspectiva Crítica: Conceptualization, Reflection, and Application of Chicana/o Pedagogy." *International Journal of Critical Pedagogy* 4, no. 1 (2012): 18–34.

González, María Cristina. "The Four Seasons of Ethnography: A Creation-Centered Ontology for Ethnography." *International Journal of Intercultural Relations* 24, no. 5 (2000): 623–50.

González-López, Gloria. "Conocimiento and Healing: Academic Wounds, Survival, and Tenure." In *Bridging: How Gloria Anzaldúa's Life and Work Transformed Our Own*, edited by AnaLouise Keating and Gloria González-López, 91–100. Austin: University of Texas Press, 2011.

Gramsci, Antonio. *The Antonio Gramsci Reader: Selected Writings 1916–1935*, edited by David Forgacs. New York: New York University Press, 2000.

Grande, Sandy. "Red Pedagogy: The Un-Methodology." In *Handbook of Critical and Indigenous Methodologies*, edited by Norman K. Denzin, Yvonna S. Lincoln, and Linda Tuhiwai Smith, 233–54. Thousand Oaks, CA: Sage, 2008.

Griffin, Rachel Alicia. "Navigating the Politics of Identity/Identities and Exploring the Promise of Critical Love." In *Identity Research and Communication: Intercultural Reflections and Future Directions*, edited by Nilanjana Bardhan and Mark P. Orbe, 207–22. Lanham, MA: Lexington Books, 2012.

Griffin, Rachel A. "Cultivating Promise and Possibility: Black Feminist Thought as an Innovative, Interdisciplinary, and International Framework." *Departures in Critical Qualitative Research* 5, no. 3 (2016): 1–9.

Gust, Scott William, and John T. Warren. "Naming Our Sexual and Sexualized Bodies in the Classroom: And the Important Stuff That Comes After the Colon." *Qualitative Inquiry* 14, no. 1 (2008): 114–34.

Gutierrez-Perez, Robert. "Warren-ting a 'Dinner Party': Nepantla as a Space In/ Between." *Liminalities: A Journal of Performance Studies* 8, no. 5 (2012): 195–206.

Gutierrez-Perez, Robert. "Brown Fingers Ran Down." In *Queer Praxis: Questions for LGBTQ Worldmaking*, edited by Dustin Bradly Goltz and Jason Zingsheim, 41–54. New York: Peter Lang, 2015.

Gutierrez-Perez, Robert. "Disruptive Ambiguities: The Potentiality of Jotería Critique in Communication Studies." *Kaleidoscope: A Graduate Journal of Qualitative Communication Research* 14 (2015): 89–99.

Gutierrez-Perez, Robert. "Question(ing) One in the Coatlicue State: A Call for Creative Engagement in the LGBTQ Movement." *Liminalities: A Journal of Performance Studies* 11, no. 1 (2015): 1–18.

Gutierrez-Perez, Robert. "Bridging Performances of Auto/ethnography and Queer Bodies of Color to Advocacy and Civic Engagement." *QED: A Journal of GLBTQ Worldmaking* 4, no. 1 (2017): 148–56.

Gutierrez-Perez, Robert. "Monstrosity in Everyday Life: Nepantleras, Theories in the Flesh, and Transformational Politics." *Popular Culture Studies Journal* 6, nos. 2&3 (2018): 345–68.

Gutierrez-Perez, Robert. "Theories in the Flesh and Flights of the Imagination: Embracing the Soul and Spirit of Critical Performative Writing in Communication Research." *Women's Studies in Communication* 41, no. 4 (2019): 404–15.

Gutierrez-Perez, Robert. "Editor's Introduction: Deconstruction as a Simultaneous Act of Reconstruction." *Border-Lines: Journal of the Latino Research Center* 11 (2019): 9–15.

Gutierrez-Perez, Robert. "I Get It from My Mother." In *This Bridge We Call Communication: Anzaldúan Approaches to Theory, Method, and Praxis,* edited by Leandra Hinojosa Hernández and Robert Gutierrez-Perez, 287–90. Lanham: Lexington Books, 2019.

Gutierrez-Perez, Robert. "Performance and Everyday Life, or a Latina/o/x in Intercultural Communication." *Journal of Intercultural Communication Research* 49, no. 5 (September 29, 2020): 433–41.

Gutierrez-Perez, Robert, "A Return to El Mundo Zurdo: Anzaldúan Approaches to Queer of Color Worldmaking and the Violence of Intersectional Heteronormativity," *Women's Studies in Communication* 43, no. 4 (2020): 384–99.

Gutierrez-Perez, Robert, and Luis Manuel Andrade. "Queer of Color World-Making: <Marriage> in the Rhetorical Archive and the Embodied Repertoire." *Text and Performance Quarterly* 38, no. 1–2 (2018): 1–18.

Gutmann, Matthew C. *The Meaning of Macho: Being a Man in Mexico City.* Berkeley and Los Angeles: University of California Press, 1996.

Haig Brown, Celia. "Creating Spaces: Testimonio, Impossible Knowledge, and Academe." *International Journal of Qualitative Studies in Education* 16, no. 3 (2003): 415–33.

Halualani, Rona Tamiko, S. Lily Mendoza, a nd Jolanta A. Drzewiecka. " 'Critical' Junctures in Intercultural Communication Studies: A Review." *Review of Communication* 9, no. 1 (2009): 17–35.

Hames-García, Michael. *Identity Complex: Making the Case for Multiplicity.* Minneapolis: University of Minnesota Press, 2011.

Hames-García, Michael. "Jotería Studies, or the Political Is Personal." *Aztlán: A Journal of Chicano Studies* 39, no. 1 (2014): 135–42.

Hames-García, Michael, and Ernesto Javier Martínez. "Introduction: Re-membering Gay Latino Studies." In *Gay Latino Studies: A Critical Reader,* edited by Michael Hames-García and Ernesto Javier Martínez, 1–18. Durham, NC: Duke University, 2011.

Hamilton, Edith. *Mythology*. Boston, MA: Little, Brown, and Company, 2013.

Harter, Lynn M. "Narratives as Dialogic, Contested, and Aesthetic Performances." *Journal of Applied Communication Research* 37, no. 2 (2009): 140–50.

Hartley, George. "The Curandera of Conquest: Gloria Anzaldúa's Decolonial Remedy." *Aztlan: A Journal of Chicano Studies* 35, no. 1 (2010): 135–61.

Heredia, Jessica. "My Path of Conocimiento: How Graduate School Transformed Me into a Nepantlera." In *Bridging: How Gloria Anzaldúa's Life and Work Transformed Our Own*, edited by AnaLouise Keating and Gloria González-López, 39–44. Austin: University of Texas Press, 2011.

Hill Collins, Patricia. *Black Feminist Thought: Knowledge, Consciousness, and the Politics of Empowerment*. New York: Routledge, 1991.

Hill Collins, Patricia, and Sirma Bilge. *Intersectionality*. Malden, MA: Polity Press, 2016.

Hobson, Kathryn. "Performative Tensions in Female Drag Performances." *Kaleidoscope: A Graduate Journal of Qualitative Communication Research* 12, no. 1 (2013): 35–51.

Holling, Michelle A. "El Simpático Boxer: Underpinning Chicano Masculinity with a Rhetoric of Familia in Resurrection Blvd." *Western Journal of Communication* 70 (2006): 91–114.

Holling, Michelle A. " 'So My Name Is Alma, and I Am the Sister of …': A Feminicidio Testimonio of Violence and Violent Identifications." *Women's Studies in Communication* 37, no. 3 (2014): 313–38.

hooks, bell. *All about Love: New Visions*. New York: HarperCollins, 2001.

Hunter, Lourdes Ashley. " 'We Need to Fix This Shit Now' Says Director for Trans Women of Color Collective." News2Share. January 10, 2015. https://www.youtube.com/watch?v=Qu1niZYDzsk.

Hurtado, Aída. "Sitios y Lenguas: Chicanas Theorize Feminisms." *Hypatia* 13, no. 2 (1998): 134–61.

Hurtado, Aída. "Theory in the Flesh: Toward an Endarkened Epistemology." *International Journal of Qualitative Studies in Education* 16, no. 2 (2003): 215–25.

Inda, Jonathan Xavier. "Performativity, Materiality, and the Racial Body." *Latino Studies Journal* 11, no. 3 (1996): 74–99.

Irwin, Robert McKee. "The Famous 41: The Scandalous Birth of Modern Mexican Homosexuality." *GLQ: A Journal of Lesbian and Gay Studies* 6, no. 3 (2000): 353–76.

Irwin, Robert McKee. *Mexican Masculinities*. Minneapolis: University of Minnesota Press, 2003.

Jackson, Ron L., and Jamie Moshin. "Identity and Difference: Race and the Necessity of the Discriminating Subject." In *The Handbook of Critical Intercultural Communication*, edited by Thomas K. Nakayama and Rona Tamiko Halualani, 348–63. Malden, MA: Wiley-Blackwell, 2013.

Jiménez, Karleen Pendleton. "'Start with the Land': Groundwork for Chicana Pedagogy." In *Chicana/Latina Education in Everyday Life: Feminista Perspectives on Pedagogy and Epistemology*, edited by Sofia A. Villenas, Francisca E. Godinez, Dolores Delgado Bernal, and C. Alejandra Elenes, 219–30. Albany: State University of New York Press, 2006.

Johnson, Chris. "Trump Administration: HIV Status Used to Justify Family Separation at the Border." *Washington Blade*, July 25, 2019. https://www.washingtonblade.com/2019/07/25/trump-administration-hiv-status-used-to-justify-family-separation-at-border.

Johnson, E. Patrick. "Introduction: Opening and Interpreting Lives." In *Cultural Struggles: Performance, Ethnography, Praxis*, edited by E. Patrick Johnson, 1–14. Ann Arbor: University of Michigan Press, 2013.

Johnson, E. Patrick. " 'Quare' Studies, or (Almost) Everything I Know About Queer Studies I Learned from my Grandmother." *Text and Performance Quarterly* 21, no. 1 (2001): 1–25.

Johnson, E. Patrick. "Queer Theory." In *The Cambridge Companion to Performance Studies*, edited by Tracy C. Davis, 166–81. Cambridge, MA: Cambridge University Press, 2008.

Johnson, E. Patrick. *Sweet Tea: Black Gay Men of the South*. Chapel Hill: University of North Carolina Press, 2008.

Johnson, Julia R. "Cisgender Privilege, Intersectionality, and the Criminalization of CeCe McDonald: Why Intercultural Communication Needs Transgender Studies." *Journal of International and Intercultural Communication* 6, no. 2 (2013): 135–44.

Jones, Richard G., and Bernadette Marie Calafell. "Contesting Neoliberalism Through Critical Pedagogy, Intersectional Reflexivity, and Personal Narrative: Queer Tales of Academia." *Journal of Homosexuality* 59, no. 7 (August 2012): 957–81.

Keating, AnaLouise, ed. *EntreMundos/AmongWorlds: New Perspectives on Gloria Anzaldúa*. New York: Palgrave Macmillan, 2005.

Keating, AnaLouis. "Risking the Vision, Transforming the Divides: Nepantlera perspectives on Academic Boundaries, Identities, and Lives." In *Bridging: How Gloria Anzaldúa's Life and Work Transformed Our Own*, edited by AnaLouis Keating and Gloria González-López, 142–52. Austin, TX: University of Texas Press, 2011.

Keating, AnaLouise, and Gloria González-López. "Building Bridges, Transforming Loss, Shaping New Dialogues: Anzaldúan Studies for the Twenty-First Century." In *Bridging: How Gloria Anzaldúa's Life and Work Transformed Our Own*, edited by Analouise Keating and Gloria González-López, 1–16. Austin: University of Texas Press, 2011.

Kellaway, Mitch K. "WATCH: Trans Leader's Speech Perfectly Explains Why We Must 'Fix Society,' Not Trans People." Advocate. January 13, 2015. https://www.advocate.com/politics/transgender/2015/01/13/watch-trans-leaders-speech-perfectly-explains-why-we-must-fix-society.

Kilgard, Amy K. "Chaos as Praxis: Or, Troubling Performance Pedagogy: Or, You Are Now." *Text and Performance Quarterly* 31, no. 3 (2011): 217–28.

Koshy, Kavitha. "Feels Like 'Carving Bone': (Re)creating the Activist-Self, (Re) Articulating Transnational Journeys, while Sifting through Anzaldúan Thought." In *Bridging: How Gloria Anzaldúa's Life and Work Transformed Our Own*, edited by AnaLouis Keating and Gloria González-López, 197–203. Austin: University of Texas Press, 2011.

La Fountain-Stokes, Lawrence. "Gay Shame, Latina- and Latino-Style: A Critique of White Queer Performativity." In *Gay Latino Studies: A Critical Reader*, edited by Michael Hames-García and Ernesto J. Martínez, 55–80. Durham, NC: Duke University, 2011.

Langellier, Kristin M. "Personal Narrative, Performance, Performativity: Two or Three Things I Know for Sure." *Text and Performance Quarterly* 19, no. 2 (1999): 125–44.

Lara, Irene. "Daughter of Coatlicue: An Interview with Gloria Anzaldúa." In *EntreMundos/Among World: New Perspectives on Gloria Anzaldúa*, edited by AnaLouis Keating, 41–55. New York: Palgrave Macmillan, 2005.

Lee, Wenshu. "Kauering Queer Theory: My Autocritography and a Race-Conscious, Womanist, Transnational Turn." In *Queer Theory and Communication: From Disciplining Queers to Queering the Discipline(s)*, edited by Gust A. Yep, Karen E. Lovaas, and J. P. Elia, 147–70. Binghamton: Harrington Park Press, 2003.

LeMaster, Benny and Amber L. Johnson. "Unlearning Gender—Towards a Critical Communication Trans Pedagogy." *Communication Teacher* 33, no. 3 (2019): 189–98.

León, Luis D. *La Llorona's Children: Religion, Life, and Death in the U.S.-Mexican Borderlands*. Berkeley and Los Angeles: University of California Press, 2004.

Lindemann, Kurt. "Live(s) Online: Narrative Performance, Presence, and Community in LiveJournal.com." *Text and Performance Quarterly* 25, no. 4 (2005), 354–72.

Lugones, Maria. "Toward a Decolonial Feminism." *Hypatia* 25, no. 4 (2010): 742–59.

Madison, D. Soyini. " 'That Was My Occupation': Oral Narrative, Performance, and Black Feminist Thought." *Text and Performance Quarterly* 13, no. 3 (July 1993): 213–32.

Madison, D. Soyini. "Performing Theory/Embodied Writing." *Text and Performance Quarterly* 19 (1999): 107–24.

Madison, D. Soyini. "The Dialogic Performative in Critical Ethnography." *Text and Performance Quarterly* 26, no. 4 (2006): 320–24.

Madison, D. Soyini. "Co-Performative Witnessing." *Cultural Studies* 21, no. 6 (2007), 826–31.

Madison, D. Soyini. "Dangerous Ethnography." In *Qualitative Inquiry and Social Justice: Toward a Politics of Hope*, edited by Norman K. Denzin and Michael D. Giardina, 187–97. Walnut Creek, CA: Left Coast Press, 2009.

Madision, D. Soyini. *Critical Ethnography: Method, Ethics, and Performance.* Thousand Oaks, CA: Sage, 2012.

Márez, Curtis. "Brown: The Politics of Working-Class Chicano Style." *Social Text* 48 (1996): 109–32.

Martinez, Amanda, and Robert M. Gutierrez-Perez, "Are We Post-Post-Race Yet? Moving Beyond the Black-White Binary Towards a Mestiza/o Consciousness." In *The Assault on Communities of Color: Exploring the Realities of Race-Based Violence*, edited by Fasching-Varner, Hartlep, Martin, Cleveland Hayes, Mitchell, and Allen-Mitchell, 49–54. Lanham, MD: Rowman and Littlefield Publishers, 2015.

Martínez, Ernesto Javier. *On Making Sense: Queer Race Narratives of Intelligibility.* Stanford, CA: Stanford University Press, 2013.

Martínez, Ernesto Javier. "¿Con Quién, Dónde, Y Por Qué Te Dejas?: Reflections on Joto Passivity." *Aztlán: A Journal of Chicano Studies* 39, no. 1 (2014): 237–46.

Martinez, Shantel. "Lessons from My Battle Scars: Testimonio's Transformative Possibilities for Theory and Practice." In *Latina/o/x Communication Studies: Theories, Methods, and Practice*, edited by Leandra Hinojosa Hernández, Diana I. Bowen, Sarah De Los Santos Upton, and Amanda R. Martinez, 355–70. Lanham, MD: Lexington Books, 2019.

McIntosh, Peggy. "White Privilege: Unpacking the Invisible Knapsack." In *Reconstructing Gender: A Multicultural Anthology*, 5th ed., edited by Estelle Disch, 78–82. Boston: University of Massachusetts, 2009.

Menchú, Rigoberta. *I, Rigoberta Menchú: An Indian Woman in Guatemala*, edited by Elizabeth Burgos-Debray, translated by Ann Wright. London: Verso, 1984.

Mendoza, S. Lily. "Doing 'Indigenous' Ethnography as a Cultural Outsider: Lessons from the Four Seasons." *Journal of International and Intercultural Communication* 9, no. 2 (2016): 140–60.

Miller, Jackson B. "Coyote's Tale on the Old Oregon Trail: Challenging Cultural Memory through Narrative at the Tamástslikt Cultural Institute." *Text and Performance Quarterly* 25, no. 3 (2005): 220–38.

Mohanty, Chandra Talpade. *Feminism Without Borders: Decolonizing Theory, Practicing Solidarity.* Durham and London: Duke University Press, 2003.

Moraga, Cherríe. *Loving in the War Years: Lo Que Nunca Paso por Sus Labios.* Cambridge, MA: South End Press, 2000.

Moraga, Cherríe. *A Xicana Codex of Changing Consciousness: Writings, 2000–2010.* Durham, NC: Duke University Press, 2011.

Moraga, Cherríe, and Gloria Anzaldúa, eds. *This Bridge Called My Back: Writings by Radical Women of Color*, 4th ed. New York: Kitchen Table, 2015.

Moreman, Shane T. "Memoir as Performance: Strategies of Hybrid Ethnic Identity." *Text and Performance Quarterly* 29, no. 4 (October 2009): 346–66.

Moreman, Shane T. "Rethinking Dwight Conquergood: Toward an Unstated Cultural Politics." *Liminalities: A Journal of Performance Studies* 5, no. 5 (2009): 1–13.

Moreman, Shane. "Qualitative Interviews of Racial Fluctuations: The 'How' of Latina/o-White Hybrid Identity." *Communication Theory* 21, no. 2 (2011): 197–216.

Moreman, Shane T., and Bernadette Marie Calafell. "Buscando Para Nuestros Hijos: Utilizing La Llorona for Cultural Critique." *Journal of International and Intercultural Communication* 1, no. 4 (2008): 309–26.

Moreman, Shane, and Dawn Marie McIntosh. "Brown Scriptings and Rescriptings: A Critical Performance Ethnography of Latina Drag Queens." *Communication & Critical/Cultural Studies* 7, no. 2 (2010): 115–35.

Muñoz, Jose E. *Disidentifications: Queers of Color and the Performance of Politics.* Minneapolis: University of Minnesota Press, 1999.

Muñoz, José Esteban. *Cruising Utopia: The Then and There of Queer Futurity.* New York: New York University Press, 2009.

Murray, Stephen O. "Mexico." In *The Politics of Sexuality in Latin America: A Reader on Lesbian, Gay, Bisexual, and Transgender Rights*, edited by Javier Corrales and Mario Pecheny, 60–8. Pittsburgh: University of Pittsburgh Press, 2010.

Nakayama, Thomas K., and Rona Tamiko Halualani. "Conclusion: Envisioning the Pathway(s) of Critical Intercultural Communication Studies." In *The Handbook of Critical Intercultural Communication*, edited by Thomas K. Nakayama and Rona T. Halualani, 595–600. Malden, MA: Wiley-Blackwell, 2013.

Noriega, Chon A., and Teresa Barnett. "Introduction." In *Oral History and Communities of Color*, edited by Teresa Barnett and Chon A. Noriega, 1–18. Los Angeles, CA: UCLA Chicano Studies Research Center Press, 2013.

Nesvig, Martin. "The Complicated Terrain of Latin American Homosexuality." *Hispanic American Historical Review* 81, no. 3–4 (2001): 689–729.

Paz, Octavio. *The Labyrinth of Solitude: Life and Thought in Mexico.* New York: Grove Press, 1961.

Pelias, Ron J. *Writing Performance: Poeticizing the Researcher's Body.* Carbondale: Southern Illinois University Press, 1999.

Pérez Huber, Lindsay. "Disrupting Apartheid of Knowledge: Testimonio as Methodology in Latina/o Critical Race Research in Education." *International Journal of Qualitative Studies in Education* 22, no. 6 (2009): 639–54.

Pérez, Daniel Enrique. "Jotería Epistemologies." *Aztlán: A Journal of Chicano Studies* 39, no. 1 (2014): 143–54.

Pérez, Daniel Enrique. "Out in the Field: Mariposas and Chicana/o Studies." In *Queer in Aztlán: Chicano Male Recollections of Consciousness and Coming Out*, edited by Adelaida R. Del Castillo and Gibrán Güido, 277–92. San Diego, CA: Cognella, 2014.

Pérez, Manuel Alejandro. "Testimonio as a Queer Puente for Healing." In *This Bridge We Call Communication: Anzaldúan Approaches to Theory, Method, and Praxis*, edited by Leandra Hinojosa Hernández and Robert Gutierrez-Perez, 17–26. Lanham, MD: Lexington Books, 2019.

Peterson, Eric E., and Kristin M. Langellier. "The Performance Turn in Narrative Studies," *Narrative Inquiry* 16, no. 1 (2006), 173–80.

Pitts, Margret Jane. "Practicing the Four Seasons of Ethnography Methodology while Searching for Identity in Mexico." *The Qualitative Report* 17 (2012), 1–21.

Pollock, Della. "Performing Writing." In *The Ends of Performance*, edited by Peggy Phelan and Jill Lane, 73–103. New York: New York University Press, 1998.

Pollock, Della. "Introduction: Remembering." In *Remembering: Oral History Performance*, edited by Della Pollock, 1–18. New York: Palgrave Macmillan, 2005.

Pollock, Della. "Moving Histories: Performance and Oral History." In *The Cambridge Companion to Performance Studies*, edited by Tracy C. Davis, 120–35. Cambridge, MA: Cambridge University Press, 2008.

Revilla, Anita Tijerina, and José Manuel Santillana. "Jotería Identity and Consciousness." *Aztlán: A Journal of Chicano Studies* 39, no. 1 (2014): 167–80.

Reyes, Kathryn Blackmer, and Julia E. Curry Rodríguezes, "Testimonio: Origins, Terms, and Resources." *Equity & Excellence in Education* 45, no. 3 (2012): 525–38.

Rodriguez, Roberto. "Chile Relleno." In *Queer in Aztlán: Chicano Male Recollections of Consciousness and Coming Out*, edited by Adelaida R. Del Castillo and Gibrán Güido, 65–70. San Diego, CA: Cognella, 2014.

Roque Ramírez, Horacio N. "Gay Latino Histories/Dying to Be Remembered: AIDS Obituaries, Public Memory, and the Queer Latino Archive." In *Beyond El Barrio: Everyday Life in Latina/o America*, edited by Gina M. Pérez, Frank A. Guridy, and Adrian Burgos Jr., 103–28. New York: NYU Press, 2010.

Roque Ramírez, Horacio N. "Recording a Queer Community: An Interview with Horacio N. Roque Ramírez." In *Oral History and Communities of Color*, edited by Teresa Barnett and Chon A. Noriega, 132–152. Los Angeles: UCLA Chicano Studies Research Center Press, 2013.

Rosario, Vernon A. " 'Qué Joto Bonita!': Transgender Negotiations of Sex and Ethnicity." *Journal of Gay & Lesbian Psychotherapy* 8, nos. 1–2 (2004): 89–97.

Rowe, Aimee Carrillo. "Subject to Power—Feminism Without Victims." *Women's Studies in Communication* 32, no. 1 (2009): 12–35.

Rupert, Mark. "Reading Gramsci in an Era of Globalising Capitalism." *Critical Review of International Social and Political Philosophy* 8, no. 4 (2005): 483–97.

Sánchez, Patricia, and Lucila D. Ek. "Cultivando La Siguiente Generación: Future Directions in Chicana/Latina Feminist Pedagogies." *Journal of Latino-Latin American Studies* 5, no. 3 (2013): 181–87.

Scholz, Linda T. M. "Hablando Por (Nos)Otros, Speaking for Ourselves: Exploring the Possibilities of 'Speaking Por' Family and Pueblo in Bolivian Testimonio 'Si Me Permiten Hablar.' " In *Latina/o Discourse in Vernacular Spaces: Somos de Una Voz?*, edited by Michelle A. Holling and Bernadette Marie Calafell, 203–22. Blue Ridge Summit, PA: Lexington Books, 2011.

Shah, Naureen. "At Detention Facilities, Legal Rights 'In Name Only.'" USA Today, October 25, 2019. https://www.usatoday.com/story/opinion/policing/2019/10/25/detention-facilities-legal-rights-for-immigrants-in-name-only/4089634002/

Shopes, Linda. "Oral History." In *Collecting and Interpreting Qualitative Materials*, 4th ed, edited by Norman K. Denzin and Yvonna S. Lincoln, 119–150. Thousand Oaks, CA: Sage, 2013.

Sigal, Pete. *The Flower and the Scorpion: Sexuality and Ritual in Early Nahua Culture.* Durham, NC: Duke University Press, 2011.

Smith, Linda Tuhiwai. *Decolonizing Methodologies: Research and Indigenous Peoples.* New York: Palgrave Macmillan, 2012.

Solis, Rogelio V., and Jeff Amy. "Largest US Immigration Raids in a Decade Net 680 Arrests." AP News, August 7, 2019. https://apnews.com/bbcef8ddae4e430 3983c91880559cf23.

Sowards, Stacey K., and Richard D. Pineda. "Immigrant Narratives and Popular Culture in the United States: Border Spectacle, Unmotivated Sympathies, and Individualized Responsibilities." *Western Journal of Communication* 77, no. 1 (2013): 72–91.

Spivak, Gayatri Chakravorty. "Can the Subaltern Speak?" In *Marxism and the Interpretation of Culture*, edited by C. Nelson and L. Grossberg, 271–313. Urbana and Chicago: University of Illinois Press, 1988.

Stavans, Ilan. "The Latin Phallus." *Transition* 65 (1995): 48–68.

Street, Mikelle. "Hate Crimes Against LGBTQ+ People Are the Highest in a Decade." *Out Magazine*, August 1, 2019. https://www.out.com/news/2019/8/01/hate-crimes-against-lgbtq-people-are-highest-decade.

Thurlow, Crispin. "Speaking of Difference: Language, Inequality and Interculturality." In *The Handbook of Critical Intercultural Communication*, edited by Thomas K. Nakayama and Rona Tamiko Halualani, 227–47. Malden, MA: Wiley-Blackwell, 2013.

Trimble, Charles E., Barbara W. Sommer, and Mary Kay Quinlan. *The American Indian Oral History Manual: Making Many Voices Heard.* Walnut Creek, CA: Left Coast Press, 2008.

Toyosaki, Satoshi, and Hsun-Yu (Sharon) Chuang. "Critical Intercultural Communication Pedagogy from Within: Textualizing Intercultural and Intersectional Self-Reflexivity." In *Critical Intercultural Communication Pedagogy*, edited by Ahmet Atay and Satoshi Toyosaki, 238–43. Lanham, MA: Lexington Books, 2018.

Upton, Sarah De Los Santos. "Communicating Nepantla: An Anzaldúan Theory of Identity." In *This Bridge We Call Communication: Anzaldúan Approaches to Theory, Method and Praxis*, edited by Leandra Hinojosa Hernández and Robert Gutierrez-Perez, 123–42. Lanham, MA: Lexington Books, 2019.

Urquijo-Ruiz, Rita E. "Coming Home." *Aztlán: A Journal of Chicano Studies* 39, no. 1 (2014): 247–52.

Warner, Michael. *The Trouble with Normal: Sex, Politics, and the Ethics of Queer Life.* Cambridge, MA: Harvard University Press, 1999.

Warren, John T. *Performing Purity: Whiteness, Pedagogy, and the Reconstitution of Power.* New York: Peter Lang, 2003.

Warren, John T., and Deanna L. Fassett. *Communication: A Critical/Cultural Introduction.* Thousand Oaks, CA: Sage Publications, 2014.

Willink, Kate. "Domesticating Difference: Performing Memories of School Desegregation." *Text and Performance Quarterly* 27, no. 1 (2007): 20–40.

Willink, Kate. "Economy & Pedagogy: Laboring to Learn in Camden County, North Carolina." *Communication and Critical/Cultural Studies* 5, no. 1 (2008): 64–86.

Willink, Kate, Robert Gutierrez-Perez, Salma Shukri, and Lacey Stein. "Navigating with the Stars: Critical Qualitative Methodological Constellations for Critical Intercultural Communication Research." *Journal of International and Intercultural Communication* 7, no. 4 (October 2014): 289–316.

Wood, Julia. T. *Gendered Lives: Communication, Gender, and Culture.* Boston, MA: Wadsworth, 2009.

Yep, Gust A. "The Violence of Heteronormativity in Communication Studies: Notes on Injury, Healing, and Queer World-Making." *Journal of Homosexuality* 45, nos. 2–4 (2003): 11–59.

Yep, Gust A. "Toward the De-Subjugation of Racially Marked Knowledges in Communication." *Southern Communication Journal* 75, no. 2 (2010): 171–75.

Yep, Gust A. "Queering/Quaring/Kauering/Crippin'/Transing 'Other Bodies' in Intercultural Communication." *Journal of International and Intercultural Communication* 6, no. 2 (May 2013): 118–26.

Yep, Gust A. "Toward Thick(er) Intersectionalities: Theorizing, Researching, and Activating the Complexities of Communication and Identities." In *Globalizing Intercultural Communication,* edited by Kathryn Sorrells and Sachi Sekimoto, 85–94. Thousand Oaks, CA: Sage, 2016.

Yep, Gust A., Fatima Zahrae Chrifi Alaoui, and Ryan M. Lescure. "Relationalities in/through Difference: Explorations in Queer Intercultural Communication." In *Queer Intercultural Communication: The Intersectional Politics of Belonging in and across Differences,* edited by Shinsuke Eguchi and Bernadette Marie Calafell, 19–45. Lanham, MD: Rowman & Littlefield, 2020.

Yosso, Tara J., and Daniel G. Solórzano. "Leaks in the Chicana and Chicano Educational Pipeline." *Latino Policy & Issues Brief* 13 (2006): 1–4.

Zukic, Naida. "Webbing Sexual/Textual Agency in Autobiographical Narratives of Pleasure." *Text and Performance Quarterly* 28, no. 4 (2008): 396–414.

Index

Critical Intercultural Communication Studies

Thomas K. Nakayama and Bernadette Marie Calafell, General Editors

Critical approaches to the study of intercultural communication have arisen at the end of the twentieth century and are poised to flourish in the new millennium. As cultures come into contact—driven by migration, refugees, the internet, wars, media, transnational capitalism, cultural imperialism, and more—critical interrogations of the ways that cultures interact communicatively are needed to understand culture and communication. This series will interrogate—from a critical perspective—the role of communication in intercultural contact, in both domestic and international contexts. This series is open to studies in key areas such as postcolonialism, transnationalism, critical race theory, queer diaspora studies, and critical feminist approaches as they relate to intercultural communication, tuning into the complexities of power relations in intercultural communication. Proposals might focus on various contexts of intercultural communication such as international advertising, popular culture, language policies, hate crimes, ethnic cleansing and ethnic group conflicts, as well as engaging theoretical issues such as hybridity, displacement, multiplicity, identity, orientalism, and materialism. By creating a space for these critical approaches, this series will be at the forefront of this new wave in intercultural communication scholarship. Manuscripts and proposals are welcome that advance this new approach.

For additional information about this series or for the submission of manuscripts, please contact:

Thomas K. Nakayama, General Editor | *T.Nakayama@neu.edu*
Bernadette Marie Calafell, General Editor | *calafell@gonzaga.edu*

To order other books in this series, please contact our Customer Service Department at:

peterlang@presswarehouse.com (within the U.S.)
orders@peterlang.com (outside the U.S.)

or browse online by series: www.peterlang.com

www.ingramcontent.com/pod-product-compliance
Lightning Source LLC
Chambersburg PA
CBHW050629280326
41932CB00015B/2582